Action, Embodied Mind,
and Life World

SUNY series in American Philosophy and Cultural Thought
———————
Randall E. Auxier and John R. Shook, editors

Action, Embodied Mind, and Life World

Focusing at the Existential Level

RALPH D. ELLIS

SUNY PRESS

Cover painting entitled "Seventeen" by Lynda Ellis.

Published by State University of New York Press, Albany

© 2023 State University of New York

All rights reserved

Printed in the United States of America

No part of this book may be used or reproduced in any manner whatsoever without written permission. No part of this book may be stored in a retrieval system or transmitted in any form or by any means including electronic, electrostatic, magnetic tape, mechanical, photocopying, recording, or otherwise without the prior permission in writing of the publisher.

For information, contact State University of New York Press, Albany, NY
www.sunypress.edu

Library of Congress Cataloging-in-Publication Data

Name: Ellis, Ralph D., author.
Title: Action, embodied mind, and life world : focusing at the existential level / Ralph D. Ellis.
Description: Albany, NY : State University of New York Press, [2023] | Series: SUNY series in American philosophy and cultural thought | Includes bibliographical references and index.
Identifiers: LCCN 2022059357 | ISBN 9781438494722 (hardcover : alk. paper) | ISBN 9781438494739 (ebook) | ISBN 9781438494715 (pbk. : alk. paper)
Subjects: LCSH: Phenomenology. | Consciousness. | Motivation (Psychology)
Classification: LCC B829.5 .E435 2023 | DDC 142/.7—dc23/eng/20230608
LC record available at https://lccn.loc.gov/2022059357

10 9 8 7 6 5 4 3 2 1

*In loving memory to my mentor, Professor André Schuwer,
who was so kind and generous in the way he opened the wonderlands
of existentialism and hermeneutic phenomenology to me
and so many other American and European students.
I still cherish the brick he saved from the old Duquesne philosophy building.*

Contents

Introduction	Interpreting Reality Presupposes an Understanding of Emotion	1
Chapter 1	The Subterranean Role of Enactive Meaning: "PANIC," "SEEKING," and the Action Trajectories of Valuation	15
Chapter 2	Focusing, Enactivity, and the Opacity of Directionality	31
Chapter 3	We're Not in Behaviorism Anymore: Panksepp and Damasio on the Enactive Structure of Motivation	47
Chapter 4	The Extended Value System and the Place of Instrumentality	65
Chapter 5	Hannah Arendt and the Curious Nihilism of Grand-Scheme Value Systems	83
Chapter 6	The Symbolic Dimension: Gendlin's Embodied Symbolization and the Limits of the Static Image	103
Chapter 7	Total Failure of Inspiration: Lessons from the Sudden Murderer and the Family Annihilator	123
Chapter 8	Lessons from Alexithymia: The Role of Phenomenological Reflection in Understanding Enactive Motivation	137

Chapter 9	The Hot-Cold Meter: Unlocking Internal Conflict by Updating Hermeneutical Worldviews	151
Chapter 10	A. J. Ayer's Stepchildren: Relativism, Truth, and the Crisis of Postmodernity	173
Chapter 11	The Hermeneutic Circle: A Story of Internal Conflict	191
Conclusions	The Embodied Mind and the "That for the Sake of Which"	209
Notes		223
References		233
Index		247

Introduction

Interpreting Reality Presupposes an Understanding of Emotion

We are living at a time when masses of people embrace dangerous conspiracy theories by managing to allow a desire to believe something to determine the content of the belief itself. This phenomenon ebbs and flows, but in principle it is nothing new. Motivation determines selective attention, which in turn affects assessments of reality. As Maurice Merleau-Ponty (1945) highlighted, we tend to see only what we are looking for. The real question is how anyone ever avoids completely drowning in the self-deceptive pitfalls of this basic dynamic. It isn't enough merely to acknowledge the existence of such a process. We can learn a good bit about the structures of our own consciousness by understanding why this tendency surges more acutely in certain contexts than others.

But can the motivational interests that preshape our thinking in this way be treated as just one more specialized "problem area" for philosophy and psychology, an ancillary appendage subjected to previously established research methods? Or on the contrary, do our methods of understanding ourselves—and even of investigating the world we experience—already depend, at least partly, on an under-the-radar operation of motivating incentives that have already determined the focus of selective attention and inattention, the choice of methodologies, the shaping of language, and the backlog of tacit presuppositions? If we then use the resulting conceptual categories, worldviews, and methodologies to understand the value-driven processes that have already prefigured them, shouldn't we expect the outcome to be like trying to implode a building while standing on its roof?

Even in the empirical sciences—in fact, even in the neuropsychology of emotion itself—experimental operations are motivated by the researcher's theoretical and practical interests. Scientists then check to see whether the operations (that is, the scientists' own attempted actions) went as planned. Did the measurements yield the predicted outcomes, or did the world resist? That is how hypotheses are supposed to be supported or rejected. As boxers learn just as quickly, everyone has an action plan until they get punched in the mouth.

But the motivation to throw this or that punch is already presupposed before the resistance can be encountered. Twentieth-century behaviorists deliberately designed research paradigms—food pellets at the end of rats' mazes, and so on—to detect hedonistic motivations (and essentially *only* those). As a result, they failed to see that there can also be nonhedonistic ones, as psychologists now are increasingly taking into account. Ironically, the arguably nonhedonistic motivator most ignored by twentieth century psychologists was the one that drove the scientists themselves—the exploratory drive, which can't be explained by rewards or punishments other than the freedom to express the exploratory behavior itself. That view didn't fit the dominant twentieth-century theories, so the research paradigms—the rats' mazes, the reinforcement schedules, and so on—weren't designed to look for it.

In the same way, the attentional biases created by our current theoretical and practical interests may not seem obvious to us now, but at some future time they will be. Someday, graduate students will be asking "How could those primitive twenty-first century scientists have not seen XYZ?"—whatever XYZ turns out to be. And yet, even at that future time, the study of emotion and motivation still can't just proceed as a specialized practical application of presupposed scientific or philosophical beliefs and concepts because, then as now, those will have been prefigured by the motivated selective attention process itself. As hermeneutic philosophers emphasize, reality isn't just perceived; it is "interpreted" through the filter of concepts, tacit presuppositions, and research paradigms. Those are shaped by earlier selective attention, which in turn is guided by motivations.

One response to this situation might be to consider at the outset that any attempt to understand anything, including ourselves, is already a way of initiating a motivated action. The blind person's stick can reveal something of the shape of the world, but first the stick has to move. When we engage in any kind of action, whether experimentally or in everyday life, the world either resists or allows the actions; we then feel that we have learned something about the world's patterns of resistance. If the underlying motivation for action is a hammer, the world will appear as "nail" or "not-nail."

This kind of approach is now referred to as "enactivism."[1] The "en-" prefix is meant to emphasize activities that we enact from within, as opposed to direct or indirect *re*actions to external inputs (granted that this "we" was already shaped by previous interactions). If understanding begins with enactions, against which reality pushes back, then the pattern of the motivation for action will shape whatever we think or feel, depending on how reality resists our punches. The patterns of valuation that motivate actions play not only an important, but a foundational role in our view of the world. Motivation—and its experience through our emotions and values—would then need to be considered at the *beginning* of any theory of knowledge, not tacked on at the end.

How Motivation Preshapes Thinking: The Enactive Approach

The neuropsychologist Joseph LeDoux, who reputedly has a snake phobia, sometimes experiences intense fear at the sight of a stick on the ground. But it is a good thing, LeDoux emphasizes, that our emotions preshape perceptions in this way. In an interview, LeDoux remarked, "You're better off treating a stick as a snake than a snake as a stick" (Boyd 1997). Emotions motivate even perceptual activities, including the brain's imaging activities. Motivational interests, in principle, prefigure all types of cognition.

White supremacist and neo-Nazi recruits aren't just reacting to what they read on the internet. They are engaged in a lifelong, self-directed project of *seeking out* information that they hope will enable some emotionally meaningful life story to unfold—some action trajectory that they can feel has value. Propagandists understand that the most effective lie is the one the target *wants* to believe. The emotion isn't just a reaction. It seeks out avenues in the world through which the target's own imagined life trajectory, a trajectory of actions, could play out. The recruits are the agents of their own deception.

The idea of "enactivism" began to gather steam at the end of the twentieth century, when philosophers and psychologists increasingly acknowledged that they couldn't explain consciousness in terms of direct or indirect *re*actions to stimulus inputs, or even in terms of some "computational" transformation of the inputs. (By "consciousness" here, I don't mean some complicated or "higher-order" cognitive process, but only the kind of experience that we don't seem to remember having had during a dreamless sleep.[2]) Enactivists point out that if the brain simply *reacted* to the retinal impressions from a picture of a cat, the resulting imitation of the picture in the matter that happens to be inside the head wouldn't explain how we understand the meaning of the picture or how we have consciousness of it (not just a physical replica), any more than if we were to implant a paper copy of the photograph into the brain. A photo sitting in a picture frame isn't conscious, so why should a physical replica of the picture be any more conscious than the original picture just because the replica is implanted into someone's brain matter? We can ask the same question whether the picture in the head is a static or a "moving" one.

Ancient and medieval philosophers already understood this "homunculus problem." Even if there were a tiny person inside the brain who could look at the physical picture of the cat etched in our brain matter, we would still need an even smaller person inside *that* tiny person's brain to see the smaller picture etched inside that brain, and a still smaller one to look at the picture in that even smaller brain, and so on ad infinitum. There would still be no explanation for how we become *conscious* of the picture. No matter how sophisticated the neuropsychology of the perceptual stream of inputs and subsequent reactions and computations, some additional ingredient is needed for perceptual *consciousness*.

Enactivism offers an alternative to the receiving-of-input model. What if we think of the stream running the opposite way? When we try to execute purpose-directed actions, and then the world exercises its veto power, we sense the patterns of limitation for our own organismic activity. As intelligent creatures, we can also *imagine and anticipate* the resistances we *could* encounter *if* we tried certain actions. This book will explore that dynamic as well.

Prior to understanding any particular stimulus in the world, we already know that we are trying to do something—press a car's accelerator or run a rat through a maze. As a result of our actions, we learn something about the car or the rat's behavior. But what is harder is to understand how the motivations for these actions shape our selective attention, our perception, and ultimately our worldview. For that, we would need ways to understand *why* we are trying to press the accelerator or run the rat through the maze. Only in that way can we get at the actual meaning of the motivated action trajectories that guide the interpretation of reality.

Once we have tried to act, reality is what says Yes, No, or Maybe to all our best-laid plans—an idea with roots in early phenomenology as well as pragmatism.[3] To a great extent, we understand what we see in terms of whatever facilitates or blocks our self-motivated actions. When the actions fail, the pattern of the failure is important information.

Granted, a hammer hitting our knee to evoke a simple kneejerk reaction does lead to painful consciousness, even though the pain seems to be primarily just a reaction. But even this reaction presupposes the biological purposes of the living organism, which are enactive and purposeful, not merely reactive.

Moreover, a newborn infant hit in the knee doesn't "understand" the source of the hit.[4] Knowledge of objects is acquired through a gradual development of structural engagement with the world, which depends on infantile experimentation—that is, enaction-then-resistance, not just reception of "sense data." In an experiment by Held and Hein (1963), kittens were strapped into carts pulled by other kittens. Without their own self-initiated movement, the kittens in the carts remained "functionally blind," until their release from the carts gradually allowed action-based navigation of their environment. They then encountered the pattern of resistances and affordances (see also Held and Hein 1958 on hand-eye coordination).

Our own failure to walk through a wall suggests that the wall isn't a figment of our imagination. The pattern of resistances to a hand movement makes us feel the contours of the movement's fine-grained limits and thus the shape of the resisting object. Even in visual perception, our eyes first search (an action) for the kind of imagery that we already feel is relevant to our purposes, and then our eye movements (also actions) either encounter or fail to encounter what they are looking for.

The Mack and Rock (1998) "inattentional blindness" experiments illustrate this point. Sometimes we fail to see what we were looking for, and the eyes have to look again. The pattern of the light fails to yield to the initial searching pattern. As Merleau-Ponty says, "We must look in order to see" (1945, 247). On a daily or even hourly basis, we can receive auditory inputs without *hearing* what is being said. Attention itself is something we enact, not simply a reaction. Even involuntary attention is driven by motivational concerns of the living organism.

But an even more fundamental starting point of this book is to understand how enactive motivation presupposes value. If action requires motivation, this motivation in turn assumes that we value something. The recipient of internet disinformation is guided down the chosen rabbit holes by a valuational life plan—a long-term trajectory of action. To be sure, propagandists know how to provide the illusion of a sense of purpose. But the values that motivate the user's need for purpose, and the attitudes that determine what can count as purpose, are already there.

It follows that the enactive understanding of reality—that is, understanding grounded in the feedback from our actual or imagined actions—depends on value-laden emotions. With no valuing, there would be no enaction, as opposed to mere reaction. And with no enaction, no knowledge of the world.

The Murkiness of Motivation

The concept of self-organization makes the action-reaction distinction possible. In biological systems, the pattern of the whole doesn't simply get determined by the causal powers of the components; the reverse is also true. The system as a whole appropriates, rearranges, and constantly replaces and reproduces the micro-constituents it needs to subserve its continuing patterns of activity.[5] These dynamic patterns, and thus the resulting agent-directed selective attention, are at least as much about long-term, self-motivated action trajectories as about external events.

But understanding the ways that value and enaction shape how we see ourselves and the world is a difficult and sometimes mine-cluttered process. The meanings of the introspective feelings through which we try to discern motivation and valuation are opaque, complicated, and hard to interpret. They are seldom if ever about just what they superficially seem to be about. "Anger" "at" another motorist is more about where I'm going, why I chose to go there, and the general difficulty of ever getting anywhere (literally and figuratively) than it is about the other motorist *per se*. Those same feelings may also be about the "dark side" of human nature in general that I fantasize to be personified behind the wheel of that other car. And implicitly, I might be worried that this "dark side" also lurks within myself. An enactive approach to emotion and consciousness can offer a crucially needed perspective on the murky and complicated motivational impulses that determine how I see this or any other situation.

"Emotion" and "motivation" aren't simply synonymous, but they are intimately related. There *can* be motivation without emotion—or at least without any *conscious feeling* of emotion (paradoxically, we often don't know what we feel or we misinterpret it to ourselves). And yet our motivations could never be consciously felt except through emotion. The motivation for action can't be logically deduced, let alone understood, merely by observing the action and without some previous understanding of what the relevant emotions "are like."

Conversely, there could be no emotion without motivation. The meaning of each emotion depends on the motivation to act.

Some would prefer to confine the term "emotion" to a short list of innate, preprogrammed responses—"basic emotions," as they are called, such as rage, fear, curiosity, nurturing, or separation distress. What I mean here needs to be broader than that if all motivation for action is to be covered. It needs to mean something as inclusive as what musicians mean by "emotion" when they speak of emotional expression in music. It *can* include items on the "basic" list (whose length has actually increased in recent research).[6] But it can also include the more nuanced, specific pang of not quite nostalgia on hearing a Chopin Ballade or the felt sense that something is "off" in a relationship. It can include a nagging feeling that I have chosen a generally bad direction for my life or that I am alienated from my culture. And it can include the curiosity or interest that determines the focus of even perceptual or scientific attention. These emotions motivate actions, which in turn determine the shape of the feedback from reality, and *vice versa*.

What makes the "basic" emotions special isn't so much their more-or-less endogenous and mutually independent status (more on that later). What is more important is that they express some of the most inevitable aspects of what is required if one is to be the kind of creature that we are. Try though we may, we can't exist other than as a conscious, self-conscious, radically finite, and necessarily interrelational form of life, and with often-frustratingly limited power and duration—including even the power to resist or escape threats to our literal survival and the need to connect with those whose interactions partly define us. These ontological necessities include inevitably emotional issues. Concerns about such inescapable parameters of our existence infect and inform the more specific feelings triggered by everyday situations in complicated ways that usually don't announce themselves in a superficial reading of an experience.

In short, feelings toward a barroom drunk are about my continuing life trajectory, not just about the drunk. Am I angry at this particular bully or at the first older boy who ever tried to bully me on the playground—or at larger facts of life that still bully me? Or are there still larger issues about why people bully each other in general? The feelings can at least partly reflect general frustrations with my ability to interact with others or sometimes with the society and culture at large. Quite a few of these already-existing areas of concern can be found unexpectedly "underneath" the superficial reading of what a feeling is about.

The *inter*active constitution of personal identity doesn't prevent action from being self-initiated. Many enactivists also emphasize interactivity (e.g., Eugene Gendlin 2018; Anya Daly 2021; Mark Bickhard 2000; Shaun Gallagher 2020; and others who will be discussed here). To be sure, Gendlin stresses that our emotional feelings, when carefully focused on, can crucially say something about what is going on in the interpersonal environment. A teacher's feeling ill at ease in the classroom might indicate, on reflection, that a particular student is having problems outside the classroom that need attention—or that the student needs more challenge, or less. Or it may signal that some of the students are feeling confused, or simply bored.

But this interactive dimension of the meaning of an emotionally felt sense doesn't erase the fact that, as a teacher, my sensitivity to the students' needs is also intertwined with feelings about a decision I made much earlier in life, to devote a good part of my life's energy to helping educate students. The current emotion has its meaning in terms of this *overall project* and the values that originally motivated it.

Am I failing the value to which I had committed myself? Was that commitment overly simplistic to begin with? Do I lack the power and capability needed to facilitate those presumably worthwhile objectives? Can any of us ever have enough power and capability in these regards? The immediate emotion poses all those questions and more. We can separate out our specific felt sense of each of the questions and focus on them one at a time, but they all figure into the initial emotion, and their meaning depends on the larger context—the overall trajectory of action.

General underlying valuational "themes" of this kind help constitute the meaning of each seemingly discrete experience along the way. Frustration with my boss is also a frustration with the *inevitable existential fact* that "everyone has a boss"—and multiple bosses, in the important sense. When we play the game of "Ain't It Awful!" with our friends, we are acknowledging that this inescapable common theme is part of what each of us individually feels. When we lose someone to death, we also grieve the *general huge fact* that reality is such as to require the person's death—the overall theme of loss, destruction, decay, and disintegration. Everyone we have ever lost, or might lose, factors into the feeling.

When these broader "existential" themes become too troubling, we are tempted simply to repress or minimize them. But if they are actually important underlying referents of our everyday experiences, then they surely must affect our interpretations of reality in major ways. For example, can I empathize with the plight of the poor while maintaining the illusion that I myself *have more power* in the ultimate scheme of things *than any of us ever realistically could have*—that I or anyone else, despite the facticity of circumstances, always have the power to "pull ourselves up by our bootstraps"? To be sure, we are the agents of our own action plans; but reality inevitably pushes back—for all of us.

The Problem of Consciousness

Modern psychology has tended to minimize the role of emotional *consciousness,* and in fact consciousness in general, by treating it as if it were, as Thomas Natsoulas (1993) puts it, a mere "appendage" to an underlying physical process. William James famously quipped that "We feel sorry because we cry" (1884, 190). But this clever turnabout doesn't refute the priority of emotion and motivation. We both feel sorry and cry (or choke up, or some other physical enactment)—all in one stroke, as two dimensions of the same process, whether we emphasize the "physical" or "mental" dimension.

James wants to prioritize the physical dimension. But even in that realm, *emotional* brain areas are the earliest to be activated—prior to the motor areas that would be necessary for an overt movement like crying. Emotional areas are even activated prior to the perceptual areas when the brain receives a perceptual input (for example, see Carl Aurell 1984, 1989; Antonio Damasio 1999; Jaak Panksepp 1998; Ellis 2005).[7] Regardless of how this problem of the "physical"/"mental" connection is resolved, what is clear is that voluntary actions, and even some involuntary ones (indirectly), have to be motivated. That is why we call them actions rather than just automatic reactions. The "We feel sorry because we cry" comment itself is motivated—by a desire to make the understanding of emotional consciousness easier than it is.

Traditionally, both empirical-scientific and philosophical approaches to motivation and emotion have tended to explain each occurring emotion primarily in relation to the external event that supposedly elicits it, as if the emotion were simply a reaction to a stimulus. As a result, each specific emotion appears superficially as if it were "about" or "directed at" the specific trigger. The enactivist approach advocated in this book emphasizes the opposite directionality. As Michael Slote (2014) aptly reminds us, the trigger is only the tip of an iceberg because emotions originate from within the intricate self-organizing process that defines a conscious and valuing creature, even though that process is also previously *inter*active.

Even grief depends on enactive understandings. Empathizing with the person is empathizing with their capacity to act. When we lose them, we feel the cancellation of their every future action. The person can never again throw a baseball, tease someone with a nickname, or walk through a door with a bottle of wine. We grieve every one of these now no-longer-possible actions. We lose all the enactions with which we had previously empathized, and all possible future ones. Staring at the "lifeless" photo, we feel the frustrated need to empathically imagine the person's actions.

I want to argue that the most basic emotions that shape our experience are *motivations for enactive processes,* and consequently they are about how we (or those with whom we empathize) could or couldn't act, including long and sometimes convoluted sequences of actions, as motivated by the meanings through which we define an ongoing action trajectory, not just a reaction to an immediate situation. This enactive sequence then shapes the feedback from worldly resistance that informs consciousness.

The implications of this point are amazingly ubiquitous. Even empirical-scientific methods with their "experimental operationalizations" (operations = actions) are a superstructure that depends on a more basic phenomenological starting point—an understanding of the motivation-action-selective-attention-then-feedback process. Phenomenology, simply put, is a philosophical and psychological discipline that doesn't simply introspect, but rather tries to refine our introspective methods to get a less superficial view of the ways in which our own presupposition-laden conscious processes inevitably affect (and somewhat distort) what we see and understand. It also acknowledges that the introspective process itself is distorted by this same interpretive problem, leading to the "hermeneutic circle"—the circular nature of self-interpretation.

Thomas Kuhn's (1962/1964) approach to science emphasizes the way theory-driven motivations prefigure the choice of experimental operations and therefore to some extent the results. Don Ihde's philosophy of technology (1998) makes this motivational dimension even more explicit. Ihde argues that we develop technologies that enable us to see primarily what the technologies were meant to look for.

For instance, consider the attempt to look for "fixes" to the problem of internet disinformation. Many internet algorithms are motivated by the designers' preference for eliciting a "Gee whiz!" response so that the user will keep clicking and reposting. The result is an avalanche of disinformation, since false stories are more likely to seem sensational. Even if a technical fix to this problem were possible, the designers might not be sufficiently *motivated to look for it.* Or their conceptual tools may not *enable* them to look for it. A resulting consensus that no technical fix is possible would then be seriously misleading. Similarly, if researchers for a drug company are to see the negative side-effects of the company's new drug, they have to be motivated to look for them—motivated, for example, by potential lawsuits, government oversight, or ethical principles.

Since the chosen experimental operations are partly driven by selective attention (which in turn is motivated), scientific understanding is not only limited, but also somewhat distorted, to an extent that is not fully determinable. The choice of what to measure and how to measure it depends on the scientist's imagination about possible intervening variables, the choice as to which theories to test, which operational definitions to use, which research projects to pursue, and perhaps most crucial, which potentially contaminating control variables to watch out for. Science presupposes imagination at every turn.

In the study of consciousness and emotion, the misleading effects of a purely empirical approach are magnified. David Chalmers (1995) and Joseph Levine (1983) have demonstrated clearly why we can't explain consciousness just by means of empirical knowledge about the brain. The fact that consciousness correlates with a certain brain process can never explain, even in principle, *why* it correlates with certain kinds of physical processes, and not with others. This "hard problem of consciousness" (Chalmers) or "explanatory gap" (Levine) isn't resolvable by empirical methods.

But that doesn't mean the study of consciousness should just write off the empirical methods. Science is an extension of ordinary enaction followed by pushback in the attempt to organize the realm of phenomena—things as they "appear" in the sense that they can and can't be affected by us. Scientists are routinely "punched in the mouth" by reality as their experimental operations fail. As Gene Gendlin was fond of remarking, we all depend on the science of aeronautics when we fly to our conferences. Consciousness is embodied in a world not dictated by our subjectivity. Merleau-Ponty too shows that the empirical sciences can help with understanding our motivated engagements with the world, if science is taken as an extension of the everyday process of action then resistance, guided by admittedly motivated selective attention.[8] Phenomenologists often refer to this world understood through action then resistance as the "life world" (e.g., Husserl 1936/1970).

Looking at a few crucial things about the brain's workings can be suggestive and potentially helpful. In this book, I use phenomenological methods—especially Gendlin's "focusing" method—but with some relevant ideas from recent research on the emotional brain. This research is increasingly consistent with an enactive view of how consciousness and emotion work. In his later philosophical works, Gendlin took an explicitly enactivist position (Gendlin 2017, 2018).

The central point I will try to make is that focusing carefully on any particular experiential event, if pursued down to its bottom level—the level of motivated attention and inattention—leads in the direction of concerns and values common to conscious and thinking creatures as such, and involving what existentialists have called the "meaning" of our values and actions. In Heidegger's terms, some of these emotional themes can even reflect "ontological" features of our form of being—themes that are inevitable aspects of what it means to be the kind of being that we are. The fact that "everyone has multiple bosses" reflects an existential theme—and to some extent an "ontological" one[9]—that affects everyone's emotions, given our inevitable interdependence. Even emotions about contingent situations—for example, antisemitism, homophobia, racism or sexism—also arise from the broad existential themes of alienation, the finiteness of personal power and significance, and the inescapable dependence on social relatedness.

There is never any apodictic certainty with these themes. We always discover more and more layers of meaning, and we often need to revise our previous understandings of a given "felt sense" in any specific context. But dispelling unwarranted presuppositions about what emotional feelings are "supposed to mean," or what they have typically been assumed to be "about," already moves us closer to their truth than we were before.

I will show that this focusing process is motivated by one of our most important driving emotions—the exploratory drive—which can be experienced subjectively, and its empirical correlates can also be found if we look. The exploratory drive motivates the attempt to understand our world, as it does for any cat or dog. For humans, it automatically puts into play a searching process that makes us want to prevent the reality of what our own emotions are about from remaining completely hidden. Yet we are simultaneously driven by competing emotions that can make us prefer not to know. These inner conflicts are always at play.

The reality that we try to understand in this book includes the most basic value-action directions that are always presupposed by any immediate "response." To understand the fundamental value issues at the bottom of the enactive process, we have to begin by studying motivation and emotion. As Frank Jackson (1986) famously argued, a scientist observing someone's brain can't know what the person feels unless the scientist already knows something of what such emotions "are like." The scientist would have to rely on earlier correlational studies, but those correlations themselves would already have depended on previous understanding of that with which the observable brain processes were being correlated—that is, the subjective feelings. The more flawed our methods of emotional reflection are, the more we end up with distorted ideas not only regarding what the emotions are really about, but also the meaning of our ongoing action trajectories, and in some cases why there is a shortage of meaning.

These enactive meanings can be both negative and positive. I will argue that the positive ones are needed to inspire action at the most basic level. The resulting value systems include but aren't limited to the long chains of "instrumentalities"—means toward other ends—that take up most of our attention.

So much energy is taken up with these instrumentalities that the experience of the more fundamental values that motivate the actions tends to get buried by the mountains of instrumentalities. The long chains of instrumental actions needed for a legislator to achieve a valued outcome might occlude or even contradict the original values toward which those outcomes were supposed to have been instrumental. Voters too might forget the original values that led to the long chains of instrumentalities that superficially *seem* to be what their political sentiments are about.

At the same time, we also can't avoid the fact that meaningful trajectory requires defining meaning in terms of the instrumentalities as well. In the lived world, the most basic values require instrumental ones in their service. We can't understand the structures of value that define these complexities in an action trajectory unless we can go beyond simply noting which concurrent event happens to have triggered a particular emotion.

Emotion is sometimes relegated to the status of a vestige from a more primitive stage of evolution. But can the elaborate growth of the prefrontal cortex now allow us to guide our lives with cognitive, rational thought, while begrudgingly placating the pesky remnants of that earlier stage of development? That view is already completely refuted by what we have said so far. Rational methods can help with constructing instrumental paths that presumably are meant to serve some purpose; but without motivation they can't provide the purposes themselves nor inspire us to pursue any purpose. And as the above observations suggest, rationality itself depends on emotion.

With no emotion, which reflects motivation, there is no purpose—hence no action and no enactive understanding of reality.

This last point doesn't make values into arbitrary emotional whims. The exploratory drive—an emotion system—makes us curious to know the truth (as best we can), aside from any ulterior rewards or punishments. Mounting evidence suggests that the exploratory drive operates independently of any emotional concern other than the inspiration to explore *per se* (e.g., Jaak Panksepp 1996, chapter 8; Ellis 2005, 2018; Davis and Panksepp 2018; Robert White 1959). But this exploratory motivation—this endogenous "love of truth," as David Hume (1740) called it—is in conflict with other emotions, and the study of emotion is needed to explore these inner conflicts as well.

This book tries to get at the bottom level of enactive meaning, the level at which our already ongoing emotional purposes define the meaning of what we are trying to do at each moment in the trajectory of our lives. The sequence in which this underlying trajectory directs selective attention then determines the contours of our perception of reality.

Philosophical and literary hermeneutics, the study of how we interpret the world—including our culture and literature—requires focusing on these underlying motivational meanings. Most crucially of all, if a relatively independent exploratory drive weren't one of our emotion systems, reality itself could be completely reinterpreted and misrepresented in the service of other emotions—as in the case of the Q-Anon and other elaborate conspiracy theories that spread through social media. Investigating the inner emotional conflicts in play here is fundamental to any hope for sorting truth from fantasy in any arena. Whether our interest is in epistemology, the social sciences, literary criticism, psychotherapy, fundamental ontology, the philosophy of science, cognitive theory, the understanding of consciousness, or even cultural studies and political philosophy, the study of emotion and motivation needs to be at the center of what we do.

I freely admit that beginning with emotion doesn't mean there aren't still problems with the "hermeneutic circle"—the circularity of self-interpretation. If we interpret reality through distorted lenses, we can't correct the distortions simply by self-reflection, which passes through the same distorted lenses. This circularity problem has to be posed for any theory of knowledge. Like anyone else, we will need to address the hermeneutic circle in this book. The point for now is that emotion needs to be taken into account at the most foundational level of any attempt to understand the world and ourselves, especially including all the disciplines just mentioned.

Chapter 1

The Subterranean Role of Enactive Meaning

"PANIC," "SEEKING,"
and the Action Trajectories of Valuation

Enactive Meaning and the Existential A Priori

There can be no doubt that my annoyance with the overbearing drunk at the bar isn't just about the drunk at the bar. The proof is that at other times I would have paid no attention. There were other drunks at other times, not perceptibly different from this one. The difference must come from what I bring with me this time. I know he must either instantiate or symbolize something more important—some larger, more daunting issue, something nagging enough to get my attention. Why this time?

Am I powerless to pay the kind of attention he both demands and blocks? Or is it my general powerlessness in many other such situations that gets triggered? Am I sympathizing with the awkward position of his poor companion? Or is it that, like his companion, I'm helplessly stuck with this uninvited crowing in the same way that I'm stuck with all the other things in my life that constantly try to trap, oppress, and maybe sometimes bully me? Plenty of those things are inescapably beyond my control—or beyond anyone's control. Was this ubiquitous theme of "being bullied" already festering? Or is it my inevitable helplessness to prevent others from being bullied; or the all-too-constant detours into distractions as irrelevant as this pointless situation? Do I see in him my own directionless stumbling through life? After all, what am I doing here at this time of night?

I can discover layer after layer of these implicit meanings, until I reach the most basic and all-pervasive ones, the ones all the specific everyday feelings presuppose. I've run into some of them before: the ones that continually recur and can't be escaped or denied. Exploring this one ridiculous episode inevitably, sooner or later, leads to those questions about the larger felt sense of a forward-moving or stalling-out life trajectory—or maybe a shortage of it altogether.

Sometimes those most fundamental motivational issues, the big ones presupposed by the little ones, can be thought of as "existential" since they literally define our mode of existence. I call them "enactive" meanings because in my view they don't just originate from something external—from someone's drunken insult, or even from general ontological structures of reality; they are primarily *en*-acted from within a valuing creature facing its inevitable smallness and finiteness in the big, daunting world. They don't just refer to the specific trigger. They arise from the overall roadmap of what we want to do with our life energy—how we intend to act, not just react. Some of these most fundamental enactive concerns are also reflected in what neuroscientists call "basic emotions"—emotions without which we can't exist as the form of life that we are.

I notice that when his alpha-male ramblings take a bullying *political* turn, an internal "Not this again!" hints that something must be reaching further. The "again" suggests the further. Preserving American democracy against authoritarian forces is a necessarily collective project, and my own being is already partly defined by this unavoidable interdependence; but what can the tiny creature that is "I" do about it?

This theme of relative powerlessness hovers under the surface every time reality pushes back. Every reminder of the spread of disinformation enflames an already-existing frustration. Every effort against it feels like playing whack-a-mole. Just as with a frustrated infant whose arms are being bound, an underlying feeling of the inevitable limitations of my own action potential also lurks somehow beneath this current situation.

To be sure, the emotion also provides *inter*-active information—in this case, about my unrequested relationship with this particular singular personage, like it or not. But beyond that, my frustration with his aggressiveness also includes, among other things, the *always-presupposed theme* of finiteness, limited power, and other enactive concerns that are already ongoing. Our definitive interactivity with others doesn't erase the theme of finiteness, but in some ways further highlights it.

In short, there is still relevance for Ludwig Binswanger's idea of an "existential a priori": "*Prior to*" the specific instance of the drunk at the bar (who isn't blocking me in any tangible way), bigger and more important obstacles have long since been looming, sounding general categories of alarm, all-pervasive "themes," which then are both exemplified and symbolized by his belligerence. These behind-the-scenes meanings stubbornly endure from one experience to another and partly shape my interpretation of each new episode (see Binswanger 1963).

The idea of an underlying "meaning" for our trajectories of action might sound like a quaint anachronism in today's intellectual climate. It can be objected that the overall purpose of our various strivings tends to remain mostly hidden, as in Heidegger's elusive "that for the sake of which" in *Being and Time*. But we can feel implicitly that there are always further-reaching aims and values guiding everyday interests—directly or indirectly. In the moment, I pay attention to the short-term of what I'm trying to do—get home or get to work on time or avoid the loud drunk's rants. But those goals' overall place in my sense of enactive meaning, or a shortage of it, is always presupposed by each of them. The purposes of action presuppose their own purposes, which serve other purposes, and so on—but the chain can't go on *ad infinitum*. An overall and further-reaching trajectory is always presupposed by each of those more specific purposes and how we understand them.

If emotions were just reactions, I would feel pretty much the same toward every aggressive drunk—not just the one who now enigmatically triggers something. On the contrary, if the drunk hadn't triggered it, something else eventually would. It would have found another occasion. The sum of motivational momentum is always already there, engaged in trying to do things, prior to any outward perception. Purposeful processes—for example, nurturing, social bonding, sexuality, exploration, and worrying about all of the above—are things we are going to do regardless of our circumstances, with or without any ulterior reward or punishment. No external "stimulus" creates their importance.

It is now almost a truism that motivation affects how we perceive things. But we need to go deeper than just acknowledging this fact. To understand our interpretations and distortions of reality, we need to get at the dynamics of this process specifically and in granular detail. We can't just think of emotion as a nuisance whose influence should be eliminated from perception. As we saw in the introduction to this book, emotion, motivation, and selective attention have their say at the bottom layer of any understanding of reality—whether accurate *or* distorted.

New Resources for Understanding Motivational Meaning

To get a better handle on the enactive and not just reactive nature of motivational and value-laden meanings, we need to understand how emotional feelings are grounded in the always already ongoing purposes of our action trajectories. To include this important grounding in the trajectory of actions, I want to apply three main avenues of recent work:

First, new emotion research presents a different picture from the behavioristic approaches of the twentieth century (although psychology had its dissidents even then[1]). "Neural plasticity" and "the brain that changes itself" (e.g., Norman Doige 2007; Walter Freeman 2012) stretch beyond the old stimulus-response models. Emotion systems like nurturing, social bonding, and an endogenous exploratory drive are increasingly taken as self-motivating, not learned through pleasure-and-pain reinforcements (Jaak Panksepp 2000, 2011; Antonio Damasio 1999; Nico Frijda 2006). Intelligent animals are hellbent on exploring, independently of any reward or punishment other than the behavior itself.

To say a mother "learns" to nurture as a result of some "reinforcement" beyond the behavior itself is now taken as absurd. The *non-hedonism* that Panksepp and others now ascribe to endogenous emotion systems like nurturing and exploration helps distinguish emotional meaning from mere pleasure or reward-seeking. Panksepp, for instance, spent his life running research labs to study "basic emotion" systems, most of which don't operate according to hedonistic reinforcement theory (e.g., see Panksepp 1998, 147–50). Basic emotion behaviors—for example, exploration and nurturing—tend to be self-reinforcing; the behavior *is* the reinforcement. These results concur with those of Freeman, Damasio, Frijda, and others to be discussed later. Each of Panksepp's endogenous motivational systems uses its own unique combination of brain processes, not dependent on any external reward.

In experiential terms, motivation to act isn't based only on the rewards of happiness, pleasure, or contented satiation. Altruism, romantic love, the nurturing of the mother, the spirit of adventure, serious musical accomplishment, to name a few examples, thrive even amidst the most miserable impoverishment. The most important art form to emerge from the United States—jazz—was invented primarily by slaves.

A second resource is the "enactivist" trend in recent cognitive theory, which offers concrete tools for thematizing meaning in terms of the action-value connection. We understand things not by making inferences from the *re*-actions of our nervous systems, but in terms of the patterns in which objects and situations afford and block motivated actions—*en*-actions as opposed to re-actions. These "affordances"—possibilities for how we could act—shape our understanding.

Enactivists explore the way even seemingly passive conscious processes like perception *proactively* seek out these action affordances of a situation (Francisco Varela et al. 1991; Shaun Gallagher 2006, 2020; Natika Newton 1996, 2000, 2017). This trend can actually be traced to Maurice Merleau-Ponty (1942, 1945), Ulric Neisser (1976), and J. J. Gibson (1986). Perception itself is motivated, not only in the sense of selective attention, but also in the sense that, in the timing of brain processes, activation of emotional brain areas always literally precedes activation of the perceptual areas when a visual stimulus is presented (Carl Aurell 1984, 1989; Michael Posner 1990; Ellis 2005). In "inattentional blindness" experiments (Mack and Rock 1998), subjects tend to see only what they direct attention to; when instructed to pay attention to a certain image, they can remain unaware of other objects even if presented near the center of their visual field.

Readers can directly experience this effect by trying out the "change blindness" demonstrations available on the internet. Selective attention and inattention can dramatically influence what we do and don't see. An emotionally meaningful image (such as a smiling-face emoji) literally attracted more of the Mack and Rock subjects' visual attention than a less meaningful one (such as a sideways smiling face or a neutral face). In the change blindness demos, something glaringly conspicuous in the image keeps changing, but we stare at the image for quite some time without noticing the change.

The white supremacist recruit not only pays selective attention but actively *seeks out* information relevant to the ongoing attempt to define meaning, flailing though it is—just as my attention to the drunk's behavior connects implicitly to my own ongoing motivations. Something about the situation appeals to some underlying motivation, whether marginal or more significant, or I wouldn't pay attention.

Enactivists also investigate the "mirror neuron system" that enables me to perceive the drunk as such. I have to understand him by imagining myself as *doing* what he is doing, involving the motor and premotor systems of the brain. He and everything he symbolizes are grasped in terms of both his and my own action affordances—the way the world affords possible actions (see Newton 1996, chapter 6, on "Understanding Persons"; also Colombetti 2014). This empathic mirroring process will be important for us here because, as we will see, empathy is one of the main components of the necessarily interactive ways that we establish the values that ground enactive meaning.

The third resource I will use here is Gendlin's "focusing" concept (Gendlin 1978, 2000, 2018), which breaks new ground toward avoiding unwarranted presuppositions when we introspect into the meaning of our own conscious and emotional processes. Gendlin proposes specific steps toward going deeper into what a feeling or felt-sense is "about"—a trickier thing than many would assume. Gendlin's approach has received support not only from rigorous introspective methods, but also hard-nosed empirical studies on emotional language in psychotherapy (Donald Kiesler 1973, 2017). It correlates with successful versus unsuccessful therapeutic outcomes (Marjorie Klein et al. 1969; Gendlin 1978), with tests of "emotional awareness" (Kiesler 1973, 2017), and even with certain brain processes (see Peter Afford 2012). But the real validation comes from introspection: We can feel the emotional change when we direct certain kinds of questions toward a given feeling.

My thesis is that focusing on specific emotions, if we stick with it, always eventually leads to underlying enactive concerns about broad life directions, including "existential" issues. Not only is my anger not really about the drunk at the bar; "anger" doesn't even begin to name how I feel with any accuracy.

Some of the most necessary themes of our always underlying struggle to define enactive meaning are ones that we all share. They are aspects of any conscious, thinking, and valuing creature who also is finite and dependent on other valuing creatures and social institutions needed to help create directionalities of meaning. Whatever else our emotions and motivations are about, they are also about these broad and inevitable preconditions for our existence and the problems they inexorably entail. Specific events both *instantiate* and *symbolize* these general thematic issues related to the broader striving to construct value systems capable of inspiring us to action.

In *Curious Emotions* (2005), I went into some detail about how a complex biological self-organizing system can give rise to emotion and emotional consciousness. In this volume, I want to focus on the conscious dimension itself. The crucial point for now is that action, unlike *re*-action, presupposes value. And value implies an underlying sense of ongoing enactive meaning. If paying attention is an action—the product of a living system—then our motivated action proclivities and their values always pre-exist our interest in any specific "input." A further complication of the enactivist approach is the paradox that self-organized action also presupposes an *inter*-active definition of what we already are. In the terms used by enactivists like Anya Daly (2021),[2] Mark Bickhard (2000), Gendlin (2018), Newton (1996, 2017), Colombetti (2014), and Gallagher (2020), we understand our world in terms of how we could act relative to it; yet those authors also acknowledge that the "me" that acts is also inevitably already an interaction.

Understanding the Meaning of Meaning through Shortages of It

One way to work toward a broad definition of the underlying sense of ongoing enactive meaning is in terms of what its shortage looks like. As in neurology, when some component has been removed, we can understand some its functions by noticing what *doesn't* happen.

Viktor Frankl, in the "Logotherapy" section of *Man's Search for Meaning*, tells of a psychiatric patient whose special-needs child prevents her from pursuing the grand career outcomes she thought could bring her happiness. Frankl asks her to imagine looking back over her life from the age of eighty-five and to imagine that she did enjoy career success and that her life has been a happy one. Suddenly a shift occurs. She realizes that what her life lacks is not happiness, but meaning, in some difficult-to-articulate sense. She then comes to feel that caring for her special-needs child is already offering her life much of the needed meaning. Not that happiness is no longer important, but she now realizes that she has been overlooking the difference between happiness and meaning.

If we acknowledge the facticity of women's economic conditions in the late 1940s, we can appreciate the difficulty of the choices she had to make. In that context, her reassessment of the options illustrates that when the foundation of a building is shifted at the basement level, all the super-structures get changed as well. Such a seismic shift can feel both frightening and rewarding at the same time.

This always-presupposed bottom-level sense of value-directed meaning—or a shortage of it—can be as *preconscious and implicit* as it is ubiquitous. Christian Picciolini (2020), a private detective and investigative journalist specializing in white supremacist cults, reports the case of a seventeen-year-old girl so confused about what her feelings were about that she chose her hate group almost completely arbitrarily. She first wanted to travel to Syria and join the Islamic State of Iraq and the Levant (ISIL), but she settled for a US-based neo-Nazi group because it seemed like a "less dusty endeavor" (18; her own words, not Picciolini's). The group's actual ideology, as disparate as ISIL's vision of the "final battle of Armageddon" and the neo-Nazis' quest for white supremacy, seemed almost incidental—a malleable vehicle to act out emotional issues without really knowing why they were there or what they were about.

Another case describes a young war veteran already mired in amorphous feelings of being "rejected" and "left behind" in some vague sense, long before he was exposed to propaganda purporting that non-white ethnicities "trying to replace him" were the real cause of his feelings (45ff.). In both cases, confusion about a pre-existing void of meaning already seeded the ground for the propaganda.

In fact, Picciolini mentions that fully *three-fourths* of his white supremacist cases referred for psychological counseling were diagnosed with an "autistic" condition (75). Why the connection to autism? Many autistic people suffer from *alexithymia*—the literal inability to know what one's own feelings are about, or sometimes even to feel emotions as such, even when the emotions are occurring and motivating behavior (this correlation is documented by Hill et al. 2004; Lombardo et al. 2007; Griffin et al. 2016; Bird and Cook 2016). The correlation doesn't mean all or even most autistic people are alexithymic, but clearly a significant subset are alexithymic enough to elicit the "autism" diagnosis.

Picciolini writes, "Extremism, regardless of whether it's motivated by a political, religious, or social doctrine, flourishes when a critical mass of people believe their lives are becoming meaningless, displaced, or disempowered" (xxi). The "meaning" dimension becomes the focus of his understanding of young people seduced into the white supremacist subculture: "Crashing into life's potholes . . . isn't solely what diverts a person toward extremism. Potholes *and* an imperiled search for identity, community, and purpose are what send us swerving" (17).

To understand the attraction to terrorist cults, white supremacist groups, Nazism, and other such totalitarianisms, we need to understand how the targeted recruit is purposefully *using* the cult and its disinformation highways to pursue a *self-directed* project of trying to define the meaning of a life path. The project is being played out in the face of extreme versions of precursor feelings that we all share to varying degrees: the sense of being "irrelevant," "disrespected," "a powerless cog in a vast, purposeless machine," "just another rat in the rat-race"—all of which, as Hannah Arendt (1968) suggests, can trigger an existential emptiness and a desperate feeling that we need some "Grand Scheme" value (as I call them), something so Grand as to instrumentally define the value of us mere mortals "in the Grand Scheme of Things"—to magically fill the void of meaning.

But as Simone de Beauvoir implies in *The Ethics of Ambiguity*, these Grand Scheme values soon run into a roadblock because they can't supply the needed meaning if they reduce human beings to merely instrumental values in service to the Grand Scheme. That would work against the feeling that being a human being has value in itself—intrinsic rather than merely instrumental value.

In fact, such a Grand Scheme immediately sets itself in a *zero-sum competition* against us. If valuing persons were allowed to embody value *for their own sake*, then they would have this same value whether they serve the Grand Scheme or not. Conversely, the more we invest meaning in our own and others' *instrumentality* toward a Grand Scheme value system, the less we feel that the *intrinsic* value of valuing creatures *as such* is enough—others as well as ourselves.

Moreover, the more we need to justify ourselves in instrumental terms, the more our fundamentally defining finiteness and relative powerlessness (in the "Grand Scheme" of things) get in the way of being able to make enough instrumental difference. To paraphrase Socrates in the *Euthyphro*, what can one small mortal do to help the all-powerful gods achieve what they can't already achieve without our help? We then wade precariously into the incoherent quicksands that can swallow the sense of enactive meaning itself. And yet, at the same time, *there is no way to avoid* orienting our trajectory of actions around their instrumental purposes. Even merely trying to stay out of the way of others' activities requires tacitly making ourselves instrumental toward those activities. A nonvote is still a vote—a vote to advance the goals of those who do vote.

These underlying questions about meaning involve conditions without which none of us can exist as who or what we are—conscious and unavoidably interdependent creatures with necessarily finite power, ability, and duration, and also with a need for an everyday minimal amount of inspiration to energize complex action directions, despite feeling that we are small and somewhat insignificant specs in the cosmos. Each new concern, besides presenting its own unique challenges, also either exemplifies or symbolizes these most basic and all-pervasive ones. It can be argued (and I will argue in a later chapter) that even our neurophysiology has evolved around them.

I don't say that these universally human issues are always the main referents of everything we feel. But I do want to acknowledge that they are always part of the meaning. And in an important sense they are the most foundational elements because the more specific feelings always include and depend on them. They are the ones inevitably implied as part of what is under the surface of every motivation. They are reflected in some of the most endogenous, "basic" emotion systems that we humans have evolved.

Panksepp, for example, identifies an entire relatively independent emotion system devoted to "separation distress," which expresses our inevitable need for interrelatedness, which also includes a basic need to experience the intrinsic value of others—the classic example being disruption of the mother's need for the infant. This same endogenous emotion system is the main substrate of the "sadness" dimension of clinical depression (Panksepp et al. 2014). In that same study, the "lethargy" component of depression correlates with suppression of a different emotion system—a separate "seeking" system, which includes an endogenous exploratory drive. These basic emotions reflect the fact that a need to explore and venture forth is a potent force, but so also are an always challenged need for interrelatedness, a general shortage of power, and a paucity of personal importance in the scheme of things, all playing a role in each specific situation.

The same challenges, in one guise or another, are *narcissistic* as well as existential ones. The normal narcissism in all of us (even without a "narcissistic personality disorder") needs to feel at least somewhat in control of our destiny. We therefore don't like to feel small, disregarded, or insignificant on the grand stage. Narcissistic disturbance—and even normal narcissism—reflects a struggle with the traditional existential issues: our inescapable finiteness and radical dependence on community and interpersonal relations; our consequent need to attract the often-fickle *attention* of others; our limited power, regardless of the specific example; and of course, the shortness of life.

But what is often missed about "existential" concerns is that the negative issues just mentioned also interact with equally potent *positive* ones. The desire to create something, to explore, to experience the intrinsic value of being, as instantiated in others as well as ourselves and our own life activities—reflected, for example, in our endogenous social bonding and exploratory drives—those are also existential values that, until recently, tended to be neglected in intellectual and scientific work, although they are always implicit in literary fiction.

To deny the significance of these inevitable and ubiquitous issues leads to the kind of absurdity once expressed by Antonin Scalia from the

US Supreme Court bench. Against the argument that the death penalty often involves execution of innocent people, he countered with the quip, "For the believing Christian, death is no big deal" (Wilentz 2002). Scalia's offhanded dismissal might sound less clever to the outnumbered soldier in the mine-cluttered outpost—believing Christian or not.

Someone might argue that the problems of death and finiteness are less important for some cultural traditions than others and for people with certain religious beliefs. But then why do soldiers who plan to live in heaven after death still fight just as hard for the survival of themselves and their buddies? When our friends are under attack, why not just say, "For the believing Christian [or Buddhist or Muslim], death is no big deal"? Obviously, we know that death is a serious impediment to what needs to be done in *this* life—the project of defining meaning—regardless of what happens in heaven. A South Asian soldier who might believe in multiple lives still fights to avoid death. We still know implicitly that we are finite and limited by the various constraints of finiteness, within which we have to define whatever meaning we do define. I can't vote, campaign, or teach my son how to kick a football from heaven or from the next life.

An even more crucial existential necessity is that we inescapably need to feel some positive value *strongly enough* to inspire us to action despite the negative emotions arising from the limitations just listed. Whatever meets this need for a minimal, baseline level of "inspiration" is what gets us through the day. As Panksepp and colleagues (2014) put it, the ability to maintain some continuous, under-the-radar feeling of "enthusiasm," if only at a relatively modest level, is required even to avoid clinical depression.

I plan to show that these basic existential questions about the "meaning" of our potential for action are always among the larger themes that prefigure the smaller, more specific emotional responses to particular situations—drunks at bars and the like. Those larger issues are crucially included in what I mean by constant or "tonic" underlying enactive meaning.

"PANIC," "SEEKING," and the "Hot-Cold Meter"

An absurdist comic film, *The Marriage of a Young Stockbroker* explores the implicit crisis of enactive meaning in the case of a fledgling Wall Street financier struggling with some surprising pitfalls of married life within the staid luxury of a wealthy extended family. A charade of artificiality seems to block real communication with his new wife. He surprises even himself by stopping after work at a pornographic movie house. "What am I doing?" he asks himself in a voiceover; "I'm not the kind of person who does this kind of thing!" Finally, he assesses that his sense of aimless drifting and dislocation can't just be blamed on his social setting. At the bottom of it all is that the family's wealth and his own are built from playing fast and loose with their trusting clients' well-intentioned stock investments. He has failed to recognize the toll these ill-gotten profits have exacted on his felt sense of meaning—the meaning of his action trajectory. The problem isn't with his marriage at all.

Unlike the alexithymic white-nationalist and ISIL followers who remain superficially oblivious to their own underlying crisis of meaning, the Young Stockbroker does feel haunted by a vague, fuzzy feeling that something is "off" with the direction of his life activities—the ongoing trajectory of his actions. There is a sense in which his "whole being" is telling him this. Gendlin (2000) suggests that the lived body, with its emotional viscera, constitutes a kind of implicit whole-body brain, which includes but isn't limited to the questioning functions of the "head-brain." Plants sense their relation to the environment, even without a nervous system. The whole-body brain uses not just the head-brain, but the entire internally motivated body of a self-organizing creature.

For Gendlin, the head-brain (which includes the emotionally crucial subcortex and limbic area and the questioning prefrontal cortex) enables us to ask questions about the meaning of an embodied "felt sense"—the "aboutness" of our emotional activity; or alternatively, it can block the questions. But the understanding also requires focusing on the precise quality of visceral feelings. Even our understanding of the "head-brain" needs to be updated to avoid reducing it to the stimulus-response model that obscures its enactive structure. If emotional feelings aren't just about reacting to specific situations, then they must be expressions of the entire self-organizing system, functioning as a whole. The head-brain, like the rest of the lived body, uses not only push-pull causality, but also self-organization (Gendlin 2018; Stuart Kauffman 1991; Gallagher 2020; Newton 1996; Ellis 2005, 2018; Ellis and Newton 2010).

The "neural plasticity" grounded in the dynamical structure of organic systems doesn't contradict the usual rules of push-pull causation, but it describes a more complex interrelation between and among them (Ellis 1996, 2005; Ellis and Newton 2010; Doige 2007). The ability to act rather than just react requires what the biochemist Stuart Kauffman calls "self-maintaining structure."[3] What Kauffman means here is essentially that self-organizing systems, such as humans and all living systems, constantly *appropriate, rearrange,* and *replace* the microlevel elements (including causal processes) needed to maintain and evolve our own patterns of organization, movement, growth, and change. The process constantly selects and re-forms its own constituents. The pattern organizes the constituents rather than only the other way around. Kauffman shows that some patterns of self-organization are much more likely than others to maintain themselves and continue.

After a concussion or stroke, the brain tries to replace the function of the destroyed cells by using other cells to play the same roles. When recreational drugs flood the brain with excess serotonin or dopamine, the brain rearranges its patterns of organization to restore its overall balance, as much as possible. It shrinks or eliminates some of the serotonin receptors to achieve the overall purpose of balance (which of course means more of the drug would have to be taken for any future "high"). Even when we eat, we are literally appropriating the components needed to facilitate dynamic patterns of organization. In each of these examples, the organism is doing the reorganization itself, rather than waiting for some external force to push the reorganization. It is acting rather than just reacting.

The Young Stockbroker's conflict isn't simply a reaction to circumstances. It is part of himself. It reflects an imbalance of the entire self-organizational structure of his life activities. The imbalance is so extreme in this case that it involves a decalibration of what I call the "hot-cold meter" (discussed in chapter 9). What I mean by this "meter" is the normal process of implicitly registering a continual preconscious felt sense that normally guides us through our daily activities without too much calculation or conscious reflection, like the GPS in a car. It registers as "getting colder" when we are getting away from what we need to be doing and "warmer" when we veer in a better direction. Chapter 9 will show that this "meter" is by no means always accurate. It sometimes, maybe frequently, needs recalibration. But we do constantly use it. Finding oneself in a bar at 4 a.m. begins to register as "getting colder," even without conscious thought.

In the example of our Young Stockbroker, one might say superficially that his main motive is to stay alive, which requires making a living—in his case, by buying and selling stocks. But under the surface, the meaning of every buy or sell is guided by the hot-cold meter, which tells him "This action is getting closer to what you need to be doing," or "No, this is getting further away." But knowing what he should be doing at any moment—whether buying, selling, or conversing with his wife—requires a grounding in the *overall trajectory* of his life. This trajectory is partly defined by a more basic choice as to *how* he is to make a living—not only what profession he should pursue, but also, how to execute that profession. For instance, he can calculate how to maximize his clients' gains with a buy or sell (with a modest commission for himself), or he can do a different combination of buys and sells to maximize his own aggregate commissions (at the clients' extreme risk). This entire part of his hot-cold meter, which normally would direct these "how" questions in each current moment, has now become decalibrated, and therefore can no longer guide him.

The "offness" felt by the Young Stockbroker—the decalibration of his internal meter—reflects what existentialists like Viktor Frankl think of as a shortage of meaning. Throughout most of the film, the Young Stockbroker has no basis for the meter ever to register as either "warmer" *or* "colder" because there is no sense of meaning in relation to which to register it. The meter is decalibrated. Initially, the "off" feeling seems to be a reaction to a circumstance—his marriage. But ultimately, he realizes that the problem goes deeper—to the underlying way in which he has defined the enactive meaning of long-term action trajectories.

For a person in a life-boat, the meter reads clearly: Figure out how to stay alive. But once on dry land, the question of what we are trying to do with our life energy—and how—immediately becomes more complicated yet is presupposed by everything else we feel or try to do.

Some of the "basic emotion" systems that neurophysiologists try to study—emotions that activate regardless of the direct or indirect effect of any reward-and-punishment reinforcements—are going to prove relevant for us, especially the ones that Panksepp (2011) calls the PANIC system and the SEEKING system. (Panksepp adopts the convention of using ALL CAPS to designate his proposed endogenous emotion systems.) The PANIC system (sometimes alternatively labeled SEPARATION DISTRESS) embodies the intensity of our fundamental need for interactive social relationship. The classic example is the unleashing of frantic neurotransmitter activity in the brain of a mother separated from her infant, and *vice versa*. Mother Nature couldn't afford for toddlers to constantly wander off into the woods. She also knew that adults need real-time interactions with others to generate meaningful action trajectories (much more on that later).

Another apparently separate and independent emotion system is Panksepp's SEEKING system. It includes among other things the feeling of enthusiasm toward action in general, a baseline, minimal level of everyday inspiration—not necessarily fireworks, but enough to motivate a normal level of activity, curiosity, and interest. This same SEEKING system also includes the "exploratory drive," which energizes us to *seek the answers to questions*, to explore our world—including ourselves—in search of understanding.

These two basic emotion systems in particular, PANIC and SEEKING, reflect some of the most inescapable, underlying long-term emotional directionalities that are presupposed by the more specific referents of passing emotional episodes. Not surprisingly, both are seriously disrupted in cases of clinical depression (Panksepp et al. 2014). The self-organizing structure of emotions is reflected in these brain systems as well as the rest of the body.

I don't automatically take these empirical results as a simple naïve realism. We also have to take seriously Thomas Kuhn's (1962) point about the selective attention process of the sciences themselves and the motivated nature of this selective attention.[4] We also should avoid jumping to any nature-nurture conclusion about the endogenous nature of the basic emotion systems. The brain of the developing infant is amazingly flexible, and the result is a huge degree of individual differences in the way all the basic emotions play out and interrelate with each other (for example, see Davis and Panksepp 2018). What makes the basic emotions "basic" isn't so much that they are innate, but that they express themselves with or without any instrumental reinforcement. They organize themselves around certain basic concerns without which we can't exist as what we are. For example, the PANIC system reflects the inescapability that our being depends on interrelations with others.

"Basic" in this context implies "endogenous"—in other words, "naturally developing from within, not dependent on learning, including hedonistic reinforcement learning." Our desire to explore isn't learned as a means of maximizing rewards (even though Mother Nature understood that having an independent exploratory drive is an advantage for survival). Understanding that these emotions aren't merely reactions to stimuli can help toward grasping some of the most important things the whole body is telling us, especially when something is "off," as in the way the Young Stockbroker was feeling.

These emotional concerns about underlying existential value-and-meaning issues are among the things that Picciolini's alexithymic white supremacists can't pay attention to. They have emotions, but they remain either unaware of them altogether, or unaware of what the emotions are "about." In my view, exploring these kinds of discomforts, if we stick with them, will inevitably lead sooner or later into the structure of the continuing action-generating motivations that constantly provide the everyday baseline of minimal inspiration and enthusiasm for whatever we decide to do in our daily lives. Those motivations determine how we direct our curiosity and what we consider worth the struggle to get done. This entire subterranean motivational process in turn both energizes and shapes our attention and our interpretation of reality.

Contemporary academic philosophy and psychology seldom propose resources designed to address this question of an underlying, always-already-ongoing enactive meaning trajectory—with rare exceptions (for example, existential philosophers and psychotherapists like Robert Stolorow 2018, Irvin Yalom 1980, and Robert Solomon 1976). But surprisingly, some of the recent biology of our lived bodies' emotional processes can now prove useful in this direction, especially if combined with the two other contemporary streams of thought mentioned above: applied-phenomenology approaches like Gendlin's "focusing" idea; and thinking about values from an "enactivist" perspective. These last two trends might be new to some, so the next chapter offers slightly fuller explications of them.

Chapter 2

Focusing, Enactivity, and the Opacity of Directionality

Of the three main resources just mentioned for studying the underlying meaning of the motivated action trajectories that affect interpretations of reality—focusing, enactivism, and recent emotion research—I would like to further flesh out the first two of those, which may be less familiar to some readers, but which I think are crucial for our purposes. This chapter describes in more detail both Gendlin's focusing technique and the enactive trend in the theory of consciousness and cognition, especially as applied to the emotional and valuational dimension.

Focusing

Forensic psychologist Louise Sundararajan told me about a patient who had flown into a fit and senselessly murdered his father; yet he literally lacked any consciousness of the enraged feelings that obviously motivated it (see also Sundararajan 2001). On measures of emotional awareness, he fell through the absolute bottom of the scale.

We can easily see the similarity between this act of murder without emotional awareness and the white supremacist's acting out of feelings with little understanding of what the feelings are actually about, or the fascist followers' misidentification of Jews or immigrants as the real cause of their own feelings of *anomie*, alienation, or powerlessness (Durkheim 1893/2013). The extreme clinical example of alexithymia, as with Sundararajan's case—the virtually complete, systematic unawareness of one's own emotions—can help us probe the difficulties of the introspective process even in more normal instances.

Gendlin's "focusing" method offers a careful, systematic approach to what Sundararajan's alexithymic murderer lacked in the extreme: introspection into the meaning of any given specific subjective process, especially an emotional one (Gendlin 1978, 2000, 2018). Like any phenomenologist, Gendlin wants to avoid being misled by mere assumptions about what our affective experiences are "supposed to" mean and to focus on the felt experience itself first, without labeling, categorizing, or "talking at" it with words. The focusing method challenges us to bypass typical preconceptions about what we would be expected to feel in a situation. Was what I was feeling really "jealousy" "of" my co-worker? Is that really what the feeling is about?

Moving past any preconceived generic emotion categories, Gendlin instead wants to work from a felt sense of the *uniqueness* of a feeling, which we first identify wordlessly as the precise way our body feels in the situation. Only then do we ask how that felt sense resonates with our best description of it, as well as the entire situation that seems to trigger it, after situating it within the broader context in our life project.

If we stay for some time with our enteroception (or proprioceptive sensing) of the specific bodily sense we are feeling, and ask ourselves various questions about it, some of the often-hidden intentionality or "aboutness" of our feelings can begin to shift away from the generic presuppositions. But this by no means provides any incorrigible or certain understanding of what the emotion is "really" about. It is only the beginning of the focusing process.

Suspending preconceptions has long been a main aim of phenomenology. Natalie Depraz and colleagues (2003), in developing the "first-person" component of their neuro-phenomenological approach—the attempt to integrate experienced consciousness with its embodied dimension—advocate a method not entirely different from Gendlin's focusing. They suggest a three-stage process: "suspension," "redirection," and "letting go." In effect, we (1) suspend all presuppositions about the experience; (2) redirect our attention to the way it actually feels in our viscera; and (3) let go of presumed explanations and judgments about the experience. Gendlin extends this process still further to try to get at a less distorted assessment of what the feeling is about, as free as possible from the typical assumptions that were "suspended" and "let go of" in the initial redirection of attention.

Gendlin wants to bypass standard presupposition-laden category words like "angry" and "jealous"—or at least move through and beyond them quickly. Instead, we find unique, one-off descriptions that can directly and precisely point attention to the uniqueness of the way it feels: "As if I were pulling a lead weight" or "Like the Dutch boy holding his finger in a dyke, and then other holes have also sprung in the dyke"—any phrase that we can feel vibrantly and specifically resonating with the way it physically feels, in the same way that a poet looks for just the right word or image to "pull up" a specific felt sense, to allow us to concretely feel it as fully and precisely as possible.

This "felt sense" sharply distinguishes itself from the stereotyped categories of feelings we might think of as typical for the given situation. We may find that "Like the Dutch boy" resonates better than "Like pulling a lead weight"—or vice versa. We know it resonates if, whenever we say the word or phrase, the feeling suddenly comes more fully alive as a concrete feeling, usually in the gut, chest, throat, or shoulders: "Yes, there it is, that's the one!" "It's as if I have to contort myself to hold back the entire sea." It refers directly to the unique feeling, which can be pinpointed and distinguished from other interrelated feelings and sensations—much as when we try out different candidates for the name we forgot, until one elicits a feeling of recognition. But for Gendlin, this is still only an early step in the focusing process.

Notice that for some people, a phrase like "The Jews are trying to replace us!" might also be accompanied by intense feeling; but those words aren't a *description of the feeling* at all. They are an assertion regarding objective reality, not a sensing of how a person feels. In the Depraz and colleagues sense, it counterproductively directs attention outwardly rather than inwardly.

If a neo-Nazi feels that immigrants or Jews are the real threat, the first thing is to bypass the assumption that the feelings are about immigrants or Jews and focus first on the actual feeling-quality at hand. Most neo-Nazis, because of their alexithymia, might be unwilling or unable to do this; but if they did, a better sense of what the feeling is about would only come later, after focusing on the actual feeling itself. Gendlin believes that even a neo-Nazi, or even a schizophrenic, can eventually *learn* to focus in this way. Focusing can't radically remake the neurophysiology of a schizophrenic, but it can help come to terms with some of the bad feelings, which in turn helps with self-management (Carl Rogers et al. 1967; Gendlin, private conversation, 2003).

So this first phase in Gendlin's method includes finding a symbolization that resonates, just as a poet would seek out the best word or image that can "hit home" with a precise felt sense. Suppose "Like the Dutch boy with the dyke" is the description that best resonates with a bodily felt emotional feeling. We can then ask questions like "When was the exact moment that I began to physically feel that gut feeling that I'm now calling 'like the Dutch boy'?" "In what other situations did I also feel something comparable to that specific 'like the Dutch boy' feeling?" "What does the Dutch boy want to happen?"

Sometimes we find ourselves surprised at the answer. Instead of "He wants the holes to be patched," we may feel our visceral response as more like "The Dutch boy is immobile in this position; as more and more holes spring open in the dyke, there is no way he can contort himself enough to continue holding back the entire sea, so he may as well just free himself by walking away from the dyke."

We can now notice that the "aboutness" has shifted. It connects to a broader horizon of implicit background conditions for the immediate situation than we originally thought. It isn't (as we might have assumed) just about the bad workday or the colleague who obstructed us, even if that is superficially what triggered it.

This method sometimes can lead to such radical shifts of perspective that it needs to be used with some caution. It can unleash potentially overpowering emotions that might initially tempt us toward rash or un-thought-out actions. For example, the "Dutch boy" experience might prompt a thoughtless kneejerk reaction like impulsively quitting a job or breaking off a relationship. That will be addressed in chapter 9, on the "Hot-Cold Meter." Readers who like to peruse books by skipping around might want to at least look at that chapter, if for no other reason to avoid dangerous oversimplifications of the implications of Gendlin's method.

One way to avoid an overly rash response to a focusing session is to go still further rounds of focusing, until we realize that sometimes what lies under the surface isn't only an accidental, contingent life circumstance. For example, we may ask: Why would I feel such venomous fury over a trivial insult if the real *meaning* of my indignation were only about the stumbling drunk in the bar who disrespected me—someone I don't even know? What troubling issues does his insult instantiate or represent for me, and why do I feel this way about all of *that*?

Some focusing experts, like Ann Weiser Cornell (2005), don't literally skip the "stock category" stage of identifying emotions, at least not initially. Cornell often does begin with the standard emotion labels like "sad" or "angry," but then moves quickly into a more nuanced description of the unduplicated *specific kind* of anger or sadness—or the more specific feelings "underneath" the anger or sadness; those too can be physically sensed in the particular situation.

In one focusing session, dealing with the failure of a young love relationship, Cornell begins with something as broad and vague as feeling "bad." The "bad" becomes more specific as she senses it in her body: "pain," then later "I sense under that, to its mood or tone. I can feel an anxiety around its edges." This description becomes still more specific as "I can feel it in my body, restless, antsy, defiant." But as soon as she says those words to herself, she suddenly notices another broad emotion category: "angry," which is quickly refined to "baffled . . . How could God/the Universe let me experience a connection that felt as good as that, and not let it continue?" (pp. 27–28) Suddenly there is a relaxation of her tension.

In this example, a particular feeling about a particular situation, as its felt sense becomes more and more specific—moving from "bad" and "pain" to "defiance"—has now counterintuitively led into a broad life question: How can the world be such that things like this can happen? This finally becomes the focus, which then leads to the question of what the feeling is wanting to be done about this unfortunate fact about "God/the Universe." The "aboutness" has shifted: It is no longer simply about the particular failed relationship—which would have left her stuck there. It now opens up to be about the nature of relationships per se, and why they work out the way they do. It invites further exploring of all the emotional meanings that were affected by the misfiring of the relationship. She is no longer stuck in the "bad/pain/anger/defiance." There is now a felt sense that maybe "God/the Universe" doesn't guarantee a successful relationship every time a connection initially "feels right." The question "What does the feeling want to happen?" now leads in a very different direction, without any deliberate effort.

Sometimes (not always, but often), this focusing process connects to the underlying question of the most basic enactive meanings that define where we are trying to go with our life activities, even if we suppose we are simply angry with our spouse or jealous of the classmate who one-upped us in money or prestige. Focusing gets us beyond those presuppositions so that we can now ask: "Yes, but *why* do I care whether someone one-ups me in these things?" Cornell similarly discovers that her feeling is about a more basic issue in our shared human life condition than someone might initially have assumed.

The important issue here isn't to reveal with some iron-clad certainty what the emotion is "really" about. In the enactive use of focusing, we don't use the felt sense to reveal "The Given," as Cornel West (1979) puts it, as if the felt sense were to unveil an incorrigible and final truth about what the feeling is about. We can always learn more and more about what a feeling means, and we can always change the symbolizations that we use. The point isn't to use the felt sense as revealing something beyond doubt, but rather as playing a role in the overall process of everyday minimal inspiration or motivation needed to provide a sense of meaning.

The difficulty of getting clearer as to what a feeling is "about" will be explored further, especially in our chapter on alexithymia. Sometimes a good part of the "aboutness" relates to general facts of life, not just the specific example we currently confront—for example, the drunk in the bar. The most basic "facts of life," of which other facts are particular ramifications, are aspects of our general human condition per se—the situation that defines us as creatures whose actions need to have some meaning, as well as the convolutions we go through to either escape or deal with the most crucial motivations within the conditions of our radical finiteness.

Enactivism

Enactivism suggests that living creatures, unlike the information processing in digital computers, understand our world through attempted and imagined actions—not just re-action to received information such as empirical perception through the five senses (for example, Giovanna Colombetti 2014; Francisco Varela et al. 1993; Ellis and Newton 2010; Gallagher 2006, 2020). We understand a coffee cup by imagining how we might pick it up and drink from it—an action. Action and action imagery (the imagining of our own actions) sharply distinguish Edmund Husserl's "life-world" as over against the world we can construct out of empirical perceptions (Husserl 1913, 1936). We understand the texture of a tree's bark by imagining how we might run our hand over it or use it as material to carve something. The empirical sciences extend and refine enactive understanding: We perform measurements and "operationalize" concepts.

The real tree, unlike an imaginary one, resists our actions: It can't be walked through as if it were a ghost. The cracked cup refuses to hold the coffee. The rotten wood refuses to hold up under carving. As Heidegger (1927) puts it, the "ready-to-hand" now becomes "present-at-hand," a reality that manifestly isn't merely subjective, precisely because it doesn't afford our attempted actions the way we wanted. This limitation of our power—the *inability* to act—helps ground our sense of truth *versus* self-deception. Granted, the result is only the truth about the realm of "phenomena"—reality as it is able to *appear to us*—not some sort of metaphysical realm of "things beyond what we can experience." But this entire enactive approach hinges on understanding "action," as opposed to "merely reacting": not an easy distinction to begin with.

When I say "action," I use the term in the same inclusive sense as Gendlin (2018, Chapter 6) and Newton (2017): I don't just mean overt motor movements. I also mean purposeful activations of *brain processes* that help subserve consciousness—processes arising from self-motivating activity rather than only from events perceived as external. Deliberately forming the image of the Dutch boy with the dyke is an "action" in this sense.

If we try to execute the act of merely thinking "Racial voter-suppression is compatible with the principles of democracy," the realities involved in these concepts resist our attempt to enact the incoherent thought. The attempted action—the attempt to maintain logical consistency within the incoherent thought—fails, just as we would fail if we tried to fly off the roof of a tall building. The failure is reflected in the convoluted system of self-deceptions needed to prop up the attempted incoherent thought, which then can lead down even more complicated rabbit holes. To be sure, other emotions might tempt us to look away from the contradiction; but to the extent that we do try to maintain logical consistency in this thought, we fail. The attempt to construct a coherent view of reality is an attempted action, against which reality pushes back.

In "The Derivation of Space," Gendlin explicates the complexity of the process in which our imagined actions help us understand the realities of the world:

> I could move that broken chair or I could carefully try to sit in it again. . . . Each object *"affords"* us many possible actions. . . . Action possibilities are *implicit, not spread out before us*. . . . How do we *have* this familiar "what we could do"? Shall we say we *know* it? Yes, but this is an odd "knowing," not something in our think-space, but rather an innumerable number. Shall we say we *feel* them? Yes, but it is a nameless "feeling," so much at once and changing all the while. . . . The implicit possibilities and their circumstances are intricately organized. Every action changes whether and how the others could be done. Some can no longer be done, but some are new possibilities. . . . An action

is not only what occurs, but also a cluster of implicit clusters, an implicit intricacy. . . . The possibilities are not separate next to each other, rather, they are implicit in each other. They are not merged but have a very precise organization. (Gendlin 2018, 155)

Maurice Merleau-Ponty's (1945) example of the football player's understanding of space illustrates this point. The need to complete a pass organizes and defines how we sense the shape of the field. In each instant, all the action possibilities are changing, and the perceived contour of the field reflects all these changes as well as potential changes. This enactive understanding of the "life-world" presupposes that we act out of our own motives—for example, to complete a pass—rather than just re-acting to stimuli. This capacity for action, as opposed to mere reaction, is a real thing, irrespective of the determinism/freedom issue.

For the terrorist recruit, each next click on the internet disinformation highway is chosen by preference over reliable sources or logical analysis. The person being radicalized is *using* the terrorist movement in the interest of a self-driven project of trying to find meaning for future actions, in light of an already ongoing trajectory.

And yet, concurrently with the recruit's self-deceptions, a conflicting drive within each person—the exploratory drive—is also trying its best to maintain a feeling of truthfulness in the project. Exploration implies seeking the truth about reality. Ironically, the motivation toward truthfulness is what leads to the elaborate conspiracy theories and weird ad hoc hypotheses—positing that Italian space lasers can control American voting machines and the like.[1] Those, at least, are *attempts* to make the incoherent thought logically consistent, even if, ultimately, they fail. This attempt too is an action, not just a reaction.

Recent neuropsychological research explicitly casts doubt on the behaviorist tradition that tended to reduce action to direct or indirect *re*-actions to previous reinforcements based on consummatory desires. Panksepp clearly emphasizes his straightforward rejection of behaviorism (1998, pp. 147–50). He and others (Panksepp et al. 2014; Davis and Panksepp 2018; Watt 2000) investigate the two above-mentioned emotion systems that will prove so interesting for our purposes—the SEEKING system, which includes the self-motivated "exploratory drive"; and the PANIC (or SEPARATION DISTRESS) system, which is one of the most important innate drives subserving our inescapable need for interpersonal relationships that are indispensable for our form of life. Later we will explore some of this research on PANIC and SEEKING, with a view to connecting them to the enactive and existential dimensions. In the final analysis, as Husserl and other phenomenologists had long ago argued, living beings understand their world through internally motivated actions, not just processing direct or indirect stimulus inputs.

Action, in turn, presupposes value. Clinical depression forces lethargic *inaction* in the same stroke that renders *valueless* every concrete action we propose to ourselves. This condition strongly correlates with long-term SEEKING system suppression (Panksepp et al. 2014). Playing music is no longer worth the effort; the action itself seems virtually valueless, no matter how much we tell ourselves we ought to do it. Yet even in the more "normal" case, even when the SEEKING system is functioning robustly, the attempt to find what is "real" about the value of our actions still resists us—as Heidegger discovered with his unresolved search for the "that for the sake of which."

Enactive Empathy

If *en*-action is at the core of what we are, then understanding others involves the way *their* actions presuppose values that define the purpose of their actions. I understand what the base runner wants—to steal a base—by imagining myself in the runner's place, executing a certain poised posture and flexing certain muscles, but masking it with deceptive nonchalance and avoidance of eye contact, in preparation for suddenly breaking toward the base. In the same way, I understand the drunk in the bar by imagining what it would be like to try to achieve whatever he might be trying to achieve by insulting people—within his own version of the quest for meaning.

As Colombetti (2014) puts it, I don't simply "simulate" what he is doing, but rather I *imagine* what it would be like to do it. The "mirror neuron system" activates some but not all of what the same system would do if we were performing the other's actions. The mirror neuron system centers in the *motor* and *premotor* areas of the brain (Gallese et al. 1996). "Mirror neuron system" really refers to an action-imagery system. It activates when we imagine what it would feel like if we ourselves were to execute a dance movement in the same way as the other is doing it. Not what it would *look like* to do it (that would be visual imagery), but what it would *be* like to perform it (action imagery). We can form this kind of "action-imagery" of ourselves executing the action—that is, we can imagine ourselves doing the action.[2]

Natika Newton (1996) elaborates the role of action imagery in all forms of consciousness and then shows (chapter 6) that we understand others through the "action-imaging" of what it would be like to execute the other's actions. The brain substrates of action imagery (as opposed to perceptual imagery) are mostly the same as what happens in our brains when we *actually execute* the movement we are imagining (Jeannerod 1997)—except that we also *inhibit* the brain signal from reaching the body's extremities, so that we only imagine ourselves performing the action without actually going through with it. In the strange clinical condition of "utilization behavior," the person is unable to inhibit the already-initiated action-commanding brain signals and so can't identify a coffee cup as what it is without uncontrollably picking it up and drinking from it (Archibald et al. 2001; L'hermitte et al. 1986).

Neuropsychologists understand that a shortage of frontal inhibitory neurotransmitters is the main physical correlate of utilization behavior. The patient remains unable to inhibit the overt action once it is initiated, yet the action has to be initiated (even if subsequently inhibited) as part of the normal process of understanding the object in terms of its action affordances—imagining how we might act relative to it.

One of the things a beginning musician finds surprisingly difficult is how to feel the beat without overtly moving the body in some way. Even as proficient a musician as Tom "Bones" Malone, the Blues Brothers trombonist known for his impeccable technique, once confided that while playing classical music, where bodily movements are discouraged, he felt the beat by slightly moving his foot inside his shoe but without allowing the shoe to move. A large body of evidence now mounts that we understand an object or situation through subliminally imagined actions (see Ellis and Newton 2010). As Gendlin puts it, the various actions that help us understand the world are mostly "implicit." We are always imagining very intricate "clusters" of them, but subliminally.

The relevance of this point is that we can get a felt understanding of others' attempted actions, not only as they try to steal bases or perform dances, but also as they face their overarching life conditions—which at the subterranean level include existential conditions. To understand a brutal hate crime, we need ultimately to imagine the panic and confusion within the offender's hopeless struggles with the shortage of meaning within their own version of the existential condition and in the face of a substantial degree of alexithymia within their own emotional life. By means of insulting people, what values is the overbearing drunk ultimately trying to achieve in his ongoing action trajectory as a whole?

We couldn't understand the action-value connection for others if we didn't find it within ourselves. Readers of Edith Stein (1916/1989) and Max Scheler (1923/1954) know this point as resonant with their pioneering work on the phenomenology of empathy. Psychoanalyst Robert Stolorow (1994, 2018) and theoretical psychologist Mark Bickhard (2000) go further, arguing that we actually exist only *in* this interactivity—that interpersonal interactions constitute our existence itself. As Gendlin puts it, "We don't just have interactions; we *are* interactions with the environment—other people, the world, the universe. . . ." (Gendlin 2018, 293). Bickhard's "interactivism" theory begins with the idea that everything, including ourselves, is a process rather than a static thing; no component part of a process can be what it is except in the context of the process, and no process is what it is except in relation to other processes. It was known at least since Galileo that even shapes, sizes, and motions have no meaning except in relation to other shapes, sizes, and motions. In the case of a complex process, the same is true on steroids.

Scheler distinguished a number of different types of empathy, and contemporary psychologists divide them into "cognitive" and "emotional" empathy—the latter including emotional concern rather than just *disinterestedly* understanding what others are feeling (and perhaps using it against them, as with the high-functioning psychopath). Even "high-functioning" psychopaths run into difficulty because they can only understand the other's motives as selfish ones since those are the only ones they can imagine.

All these forms of empathy involve using the mirror neuron system—an action imagery system—to imagine the other's attempted actions and implicitly the values that motivate them. This is how we understand what the base runner wants. We imagine doing those same actions ourselves.

If we take valuing creatures themselves to have *intrinsic* value—value *in their own right* or *for their own sake* rather than merely serving some ulterior purpose—then empathy and its complications must also play a crucial role to facilitate or thwart *our own* experience of the intrinsic value of valuing creatures as such. Experiences of intrinsic value, in turn, are implicitly needed to ground whatever *instrumental* values we find motivating. Instrumental values, by definition, serve something other than themselves, something toward which they are instrumental.

I plan to argue later that our own experiencing of the most obvious locus of "intrinsic" value—the value that we place on valuing creatures *as such*, where empathy provides a crucial portal—plays a key role in grounding the inspiration for our own action. If we then kill enemies in combat or lock up criminals in prison, it isn't that we don't still acknowledge their intrinsic value qua valuing creatures, but rather that this value is in conflict with other values that we also consider important. This process will be explored in more detail as we proceed.

A Crucial Problem: The Intrinsic-Instrumental Conflict

Other than a few extreme psychopaths, we can experience other valuing creatures as "intrinsically valuable"—valuable for their own sake, not merely valuable as instrumental toward some other purpose. And we don't feel that our own emotion of "valuing" them is what gives them their intrinsic value. We don't feel that their value would disappear if we ourselves were to die and if we thus were no longer in a position to value them. The value seems to be there, independent of us. Acknowledging this intrinsic value presupposes the ability to empathize by using our own "mirroring" action imagery. More on this complex set of dynamics as we proceed.

I grant that, during childhood, this empathic acknowledgement of the intrinsic value of others may be limited to select individuals with whom the child is in immediate relationship. We can't automatically leap from mirror neurons to some sort of moral system. Establishing empathy requires an attentional focus that can be *selectively avoided* if we choose to do so in given instances. This selective inattention seems to come fairly easily for many people in many contexts.

However, I plan to show that, as a result of an extensive developmental process in humans, we end up implicitly extending the status of intrinsic (not merely instrumental) value, not just to specific individuals, but to valuing creatures per se, at least to the extent that we are able to establish feelings of empathy. Ultimately, in order to resolve various *internal* conflicts that are especially pronounced for animals with our mental capacity, we have to admit to ourselves, even if only implicitly, that intrinsic value applies to creatures simply *by virtue of* the property of being a valuing creature as such. Whatever value they have by virtue of any other property would become merely an instrumental value. This intrinsic value of valuing creatures, including ourselves—whether universalized or extended only to a narrow group—is one of the main intrinsic values that motivate our own instrumental actions, if not in fact the main one.

But this valuational dynamic, whether experienced toward all valuing creatures universally or only toward a narrow group, makes certain internal conflicts inevitable. Crucially, it creates a situation in which experiencing intrinsic value by itself is never quite "enough"; we also need to invest energy into chains of *instrumental* values, presumably in service to the intrinsic ones. Most of what we do in life *is* instrumental in this sense. We focus attention on getting to the top of a hill so that we can win a battle, so that we can win a war, so that . . . and so on . . . while at the same time adhering to the rules of engagement, so that we can meet the conditions of "just war," so that we can avoid military disciplinary action, so that . . . and so on. Our attention is usually focused primarily on instrumental values of this kind.

Why does this create a conflict? The problem is that instrumentalities inevitably become a *necessary* component of enactive meaning. The meaning of my actions requires that I am a competent and effective soldier, father, citizen, worker, and so on. But then it is no longer *sufficient* that the value of valuing creatures themselves is "intrinsic"—valuable *just for their own sake*, simply by virtue of being valuing creatures per se and regardless of whatever instrumentalities they do or don't serve. If sheer intrinsic value were "enough" to ground the sense of meaning for our actions, then nothing else would be *necessary*. But our instrumental values *are* necessary for our sense of meaning. Evaluating ourselves or others in terms of our instrumental value can therefore undermine the always implicit sense that the intrinsic value of valuing creatures, *all by itself, with or without any instrumentality*, is "enough" to ground a sense of meaning for everyday actions.

If a child chooses to leave the family business or drops out of medical school, we don't cease grounding our feeling of everyday inspiration in the implicit sense of the child's intrinsic value. But at the same time, we don't encourage the child to stop looking for avenues to do something useful. We understand that the child's own sense of enactive meaning depends on being able to serve instrumentally worthwhile purposes. Yet we can't allow the child's value to depend on these instrumentalities. The more it does, the less sufficient is the child's intrinsic value to ground a sense of enactive meaning. With no feeling of intrinsic value, there would be no point to the instrumentalities. This dynamic creates a constant tension between the intrinsic and the instrumental, in each person's motivating value system.

In short, if everyday actions are to have meaning, it isn't enough to just sit back and experience the intrinsic value of ourselves or others. If the SEEKING system is to rise to the needed level of inspiration to counterbalance life's necessary travails (including existential ones), we will sometimes need to set up complicated projects and struggle to make ourselves effective instruments in their service—what I call in chapter 4 an "extended" value system, including complicated structures of intrinsic and instrumental values.

But the danger here is that we lose the feeling that valuing creatures can have "enough" value simply *by virtue of* being valuing creatures per se—that is, in the intrinsic sense. Lacking a strong enough feeling of this intrinsic value, we could be left in limbo, desperately flailing in search of something, anything else that might promise to fill the void of intrinsic value now vacated through the reduction of valuing creatures themselves to their instrumentality. We would be left implicitly with a shortage of intrinsic value and therefore of enactive meaning.

The resulting shortage of enactive meaning thus potentially invites seduction by anything that seems as if it could be valued not just as an instrumental, but as an intrinsic value—Heidegger's "that for the sake of which." Cult leaders, authoritarian movements, hate groups, potentially infinite financial greed—and, yes, as the young James Baldwin discovered, even many religious systems that don't ground themselves in the intrinsic value of valuing creatures ourselves—might seem to propose a "Grand Scheme" value that promises to offer an intrinsic value, although the promised meaning ultimately proves illusory. The danger is that the Grand Scheme reduces valuing creatures to instrumental values, thus undermining the sense that their intrinsic value is sufficient for enactive meaning. In that case, the Grand Scheme not only doesn't serve the stiving for meaning; it actually undermines it.

Navigating this tension between the intrinsic and the instrumental value of ourselves and others—all of which is necessary for defining meaning—can be tricky. When our instrumental efforts fail or are insignificant, how can it still seem *sufficient* that we at least have intrinsic value, simply qua valuing creature as such? Given the need for instrumentalization, and given our inevitable finiteness, we might then feel that our life project, to the extent that we define it in terms of the instrumentalities, becomes like emptying the ocean with a spoon.

To sustain a strong enough feeling of everyday inspiration implicitly grounded in the intrinsic value of conscious creatures as such (especially human beings) becomes still more challenging when we read the daily political news, the crime statistics, or the routine reports of human exploitation and cruelty to each other and to other animals. Who can avoid noticing that some type of fascism, often even genocide, clouds every century of human history and that our innumerable human lies invariably travel faster than truth? The migration of early humans is sometimes traced by the patterns of extinct species left in their wake. Humans always seem to obliterate their own habitat, and every generation launches its own senseless wars—to name just a tiny sampling of scars on the dignity of humanity. How much meaning can we ground in the intrinsic value of such a bumblingly destructive creature?

As Charlie Harvey (2016, 2020) so eloquently makes the case, all these issues impede our ability to feel inspired by the intrinsic value of humans per se. In fact, in terms of population dynamics, aren't there already just too many of us? Think of the billions of chickens, cattle, and pigs slaughtered and inhumanely treated, the thousands of square miles of rainforest obliterated, the oceanic species suffocated by pollution, entire seas dead from it, just to support and make room for us!

To complicate further this challenge to our feeling of intrinsic value, Alfred Adler (1961) stresses that many of us to greater or lesser extents suffered exaggerated belittlement and disempowerment during childhood—the diminishment of being beaten, neglected, or told that we were stupid or inadequate in various ways. This diminishment would have cut into the ability to feel that we have intrinsic and not just instrumental value. It would shift the focus toward proving ourselves in purely instrumental terms. Yet at the same time, the diminishment itself makes us feel powerless to achieve enough *instrumental* worth to "make a difference." We then become hypersensitized to potential retraumatization by any feeling of powerlessness, smallness, insignificance, or interpersonal alienation—the very problems that define the most necessary parameters of our existence.

While these inevitable concerns about the meaning of our actions can be intensified by unnecessary childhood traumatization, Stolorow (2018) emphasizes that the problems themselves aren't just a function of contingent traumata or neuroses. Even the simple threat of death highlights all the issues of smallness and insignificance in the overall scheme of things—that we "strut and fret our hour upon the stage and then are heard no more." This intrinsic-instrumental conflict will be discussed in more detail in our chapter on the "extended value system."

Any of these existentially necessary concerns about enactive meaning can disturb or jolt, but possibly more perilous is failure even to credit their insidious presence, as initially was the case with the Young Stockbroker. Lurking vaguely at the horizon of a murky, almost inarticulable felt sense, the fuzzy referents of these sentenceless question marks are hard to nail down, like the monster in the closet we don't want to look at—just as we fear, and probably have good reason for fearing, to look within ourselves. Given this murkiness, it might be best to allow the meaning of "enactive meaning" to unfold methodically and stepwise, through a series of phenomenological investigations. In the final analysis, on a daily basis, some minimal sense of meaning is needed to inspire action. And we are fundamentally enactive creatures.

Why does so much internal emotional conflict get in the way of this everyday inspiration to action, leading us instead to lapse into lethargy or to concoct so many illusions, destructive ideologies, and cults of personality, or simply self-denigration, in our attempts to define and read the meaning of our own actions? Gendlin's focusing concept and the enactivist viewpoint will be explored further as we proceed. But first, as perhaps an even more basic groundwork, it will be helpful to consider, in our next chapter, some important changes in understanding offered by some of the recent neuropsychology of emotions per se.

Chapter 3

We're Not in Behaviorism Anymore

Panksepp and Damasio on the Enactive Structure of Motivation

There was no "us versus them" between empirical research and introspective methods like phenomenology in the pioneering work on "emotional awareness" by Eugene Gendlin, Don Kiesler, and other associates of Carl Rogers. To be sure, they were fully aware of the fallibility of empirical methods. But Kiesler wrote the "bible" on statistical analysis in empirical research on psychotherapy (Keisler 1973/2017). The focusing method's effectiveness was studied empirically by correlating it with scores on the earlier Carl Rogers Experiencing Scale (Rogers 1959), as well as with psychotherapeutic outcomes (Gendlin 1978), and with changes in brain patterns.[1] Degrees of emotional self-awareness were diligently measured by comparing the Experiencing Scale with the scores of "raters" listening to the precise wordings of therapeutic interactions, and the ratings themselves were validated by means of statistical "inter-rater correlations." That is, the raters' ratings all correlated highly with each other, suggesting some degree of objective validity.

Early in life, Gendlin worked with Rogers as one of those "raters," scoring therapy clients on their use of emotional language. Marjorie Klein, Gendlin, Kiesler, and Mathieu (1969) consolidated their work with the updated "Experiencing Scale," and Gendlin finally developed this approach into a systematic focusing "method" (Gendlin 1978). Further empirical work in the 1980s showed brain changes that occur while focusing (updated by Peter Afford 2012).

It is true that Gendlin and his associates were somewhat circumspect about empirical research on the emotional brain. They didn't want to encourage people to think of emotional awareness as simply a conscious "reading off" of physiological emotional processes, as if the emotions could play out physically with or without consciousness—a simplistic assumption often encouraged by cognitive theorists caught up in the computer analogy. Emotional consciousness isn't just a "readout screen." Being aware of what our emotions are about, or unaware of it, shapes and reshapes the way we feel and act, even at the brain level (as Afford explains in some detail).

In recent years, Gendlin renewed his interest in the brain and was working on a follow-up to an earlier article on the mind-body/mind-brain problem (Gendlin 2000); some of that new work went into the last book completed during his lifetime, *A Process Model* (2017). Other recent phenomenologists like Gallagher (2006, 2020) and Depraz and colleagues (2003) have also connected their work to brain research in the form of "neuro-phenomenology." Meanwhile, new empirical research has been acknowledging that the most basic emotions, even in their physical manifestations, aren't reducible to stimulus-response mechanisms. The most basic emotions are self-initiated, yet interactive—complex, nuanced, and internally conflicting, not just "responses."

Some of this recent emotion research can be helpful in exploring the most all-pervasive affective processes related to enactive meaning trajectories. The most "existential" emotions are aspects of *what we are,* as enactive, not just reactive creatures. Some of these processes can also shed light on the inevitably intersubjective and interactive aspects of what we are. In this chapter, I want to put a few relevant themes on the table, taken from some of the emotion research I would consider resonant with an *en*-active rather than re-active approach to the always-presupposed meaning trajectory of our human life world.

It Isn't Your Grandfather's Emotion Research: The Interplay of SEEKING and PANIC

Ordinary house cats don't need to be instrumentally reinforced for exploring. How did the hedonistic tradition from Thomas Hobbes (1651) to B. F. Skinner (1968) miss this fact? The cats don't need to learn to explore by being rewarded for it. They will endure considerable hardship to be allowed to explore, and still more to protect their young or their mates.

As humans, we can notice through careful introspection that we value exploration even without any direct or indirect reward other than the exploratory behavior itself. The same effect can be seen empirically.[2] Robert White (1959) observed that behaviorists of the twentieth century might have been more amenable to an independent exploratory drive, not conditioned directly or indirectly through pleasure-pain reinforcements, if they had only reflected that this drive personally spurred their own grueling lab work, often into the wee hours.

Another historical precursor for a less hedonistic way of thinking about basic emotions was the psychiatrist Otto Rank (1929, 1936). Working from his patients' introspection more than empirical methods, Rank saw life as a constant inner conflict: on one hand, a fear of newness and the unknown; on the other, a fear of "entropy"—of being suffocated by a loss of vitality, a low-energy condition that in his view can kill what he called the "creative" process that is needed to achieve a workable balance between his proposed opposing tendencies. Almost a century before Panksepp's SEEKING system, Rank was speaking of an inherent tendency toward newness, adventure, and exploration, with a correlative "fear of death," in which he included fear of any kind of entropic condition—whether in literal death, or in the quasi-death of lethargy or merely dull plodding.[3]

Rank proposes that both of these opposing tendencies are always in play, even when bad times force a struggle for sheer physical survival. We can still engage the struggle toward more expansive values—as when the poor serve meals to the even-worse-off and learn to play musical instruments. Or we can do it in an entropic, deadened frame of mind, as in the dull comforts meant to distract from what may seem like a dead-end job or an endless monotony of daily drudgery. We will see in this chapter that this lethargic condition strongly correlates with suppression of Panksepp's SEEKING system (Panksepp et al. 2014).[4]

Even for lower animals, motivation isn't reducible to reduction of hedonistic drives alone, or even survival. In fact, as Rank pointed out (following up on Freud's *Beyond the Pleasure Principle*), reduction of consummatory drives alone would ultimately mean reduction of all the electrons in all the atoms of our bodies to their lowest possible energy state, which would literally be death. If complete consummation of all drives were to mean that all electrons in the system cease flowing, the result would be complete stasis. It would mean that half of Rank's picture of the internally conflicting motivational push-and-pull had completely won out over the other half—which strictly speaking isn't even entirely possible if a being is to continue living.

To understand why activities like exploration and nurturing of the young can be meaningful for cats or for humans, with or without any ulterior rewards (other than the behavior itself, whether "pleasurable" or not), we can profit from some groundbreaking research on the emotional brain that is remarkably congruent with the phenomenological reflections of the previous chapter. Scientists like Panksepp (1998, 2000), Antonio Damasio (1999), Nico Frijda (2006), Doug Watt (1998, 2000), Panksepp and colleagues (2014), and Davis and Panksepp (2018), among others, have broken substantially from the tradition of behaviorism and consummatory reinforcement theory.

Damasio (1999) sees emotion as the key ingredient of all types of consciousness. Whenever a neurological impairment knocks out some cortical area, certain *cognitive skills* are lost, but *consciousness* remains and can often be subjectively remembered later. But with impairment further down in the brain—especially the midbrain, periaqueductal gray (PAG) and ventral limbic areas, which are important *emotional* areas—subjective consciousness itself is lost. The lower in the brain the damage goes, the greater the loss of consciousness. These subcortical areas are the ones that are inseparable from the feeling of emotions, suggesting that emotion is a crucial requirement for any conscious process. Certainly, if enactivists are right about action-understanding, then we need motivation to gear up those actions, even in cases where the actions are only imagined.

Granted, these "basic" emotions, rooted in the structure of our emotional brains, are only a part of our overall affective life. But Damasio shows that the emotional brain areas are the crucial requirement for consciousness itself. Doug Watt (2000) explores the contributions of the emotional areas of the deep subcortex, such as the PAG, to even the most sophisticated cognitive processes. Even a mathematical calculation or an act of logical deduction requires motivation. Frijda (2006) interprets emotions as including an internally motivated "readiness for action," waiting for an opportunity to express itself—a view highly consistent with the enactive approach. Damasio, Watt, and Frijda all agree that emotion is the most necessary underpinning for any type of conscious state.

What is revolutionary, for Western ways of thinking, is that these basic emotions don't just seek pleasure or happiness, or to avoid displeasure, unhappiness, and punishment—as the curious cats understood all along. Of course, we are happier if the environment is friendly to our basic emotions, but we feel those emotions either way.

Panksepp finds that if we include the "PLEASURE/PAIN" system as just one motivational system among many (as in his major work, *Affective*

Neuroscience of 1998), there are at least eight mostly independent and separable emotion systems, as seen by observing the brains and neurotransmitter activity of humans and various other mammals. (For Panksepp, emotion and motivation are always correlated.) Here is a list of the eight systems he was able to identify.[5]

The PLAY system
The RAGE system
The FEAR system
The CARE (or NURTURANCE) system
The PANIC (or SEPARATION DISTRESS) system
The LUST system
The SEEKING system (including the curious cat's exploratory drive)
The PLEASURE/PAIN system

Panksepp acknowledges that these "basic" systems don't cover everything we feel; but they are inescapable facets of what we always already are, separately from anything learned through reward, punishment, or even exploration.[6] There is no need to go into the specifics of the neurophysiology in this context, except to note that each system uses a uniquely different combination of brain areas and neurotransmitters—distinguishable from each other, and not dependent on reinforcements.

At least two of those systems are crucial for our purposes—the SEEKING system and the SEPARATION DISTRESS system, which Panksepp later labeled the PANIC system (he uses "PANIC" interchangeably with "SEPARATION DISTRESS"). We saw already that the SEEKING system has a special status for our purposes: It includes, among other things, the "exploratory drive"—an independent desire to search for the truth of what is there, just for the sake of knowing, and not necessarily to serve some ultimately hedonistic purpose. But beyond that, a suppressed SEEKING system also reflects a lack of inspiration or "enthusiasm," a deficit of the feeling that our actions have much value, as in cases of severe depression (Panksepp et al. 2014). For that reason, SEEKING plays a special role in the underlying trajectory of enactive meaning.

PANIC too plays a crucial role in the underlying sense of meaning. If action requires motivation, which entails value, then we need to feel, at least implicitly, that there is an intrinsic value for the sake of which our instrumental values have their meaning. One of the most likely candidates for intrinsic value is the value of valuing creatures themselves. PANIC reflects the inevitable existential need for relationship with other valuing creatures; it is a primary way in which we experience this value, or a deprivation of it. The underlying emotion is an "existential" one both because we can't do without it, and also because, as Gendlin puts it, we don't merely "have" interactions, but in fact we *are* these interactions. Given our inexorably interrelational form of existence, the PANIC system is going to be pivotal for us. Let's examine it in a little more detail.

PANIC

The PANIC (or SEPARATION DISTRESS) system is the one that most specifically connects to the potentially cataclysmic felt sense of our need for social interaction, which has been studied by phenomenologists like Emanuel Levinas (1969), Edith Stein (1916), Max Scheler (1929), and others (but without using Panksepp's neuropsychological terminology).

Panksepp's PANIC system includes a uniquely specifiable combination of brain areas and neurotransmitters that predictably activates in a screaming infant's separation from the mother, or the gut-wrenching sobs of a grieving widow—or even in the quasiseparation of lovers' spats. The more invested we are in a relationship, the more easily the PANIC system can be stirred up. In sensitive individuals, even a rejected manuscript can trigger it. If a harsh word from a friend or co-worker shakes us, what we are feeling involves at least in part an eruption of the PANIC system. We will see later that a sense of extreme alienation from the community can also be relevant to it.

Constant small disturbances of the PANIC system can help keep everyday relationships calibrated. We feel a slight disturbance when the other begins to seem alienated, and normally we correct for it without much conscious awareness. Panksepp studies the empirical manifestations of the system, but we can also regularly feel it subjectively.

To be sure, these feelings are mixed with more subtle and nuanced felt senses that can't be reduced to any "basic emotion system." For my own part, a rejected manuscript involves not just PANIC, but also a threat to my natural laziness. I don't fondly look forward to being told I have still more work to do, including learning whole new lines of research—a daunting workload added to an already busy schedule. My viscera quietly shout, "Many more holes have sprung in the dyke!" And we could explore other nuances of the felt sense.

But part of what I feel can be traced directly or indirectly to the PANIC system and to feeling alienated from others or a community of others. Rejection is one of the classic reminders of the threat of alienation. "No one likes my work." "I can't connect with them!" "Am I wasting my time by even trying?" The feeling is similar to the preteen's "Nobody ever asks me to dance!"

PANIC can even trigger something as seemingly unrelated as political violence. As Picciolini notes, white supremacist recruits' feelings involve an underlying feeling of being rejected by the community, "left behind"—culturally more than economically. This amorphous PANIC has more to do with what the feeling is about than any specific issue the cult can induce its followers to focus on—"being replaced by immigrants," "losing our country," and so on. The recruiting group is enflaming an already underlying PANIC while at the same time encouraging the recruit not to interpret the feeling as being "about" what it is about.

One year after the January 2021 insurrection at the US Capitol and two years into the Covid-19 pandemic, a poll revealed that 34 percent of Americans had come to believe that physical violence against the US government is justifiable (Kornfield and Alfaro 2022). How many of those angry people would connect their underlying PANIC to the feelings of alienation exacerbated by two years of social isolation by the pandemic? The tendency instead is to interpret feelings as being "about" whatever trigger stimulus is presented—"immigrants taking our jobs," elections being "stolen," and so on.

The paramount eruption of PANIC that results from death or separation from a loved one—the classic and most extreme example—isn't simply "a feeling." It continues as an underlying *theme* for which every subsequent emotional episode might be experienced as only a passing modification. After a major loss, any ensuing laughter at a comedy skit or guilt over being late for a meeting is largely a mere footnote to the underlying grief. Each new interpersonal disturbance introduces slight modifications of the ongoing feeling of loss in the same way that Baroque composers added embellishments to a melody. Years after a major interpersonal trauma, a newly occurring anger at a motorist can be more about the underlying PANIC than the specific motorist—the feeling of being alienated or estranged from needed social connection. The general theme of alienation is one of the inescapable emotional issues for beings like humans. It is therefore reflected in an entire basic emotion system, the PANIC system.

When Panksepp uses the term "PANIC," we shouldn't confuse it with a separate FEAR system, which not only feels different subjectively, but also uses a clearly different combination of brain processes. PANIC specifically refers to the pain of social separation or estrangement. Since social alienation is one of the core existential issues, PANIC will prove at least as relevant for our understanding of the sense of enactive meaning as FEAR, if not more so; and its brain correlates are clearly different from FEAR.[7]

In existential terms, we need to enact our form of being in relation to others in order even to be what we are. Stolorow (1994, 2018), as well as Kiesler in his later work (for example, 1996), and also Gendlin (2018), argue that actualizing and enacting the adult form of our being requires not just developmental nurturance, but also real-time interaction with a community of others, beginning with the mother, but extending ultimately to friends, colleagues, and society as a whole.

Our tenuous understanding of the neurophysiology of these basic emotion systems will evolve and change through history; we shouldn't pin too much of our understanding on rapidly changing empirical research. But the existential issues reflected in Panksepp's basic emotion systems will remain as long as there are humans.

Underneath PANIC, and presupposed by it, is a more positive felt sense. Real-time emotional relationships, at least implicitly, involve a feeling of the *value* we place on other valuing creatures. The nurturing of a mother reflects that the children are felt as intrinsically valuable—valuable in their own right, not just for the pleasure they bring to the mother. The proof is that she sacrifices on their behalf.

From the standpoint of a mother, or a mate or a friend, we feel that, even if we were to die tomorrow, there is a sense in which that other person would still be worthy of being valued. Their value isn't felt to be dependent on whether I value them or not. In losing someone, we lose the opportunity to celebrate the value of conscious existence as particularly instantiated in that person; this loss, or the threat of it, hyperactivates the PANIC system. So much value and meaning have been invested in a person or group that the least disturbance can send the PANIC system into hyperdrive.

Some might try to interpret this social bonding need as derivative from hedonistic reinforcement. It might be assumed that the child's happiness makes the mother happy, and therefore, it is "reinforcing." But this would not be true if the mother didn't already value the child qua intrinsic value in the first place. She doesn't do the nurturing in order to obtain the pleasure of it, but just the reverse: It is pleasing only because she wants to do it. It isn't as if a suitable quantity of some other pleasure could substitute for it. And the nurturing behavior doesn't require any reinforcement other than the behavior itself.

Stolorow especially explores the way trauma, such as loss through death, can exacerbate subsequent instances of this effect later in life. The PANIC system in this case has been hypersensitized. In later chapters, we will see that many subsequent emotions are as much about that original loss, or about alienation or threat of alienation, as they are about the specific trigger incident at hand—if not more so.

Because the interpersonal dimension is so indispensable, we come already equipped with a nervous system that is susceptible to orchestrating acute disturbance when disrupted by loss of the very grounds of important relationships—or even the acute threat of their loss. Emotional processes, like all forms of consciousness, have to be physically embodied.

In sum, the feelings associated with the PANIC system inevitably play into our feeling of the intrinsic value of human existence, in three different ways:

First, we experience others *as* intrinsically valuable—valuable in their own right, not just instrumentally toward some other purpose. (Whether we universalize this experience of others' intrinsic value to cover *all* others will also become important for us later.)

Second, others' devaluing *of us* can lead us to doubt our own intrinsic value, and thus the value of our life activities—and consequently (I will argue later) we implicitly doubt the value of humanity per se; this in turn leads to still further devaluing of our own actions since some intrinsic value is needed to ground the experienced instrumental value of our actions.

And third, others' perceived devaluing *of us* can block the various avenues through which we appreciate positive value *as instantiated in them*—hence still further hyperactivation of the PANIC system.

However, the social bonding feelings associated with motivations like PANIC and CARE (or NURTURANCE) couldn't effectively guide our interpersonal interactions if we weren't also driven, independently, by an exploratory drive, which is part of the SEEKING system. The exploratory drive reflects our curiosity, our desire to know what is true, in addition to how we happen to feel about specific people on specific occasions. Most of us consider it wrong to kill *anyone,* regardless of how little empathy we feel for them at the moment. Arbitrary, accidental feelings aren't enough to ground coherent social, moral, and political interaction. This contribution of the exploratory drive, in my view (Ellis 2018), is the missing link that needs to be added to "sentimentalist" approaches to ethics and political philosophy (as Slote 2014 also implies). And beyond the effects of the exploratory aspects of the SEEKING system, the same system as a whole has to be activated in order to feel inspired by the value of any action whatever—even the most banal everyday ones. SEEKING activation therefore is indispensable for any sense of underlying enactive meaning. Let's consider it in a little more detail next.

SEEKING

The SEEKING system works to facilitate curiosity, interest, exploration, and the impetus to voluntary and self-motivated action. Its functioning subserves the tendency of cats to explore their world regardless of any reinforcement for doing so. We can then condition *other* behaviors by rewarding a subject *with* an opportunity to explore (as Harry Harlow already demonstrated with monkeys as early as 1950; the monkeys work for the reward of looking out the window). But the new research shows clearly that the exploratory behavior *per se* (for example, looking out the window) is *its own* reinforcement.

In his seminal volume *Affective Neuroscience* (1998), Panksepp characterizes the experiential side of the SEEKING system in this way: "This harmoniously operating neuroemotional system drives and energizes many mental complexities that humans experience as persistent feelings of interest, curiosity, sensation seeking, and, in the presence of a sufficiently complex cortex, the search for higher meaning" (145).

In clinical depression, a major hallmark, maybe the crucial hallmark, is a long-term dampening of the SEEKING system—a consistent pattern reported by Panksepp and colleagues (2014). In this case, we just don't feel like doing anything. Someone previously obsessed with music now finds taking the instrument from its case to be a deadening experience. As Panksepp and others put it, we become incapable of feeling "enthusiasm," even to a modest extent. The study shows that long-term dampening of the SEEKING system correlates with clinical depression, by means of brain scans, clinical diagnosis, and observation of neurotransmitter levels. A caveat is that the system is widely distributed, and parts of it can be hyperactive even while other parts become underactive.[8]

The SEEKING system includes the "exploratory drive" and therefore plays a crucial role, in humans, for energizing any kind of introspective curiosity—including curiosity about the interpretation of emotional meaning. Exploration includes a search for the truth about reality. It involves the inherent motivation to ask questions. All animals, especially mammals, come equipped with a powerful exploratory drive, but for humans, one manifestation is the need to ask *ourselves* questions. For example, we can ask ourselves whether we value something for its own sake, regardless of any other outcome (intrinsic value), or whether we value it by virtue of its facilitating some further outcome (instrumental value).

Granted, animals do try to maintain *predictability* in their environment and life activities (Bitbol 2019); yet there is also a contrary built-in tendency toward curiosity, adventure and discovery. Mother Nature knew that a robust exploratory drive could create an advantage for survival, but from the individual's viewpoint, it is simply a built-in desire, valued for its own sake, without the need for some ulterior outcome. In fact, exploratory behavior is so crucial for intelligent animals that Mother Nature needed for it to operate as a *primary* motivator—independent of other motives and without any external reinforcement. Hsee and Ruan (2016) found that inherent curiosity sometimes can even be a *stronger* motivation than hedonistic rewards or punishments. Their subjects preferred the sheer satisfaction of curiosity over more hedonistic rewards.

Understanding the architecture of the complex edifice of the intrinsic and instrumental values that motivate action requires looking at the interplay of SEEKING and PANIC. SEEKING requires that we value something with a positive valence, strongly enough to motivate action. Its dampening correlates with the lethargy of depression. But PANIC reflects the crucial importance of the most obvious basis for intrinsic value per se: the value of other valuing creatures themselves. When the PANIC system is thrown into chaos, so is the underpinning of the feeling that anything at all is worthwhile since instrumental values depend on the underlying intrinsic ones. PANIC reveals this need to take others as having intrinsic value. The resulting threat of valuelessness is then reflected in SEEKING system suppression.

Limits of Empirical Correlations and the Need for a Deeper Level of Analysis

This brings us to several crucial caveats about the role of the brain here. First, "basic" emotions refer only to a subset of our overall affective life. Neither Panksepp nor Damasio nor Frijda nor Watt argues for a "nothing but" reductionism of the meaning of emotions. They are not saying, when someone falls in love, "Oh, that's nothing but an interaction of the LUST, NURTURANCE, and PANIC systems." The inevitable explosion of PANIC when we lose a romantic partner or military comrade doesn't predetermine whether or with whom we fall in love or affirm a strong friendship. Those emotional processes are intricate, subtle, and full of the complexities of individuality, life circumstances, and internal conflicts.

Even FEAR and RAGE can't be seen as just a result of "amygdala hyper-activation." Doug Watt (1998, 2000), in agreement with Panksepp, shows that these emotional processes are widely distributed and holistic, including many brain areas and especially the periaqueductal gray (PAG) area of the brain stem, and of course the activity of the viscera and the entire body. The tiny amygdala acts mainly as a habit-driven storage device for our knowledge of things *toward which* we have learned to feel anger or fear (and in some cases have inherited a tendency to do so). Like the switch in a light fixture, the amygdala triggers the wider RAGE and FEAR systems to activate. But those systems are much more widely distributed than just the amygdala. Their activation, as well as their actual *feeling* dimension, always involves the deeper subcortex, the viscera, the prefrontal regulation, and the entire body (Watt 2000; Panksepp 2011, 2014).

A second caveat is that as Gendlin cautions, when we reflect carefully into a felt sense, what we find is much more nuanced and specific than the broad category labels that Panksepp is using—for example "FEAR" and "RAGE." But the specific felt senses of our daily lives do *include*, among other things, activation of the systems that Panksepp highlights. The fact that the feelings of depression correlate so strongly with SEEKING-system suppression illustrates this point. To be sure, we wouldn't make much progress in psychotherapy by describing feelings with such simplistic categories as "panic," "fear," or "rage." We need more specificity than those broad category labels would suggest. But they do seem to interact and overlap with more specific felt senses, if we respect the complexity, nuance, and interrelatedness of the various emotions involved.

A third caveat is that since emotion systems are widely distributed, discussions of their "dampening" or "inhibition" should respect appropriate nuance. Some parts, or some functions, of the SEEKING system can be hyperactive, while others remain quiet or even inhibited (for example, see Alexander et al. 2019 and Zikopoulus et al. 2017 on the intricate complexity and adaptability of these brain systems). This *compartmentalization* becomes especially important in understanding the emotional effects of confirmation bias and authoritarian tendencies, discussed in later chapters. In those cases, SEEKING suppression is deliberately contextualized and then habitually selective, much like selective inattention.

And fourth, again because these systems are so widely distributed, they are expressions of the whole organism, working toward the purposes of the entire self-organizing creature. Unless there is a very localized malfunction of a specific brain area, such as prefrontal injury (crucial for impulse control and understanding the "aboutness" of feelings), I can't just insist that my emotions are "not really mine, only a product of my brain systems"—except in the loose sense in which none of us got to choose our physical bodies with their various necessary limitations (part of Heidegger's *Geworfenheit*, or "thrownness"). As Bill Faw (2000a) colorfully puts it, I can't use the criminal defense that "my amygdala-orbitofrontal circuit made me do it." In a sense, it might not be "my fault" if I turn out to be a psychopath due to what is going on in my brain; but the neurophysiology is the empirically observable dimension of my own conscious processes. Those are still "me."

A related qualification is that interaction with the environment, as a child develops, profoundly affects the way the brain's emotion systems are organized. Neurologists now are fond of saying that the nervous system is "plastic," or malleable. Self-organization means that the various parts work in dynamic and flexible interaction with each other, constantly tuning and retuning, even amidst internal conflict between different parts and aspects of this "me." Brain systems like PANIC and SEEKING are empirical manifestations of subjectively experienceable conditions of existence. Some version of the "basic" emotion systems inevitably develops because they reflect existential necessities for beings of our kind.

The ability to formulate questions is what allows an "I" (some would call it a "transcendental ego") to stand back and ask myself about what a particular aspect of me is feeling and what those feelings are trying to say, what they are "about." Phenomenologically, a *question* is a type of *emotion*: It is a targeted *feeling* of curiosity prompted by incomplete understanding of something. So a special use of the SEEKING system, in its "exploratory drive" aspect, actually fuels Gendlin's focusing process.

For our purposes, what is most striking about these "basic" emotions is that we can't escape them. They don't happen *to* us, but rather are aspects of what we are. They always play a role in our value feelings, even if we try to ignore them. In the case of SEEKING, one of its roles is veritably as a driver and energizer of the search for truth itself. It pushes back *from within ourselves* against our own self-deceptions and delusions.

SEEKING-System Imbalance in Clinical Depression: Happiness versus Meaning

Clinical depression manifests itself in the empirical dimension with a marked dampening of Panksepp's SEEKING system (Panksepp et al. 2014). The depressed person's initial response to every situation resembles the response of Melville's Bartleby the Scrivener: "I prefer not." Although this emotional situation sometimes can be triggered by hyperactivity of the PANIC system, the SEEKING-system suppression remains the central and definitive hallmark of severe depression. "Social rewards" alone can't pull us out of it. "He shuts me out!" is a typical response from a spouse or family member. Social relationships afford as little energizing effect as anything else. Life goals might be well underway, but achieving the goals *per se* offers too little value or meaning to inspire further activity.

In short, everything is going great, but everything is terrible. The person would very much like to get motivated to do something but can't—reminiscent of the bank robber's famous remark: "I wish I didn't want to rob banks, but I do want to rob them." It seems counterintuitive to want what we don't want.

Part of this depressive double paradox relates to Viktor Frankl's (1959) sharp distinction between meaning and happiness. During Frankl's years of captivity in Nazi concentration camps at Theresienstadt and later at Auschwitz and Dachau (Pytell 2017), his fellow inmates could hardly hope to be "happy." They certainly couldn't hope for much "positive reinforcement," and even their chances of long-term survival weren't good. Yet some managed to find some meaning in their struggle or in their lives within the struggle—if only by preserving the hidden photo of a loved one or helping a friend acquire half of a cigarette.

This experience led to Frankl's "logotherapy"—from the Ancient Greek word *logos*, or "logic of meaning," used by the ancient Stoics. The central premise of logotherapy is that "happiness," in the everyday modern sense, is a separate dimension from *meaning*. (The ancient Greek *eudaimonia* didn't mean "happiness" in the modern sense; it would have been better translated as something like "healthy soul" or "well-spiritedness.") For Frankl, happiness, especially in the simple "feelgood" sense, differs fundamentally from feeling that our life activities are *meaningful*. Happiness in the modern sense depends on good outcomes (even if the outcome in question is only the carefreeness of nirvana). Meaning, by contrast, doesn't depend on the outcome; it requires only that we take something to be valuable enough to warrant our daily struggles in the first place—separately from how we feel when we achieve it or don't achieve it.

Some of the contemporary "happiness" research tends to blur this distinction. The meaningful experience of intensely valuing something is a different thing from being *successful in achieving* whatever we value. The act of demonstrating against a war can overtly symbolize and thus intensify our affirmation of the value of peace, which is felt as *meaningful*, even as we remain *unhappy* about the continuation of the war—the failure to achieve what we value. Panksepp and colleagues find that the "sadness" dimension of depression—the negation of happiness—correlates with the PANIC system, whereas the lack of "enthusiasm"—the lethargy and shortage of *meaning*, the failure to feel motivating values very strongly—correlates with SEEKING suppression. Those are two different emotion systems.

Not only can we value something without being happy that we have achieved it, but the converse can also be true. We can be happy that we have succeeded at something and yet fail to intensely enough feel that what we have achieved is very valuable in the first place.

Another aspect of the depressive paradox relates to the idea of "blockages" to action. Inaction can result from an inner conflict. One part of us wants to act, while another resists the action. Ann Weiser Cornell (2005) addresses this inner conflict from a focusing perspective. We can first focus introspectively on the actual felt sense of the desire to act (What does the desire to act feel like when it gets blocked?); and then also focus on the concrete feeling of the desire to hold back (What does the holding-back want to protect me from? What are the reasons for its fear?). When we focus carefully on the bodily emotional feeling of both conflicting impulses, one at a time, the block against action sometimes tends to begin a slow process of resolving itself either for or against the action, or toward some third way, without any deliberate effort.

Our interest here is less in understanding *blocks against* action as to get at the underlying motivation-to-act half of this situation in the first place. What are the values that can inspire us to action and define the meaning of what we are trying to do in the first place? The idea that the SEEKING system is what gets dampened in the absence of inspiration or "enthusiasm" (Panksepp's word) seems to offer a promising clue.

In most instances of depression, *negative* value feelings obviously do rise to an intense level, for example when focused on loss of a loved one. We might even "revel" in the agonizing feeling. It is, at least, an experience of value. But a more positive value experience would be needed to inspire action—not just pleasure or achievement of outcomes, but rather a feeling of the value *of* some possible action, in a positive way.

A general dampening of the SEEKING system, as Panksepp and colleagues show, is the main brain correlate of this lack of enthusiasm and zest for life. There is a feeling of deflated meaning in something similar to Frankl's sense—a lack of intensity in valuing any potential action, other than in a negative and uninspiring way. To be sure, a good bit of frantic energy, sometimes undirected and chaotic, can occur *initially* from a triggering of the PANIC system; but then comes long-term SEEKING-system suppression.

Panksepp and others (2014) therefore sharply distinguish between the lethargy through dampening of SEEKING and on the other hand what they call the "sadness" component of depression. The "sadness" dimension correlates with the PANIC system, whereas the lack of "enthusiasm" correlates with a different system—the SEEKING system. The interconnection between these two dimensions needs to be explored further as we proceed since they both play such an indispensable role in the motivation for action.

But noticing these objective facts about the brain offers little guidance in how to execute the *subjective, conscious* processes that might enact the needed brain activity—especially for a conscious creature as complicated as humans. Drugs can physically stimulate energy and some relief from sadness, but not a sustainable sense of enactive meaning: The simpler drugs (those that only elevate dopamine) often lead to reckless hypermania, sometimes suicide, or even murder (e.g., see Gabbay et al. 2013; Davidson et al. 2007; Retz et al. 2004). More sophisticated drugs allow the organism to fuel its own balance by indirectly *preventing suppression* of the natural SEEKING system (such as serotonin reuptake inhibitors, which rely on the body's natural neurotransmitters). Even then, there are temporary eruptions of either PANIC or lethargy (SEEKING-system suppression), and the system may eventually restore its own balance in a way that resists the drug's effectiveness.

Robert Stolorow (1994, 2018) follows up on Frankl's ideas about the role of existential meaning for psychiatric problems like depression and anxiety. Stolorow with his intersubjective existential approach sees everyday anxieties as instances of concern about larger issues. Marital discord can be a way of channeling a basic "PANICKY" feeling involving our necessary dependence on other people for meaning—an acute concern over actual or potential alienation, which Stolorow emphasizes can also be further sensitized by earlier instances of the same concern. Ironically, in petty arguments between close friends or relatives, each individual's PANIC over the potential for alienation flares up, eventually leading to *real* alienation, hence further activation of PANIC, and so on in a vicious circle.

PTSD can be connected to both PANIC hyperactivity and SEEKING suppression, as well as other basic emotions that relate to the always presupposed sense of ongoing enactive meaning: Fear and anxiety reflect, among other things, the basic worries about the shortness of life and our own relative powerlessness and smallness; PANIC relates to social alienation. Combat veterans trying to re-enter the civilian economy in the wake of devaluation of human life and hypervigilance against the ever-presence of death, only to face a sense of being culturally and economically "left out" or "superfluous," face all these existential challenges.

Like Irvin Yalom (1980), Stolorow traces many everyday emotional problems to the more all-pervasive and potentially terrifying existential problems that we discussed earlier: death, ever-potential alienation, the smallness of our own personal significance in the bigger picture, and our necessarily limited power over circumstances and destiny. These concerns can trigger basic emotion systems like PANIC and SEEKING. By suppressing awareness of these recurring underlying themes, in the view of the existentialists, we might misconstrue what our feelings are about, attributing them only to smaller everyday problems that represent *less-terrifying instances* of the larger ones.

In Stolorow's view, any major trauma can exacerbate these existential concerns even further. This would include not only the devastation of loss through death, but also childhood traumatization by acute powerlessness or feelings of insignificance, including repeated humiliation by being labeled as "stupid" or "useless." Paradoxically, the same experiences can force *repression* of the very existential concerns that they trigger, as too terrifying for surface consciousness. Lingering childhood feelings of "smallness" and "uselessness," as well as adult traumatic experiences, can connect in hidden ways to the larger existential challenges of basic finiteness to which the existential psychologists would want to trace them. Plagued by illnesses toward the end of his life, my father, R. J. Ellis, described this odd congruence between small, everyday problems and the larger existential ones with the following poem:

> I wait to meet the matador,
> And lo am slain by a picador.

∼

Frankl often speaks of the need for "purpose" as part of the underlying sense of meaning. This actually complicates matters further: As hinted earlier, instrumentalities are required for this idea of purpose. We have already seen the inevitable conflict between instrumental values and the most foundational intrinsic value—the value of valuing creatures per se. The existential *necessity* of a feeling of instrumental "purpose" can cut against the *sufficiency* of the intrinsic value of valuing creatures as such, simply for their own sake.

A predominance of instrumental over intrinsic value is illustrated par excellence in "Grand Scheme" value systems like totalitarian and cult followings, where all other needs and interests are subordinated to the Grand Scheme and where entire categories of people who are perceived as outsiders to the group, or even who are not sufficiently loyal to the cult, can be severely devalued. Everything and everyone begins to be evaluated only insofar as they serve as instruments in service to the Grand Scheme.

But even in the most normal everyday life process, most instrumental values serve in turn other instrumental values, and so on, leading to long chains of instrumental values, like the ancient trade routes that extended to the furthest frontiers of prehistoric Scandinavia, or like the supply chains for Napoleon's army in Russia. Any disconnect between any one point in the chain and the chain's source can disrupt the entire chain. And if the frontiers go to war against their own source (like the Russian army of 1917), or vice versa, the entire edifice tends to collapse. In the next chapter, we try to get a handle on how these chains of instrumentality serve the function of enactive meaning, and how they sometimes block that same function.

Chapter 4

The Extended Value System and the Place of Instrumentality

Consciousness isn't a metaphysical ghost floating in the sky somewhere. It needs to be physically embodied through action. Action, or even imagined action, can perform a "symbolizing" function, in Gendlin's sense, serving to intensify our conscious valuing of things, independently of whether we achieve the valued outcomes or not. We symbolize commitment to a political cause by taking action—campaigning, organizing, and voting. In this way, we feel the commitment in a concretely embodied way.

A line of poetry might move us only mildly when read silently, whereas reading it out loud chokes us up. The physical act of saying the words makes us feel them more intensely. Motivations and values too are intensified by the expanded embodiments that symbolize them.

Many actions that inspire us by intensifying value feelings don't connect directly to any *intrinsic* value—any "for the sake of which"—such as the intrinsic value of valuing creatures themselves. Our lives tend to revolve around instrumental values like working effectively, improving an athletic technique, or voting and campaigning for a political cause. After all, don't we get a good part of our inspiration from work and from other activities whose purpose is to serve some longer-term end? For most of us, life would seem flat and dull without numerous activities of that kind. We have "extended" our value system to include these instrumentalities within the sense of enactive meaning. The instrumentalities give us a sense of "purpose."

But treating ourselves as instrumental values in the service of such purposes is in tension with the more important intrinsic value of ourselves and others, which needs to exist irrespective of whether we serve such "larger" purposes or not. By putting oil in the car, *in order to* get to work, *in order to* earn some money, *in order to* serve the needs of a family, I implicitly affirm the more basic value that grounds these instrumental ones: the intrinsic value of the valuing creatures themselves. But there is also a tension here. If I lose the job, I lose some of the sense of meaning that this instrumentality facilitated, and the feeling of my own intrinsic value can easily be diminished as a result.

The need to find some instrumental value that we can serve is an unavoidable consequence of intrinsically valuing anything. We therefore feel a need to serve something whose value further extends the instrumentalities that follow from whatever (or whomever) we take as having intrinsic value. This makes us want to serve some process that goes beyond ourselves or any one individual—the perfecting of a professional craft, the preserving of a republic, the well-being of an extended family, the tradition of legal ethics, or the ongoing project of philosophy. We construct a good bit of the meaning of our actions around such instrumentalities or "purposes"—being a good musician, an effective teacher, a good parent, and so on.

In short, the enactive meaning of our actions *needs* instrumentality just as much as it needs intrinsic value, despite the implicit conflict between them. The demands of life within a finite existence require buckling down, pushing ourselves, and reflecting critically on our shortcomings with tasks and purposes we have set for ourselves. Young athletes can't just admire what is good about their own performance: Self-critique and diligent striving are necessary. The Young Stockbroker, at the end of the film, realizes among other things that he needs to "find something useful to do."

The more we feel our own and others' value to be instrumental toward various purposes—and the more *necessary* these instrumentalities become for the sense of enactive meaning—the less *sufficient* the intrinsic value of valuing creatures themselves becomes for the meaning of our actions. As a crucial component for an understanding of the overall project of creating these meaning trajectories, we should take a moment to reflect specifically on how this more "extended" value system comes about.

The Extended Value System

When the alarm clock rings, we might feel that we are waking up because we "have to" get to work or buy groceries. But feeling this "have to" strongly enough to energize us to confront the slings and arrows of the day presupposes a certain baseline level of inspiration—not fireworks, but enough to avoid Bartleby the Scrivener's "I prefer not." Regardless of what we "have to" do, such lethargy, as we saw in the last chapter, would characterize SEEKING suppression, and thus clinical depression or severe inaction.

The values that motivate this tonic background feeling of everyday inspiration go somewhat beyond friendly interactions with the convenience store clerk or the occasional charitable donation—although those are clearly meaningful in the sense that they do affirm the intrinsic value of the most basic intrinsic value: valuing creatures themselves. Beyond that, there is a sense in which we seek a purpose that isn't served just by everyday interactions with other valuing creatures, intrinsically valuable though those might be.

The paradox here is that the underlying feeling of the meaning of our actions doesn't always come directly from real-time interactions with people—even though those valuing creatures are the most obvious candidates for something that is intrinsically valuable.

This paradox stands out as if in a controlled experiment if we take an extremely introverted personality as example. Even for an introvert, the friendly interactions do occur, but on a more limited basis. How does the introvert sustain the feeling of everyday inspiration with so little access to the most basic intrinsic value—the value of other valuing creatures? One of the most consistent findings of factor-analytic personality research is that introversion-extraversion *doesn't* particularly correlate with either "agreeableness" or "negative emotionality" (for example, see Davis and Panksepp 2018). How is it possible that introversion doesn't lead to devaluation of others or a deficit of an enactive meaning trajectory?

The Russian composer Serge Rachmaninov, clearly an introvert, confided in very few people and wasn't particularly thrilled by the process of public performance, despite his brilliant technique and ease of execution. He wasn't the least bit nervous about his actual performance, but he did shy away from the degree of *socializing* involved in touring. Even with close friends, he was private and guarded in communicating personal thoughts and feelings. His musical work was so important to him that his psychoanalyst, Nikolai Dahl, in helping him out of a bout of depression, famously resorted to posthypnotic suggestion to motivate Rachmaninov to revitalize not his interpersonal relationships, but rather his composing work—resulting in the celebrated *Piano Concerto No. 2*.

In short, the inspirational dimension for Rachmaninoff seemed separate from the interpersonal realm. But how can that be possible, in light of the interactive constitution of what we are, and given the foundational role of the intrinsic value of valuing creatures? Why wasn't Rachmaninov's PANIC system always in hyperdrive?

Like any composer, Rachmaninov spent incalculable hours practicing his instrument and trying out musical ideas, not for an audience of particular listeners, but for an indeterminate number of *hypothetical* listeners, whose specific life circumstances not only *were,* but actually *needed to remain* undefined, various, and unpredictable. The music had to speak to as many of those hypothetical people as possible. But the music could speak to them only because they were, at the most basic level, valuing creatures, even if only imaginary ones.

Rachmaninov's trajectory of actions had meaning, not simply because specific valuing creatures were valued by him, but because there was a more elaborate *system* of value built on the initial foundation of the value of hypothetical valuing creatures qua potential listeners—the "very idea" of a subjectively emotional listener. Like a novelist, he lived his daily life interacting with imaginary characters—but those characters stood for the universal idea of "valuing creature," just as a concrete individual would.

This abstracted and universalized system of values, grounded in the value of valuing creatures as a general idea, beyond any specific interaction, was the source of the "something more" needed to wake Rachmaninov up in the morning. It served as the source of the normal level of inspiration presupposed by "meaningful action." Imagining how a variety of potential valuing creatures would hear the music was the foundational criterion for what worked or didn't work in his music. Any chord or musical phrase would have to be rewritten if it didn't work in terms of the imagined effect on the listener. This crucial reliance on his relationship with an imaginary listening audience was why Rachmaninov's psychiatrist knew that composing music would be the thing to lift him out of his depression.

Rachmaninov's example suggests a way in which the *universalization* of the value of valuing creatures can not only become helpful but actually might be implicitly necessary for the sense of meaning. The next section further explores this role of implicit universalization in the extended value system.

The Role of Implicit Universalization

We have already seen that value systems are at least partly grounded in the nuts and bolts of specific feelings toward specific individuals, as reflected in the PANIC, CARE (or NURTURANCE), PLAY, and even the LUST systems. Even sexual intercourse releases oxytocin, one of the main neurotransmitters of the CARE system, irrespective of gender or sexual identity. But these valuing experiences, hinging on the intrinsic value of valuing creatures, eventually get extended and fleshed out by further exploration.

The motivation for this exploration of the valuational realm, beginning with early childhood, is reflected in SEEKING system activity, which is just as endogenous as the specific social bonding systems. In the naturally motivated search to understand our world—and specifically the need to understand interpersonal reality as we grow up and mature—we learn to universalize our caring about valuing creatures in general, since we can't deny that their intrinsic value is simply *by virtue of* being valuing creatures per se. We notice that all valuing creatures share that very same property. If the value were by virtue of some other purpose served by the creature, it would be instrumental, not intrinsic value.

Motivation to develop a value system as we mature through childhood depends crucially on the exploratory drive. There is an implicit searching for truth in this development. If we don't value people simply by virtue of the fact that they are valuing creatures, then we are valuing them in a way that depends on instrumental functions that they serve—that they please us personally, enhance our own happiness, achieve great outcomes, or serve a cause such as The Revolution or The Fatherland.

We therefore begin to realize that to reject anyone's intrinsic value (at least in the *prima facie* sense) would weaken the feeling that being a valuing creature per se is enough to give someone value. If we were to reject the intrinsicness of people's value, we would implicitly reduce them to merely instrumental value. But then there would be a void of intrinsic value in our own valuational and motivational system.

When we acknowledge someone's intrinsic value in a *prima facie* sense, we allow that this value sometimes has to be balanced with other values, such as the intrinsic value of *others'* well-being. Even a serial killer has *prima facie* intrinsic value, but when we balance this *prima facie* value against competing values, such as the safety of potential victims, we have to punish the killer. We do devalue serial killers in the *instrumental* sense. The fact that we don't reject their intrinsic value is reflected in our repugnance against the idea of mercilessly torturing criminals. For any of us, unless we are complete psychopaths ourselves, there is some limit to the amount of suffering we would be willing to inflict on a valuing creature, no matter how bad they are in the instrumental sense—in the sense that they cause harm.

If we lose the sense of the intrinsic value of valuing creatures as such, we are then tempted to fill the void of intrinsic value with Grand Scheme fantasies. For example, authoritarianism and cults of personality try to fill this void by subordinating intrinsic value in favor of instrumental ones in one of two ways: They either (1) make us all into mostly instrumental values in the service of the Grand Scheme, so that some have more of this instrumental value than others; or (2) they try to limit the realm of intrinsically valuable creatures to a small subset—close friends, family, the tribe, those who are "like us."

Even though the second option does attempt to preserve the intrinsic value of some, it requires constantly ignoring the realization that when the realm of valued creatures is limited to a subclass, they aren't being taken as having intrinsic value *as such*. If their value were *by virtue of* being valuing creatures as such, then all valuing creatures would have intrinsic value. If we value them only as family members or countrymen—their *instrumentality relative to us*—then they aren't valued just by virtue of their humanity, consciousness or subjectivity—the kinds of things that make us valuing creatures.

We then live with constant internal contradictions and cognitive dissonances. Without some sense that valuing creatures have intrinsic value, not much inspiration can even be drawn from the *instrumental* values that depend on it, because then there is too little intrinsic value *toward which* the remaining instrumental values *are* instrumental.

But what if an inspiring realm of science, philosophy, art, or sports *isn't* motivated by its instrumental usefulness for valuing creatures, but is simply "fun," or of purely theoretical interest, like pure physics research, appealing directly to our exploratory drive and our PLAY instinct? Even then, such interests still have to be balanced in our lives with other values that do involve connection to the value of valuing creatures. Universalization of the idea of "valuing creature"—as in hypothetical audiences or potential users of a new medical treatment—can fuel the enthusiasm of the SEEKING system by allowing a feeling that the value attaches to creatures simply qua valuing creature per se, and not because of some accidental property or some particular relationship to us personally—which would give them only instrumental value.

To be sure, when we immerse ourselves in an activity like music, we normally don't focus attention on the indirect connection to valuing creatures, including hypothetical or imaginary ones. But in Heidegger's terms, there still needs to be some implicit "for the sake of which," even if we aren't currently directing our attention to it. Even when we turn a screw at an assembly line, we implicitly affirm the value, not only of the user of the product, but also of the next worker on the line who depends on that screw being in place.

Because the hypothetical users of our products are imaginary and indefinite, they are also *universalized*. Their subjectivity is accepted as valuable simply by virtue of the fact that we imagine them as subjective creatures. Some may evoke easier empathy than others, but the intrinsic value that the empathy acknowledges doesn't depend on a person's instrumentality relative to us or to any Grand Scheme.

When a musician loses respect for the listening audience, the performance misses its inspirational power *even for the performer*. The attitude becomes "I'll have to churn out some simplistic, popularized schlock for the dumbed-down tastes of the masses." As a result, the artist loses the feeling of inspiration. By contrast, a concert pianist once told me he found his inspiration by imagining someone in the audience hearing the Schumann *A-Minor Concerto* for the first time. He didn't know who this specific listener was, but he imagined it.

For any artist, it is true that the limitations of the audience's tastes present a problem. The current popular taste sets one of many *limits* within which the creative work is constructed—just like the dimensions of the canvas, the number of beats in a sonnet, the medieval demand for religious subject matter, or the available instrumentation for the music. Art is constructed within those limits—and the limits usually do include the somewhat culturally relative popular tastes of the listeners and the current orientation of the music critics. But if no possible listening audience is felt to have *value*, then neither can the music.

Many individual differences create various difficulties in feeling the intrinsic value of the "listening audiences"—or analogous representations of universalized humanity for the scientist, craftsman, politician, or even mathematician—those in relation to whom we are doing what we are doing. But each of those difficulties connects in one way or another to two basic emotion systems—PANIC and SEEKING, for two crucial reasons:

1. SEEKING suppression interferes with the exploratory drive and thus reduces the ability to comprehend that the value of valuing persons is implicitly universal—whether the SEEKING suppression is targeted (as in the deliberate blind spots of authoritarian, xenophobic, and ultraconformist attitudes), or whether it is involuntary and global (as in depression). It either dampens enthusiasm altogether, or it *selectively limits* the natural deployment of the exploratory drive, and thus our curiosity about value issues themselves. In this latter case, the

step from specific social bonds to universalization of human value may not be taken even as we reach adulthood. We remain alexithymic to the value of strangers or those who aren't "like us."

2. PANIC-system disturbance can easily dampen the experience of the intrinsic value of others. PANIC can be reflected in hyperactivation of feelings of grief, social alienation, abusive personal relationships, humiliation, or the loss of or separation from loved ones. Value-affirming social bonding emotions can also be disrupted by convoluted defenses *against the sheer risk* of exposure of the PANIC system, as in specific emotional disturbances that clinical psychologists see routinely. Any of these problems—a matter of degree for most of us—can subtract from our access to the concrete feeling that there are intrinsic values worth constructing instrumentalities around and therefore dampen our everyday tonic feeling of a normal level of inspiration to action.

PANIC, SEEKING, and the Enactive Inspiration to Instrumental Action

Investment in the "extended" value system can create mazes of complexity in trying to balance achievement of instrumental excellence against the intrinsic value of either ourselves or others. Sometimes we set overly grandiose goals precisely *because* the simpler ones fail to motivate the needed action. "Perhaps an even more magnificent outcome could inspire me to act." The grounding of even the instrumental value then gets lost if the instrumentalization occludes the intrinsic values that ground it—especially, in this case, the intrinsic value of ourselves.

In this case, we become merely "instruments"—whether successful or failing ones. With a shortage of the feeling of intrinsic value, SEEKING becomes suppressed, unbalanced, or too narrowly directed (as in the case of addiction). With the resulting dampening of the capacity for "enthusiasm," the idea of initiating action per se arouses less and less energy or motivation. It is almost as if we had become passive rather than active creatures; yet the ability to deliberately act is what distinguishes animals from the inanimate.

The famous football quarterback Terry Bradshaw experienced this loss of inspiration. Even during his record-setting four Superbowl victories, he suffered from severe depression. He later described himself as having wished his football career would just hurry and get itself over with (see Bradshaw's *Chicago Tribune* interview with Don Pierson, 2003). It wasn't that he didn't have good interpersonal relationships with his teammates. He even did a weekly radio show with his friend and backup quarterback, Terry Hanratty. But he found himself unable to feel very inspired by the value of any action he might take, although he could *re*-act to environmental circumstances with some effort. He couldn't just play for the love of the game. Ultimately, only the fear of failure and the discipline of his coaches' practice routines—the demand to serve instrumentalities—kept him going. He feared failure to achieve these instrumental outcomes, and thus he was motivated just enough to comply with the external demands of training.

In an abstract way, the depressed person is strongly motivated toward one goal: to *stop* the suffering and lethargy. But there is no specific action toward which much enthusiasm can be mustered. Even Bradshaw's impressive achievement of goals couldn't add up to an enthusiastic motivation. He managed to avoid complete surrender to the depression by stoically forcing himself to keep up his physical training. Physical activity can release just enough dopamine to wake up the SEEKING system, at least to an extent.

An overly facile understanding of the difference between "normal" grief and depression would be that a grieving person experiences "realistic" sadness, whereas the depressed patient's sadness isn't based on any real misfortune. After all, Bradshaw won four Super Bowls and was married to three wonderful women (by his own description). But there was nothing "unrealistic" about his sadness and lethargy. If no amount of career success or affirmative relationships can make any particular action seem worthwhile, then it *really doesn't* make much difference whether things are going well or not. We might labor under the illusion that "if only I could achieve X or Y, then I wouldn't be depressed." But the illusoriness of these values is revealed when X or Y *is* achieved, yet we still feel depressed. Success in attaining what we want in life is a different dimension from experiencing the value *of* whatever we value, intensely enough to make us feel enthusiasm for it.

To be sure, feeling depressed does allow focusing attention in a *negative* way on important values—by lamenting all the suffering and potential suffering in the world. What depression prevents is much intensity for the feeling of the *positive* value of taking action. The PANIC system may have been disturbed through childhood abuse or neglect, or the early trauma of loss of a loved one, or just too much social rejection (for example, see Bryer et al. 1987; Judith Herman 1992; Yehuda et al. 2001). Sometimes there are neurophysiological reasons, such as an innately sensitive PANIC system. The person's brain configuration may make them hypersensitive to even a slight degree of social rejection or alienation. Again, this PANIC can trigger depression because it blocks access to the intrinsic value that could motivate us—the "in-principle-universal" valuing of other valuing creatures, at least at an implicit level. The result then is suppression of the SEEKING system, which requires value feelings for the sense of everyday, ordinary inspiration. We then suffer from a deficit of motivation for action.

But even without severe depression, we can all notice on reflection that the strength of our valuing of desirable outcomes varies from time to time. "There are already so many excellent virtuoso violinists in the world; does it really make a great difference whether I add one more?" In the "Big Picture of Things," is this outcome itself really meaningful enough to inspire all the grueling everyday practice? Bradshaw always wished he could just quit playing football, even as he kept winning Super Bowls.

Bradshaw's case illustrates that depression isn't alleviated by attaining valuable outcomes. We can't write off this strange fact by remarking, "Yes, it's amazing how irrational people can be when in the throes of depression—the birds are singing outside, it's a nice spring day, they have their friends and family and are successful at what they do, etc., yet they feel depressed—how irrational!" The real problem isn't that depression is irrational. The problem is that even if we have had success (or good luck) in attaining the things we want, we may not have had good luck in being able to intensify our feeling *that attaining those things is all that much worth doing*.

This is where the problem of enactive meaning becomes acute. The problem is not so much of attaining valued outcomes, but of *valuing* those outcomes in a strongly motivating way in the first place—feeling their pull to action with some degree of intensity, and with a positive valence.

In sum, instrumental values need to maintain some sort of connection to the most crucial intrinsic value itself: the value of *us conscious creatures*—even if the connection is extended by many intermediate values (as in Rachmaninoff's case). Meaning needs a sociality dimension. Bradshaw in his *Chicago Tribune* interview refers repeatedly to always feeling "alone," despite his famously gregarious personality—clearly an expression of the PANIC system. His worst bouts of depression were triggered by the dissolution of his three marriages. We will soon have to get back to the interconnections between the social dimension (PANIC) and the enactive-exploratory dimension (SEEKING).

If SEEKING-system suppression is the hallmark of clinical depression (even when triggered by PANIC), it would seem to follow that SEEKING activation is a fundamental dimension of the trajectory of felt meaning for any particular action. And the meaning of those action trajectories, in turn, is a crucial component to the meaning of any specific emotion that deceptively *appears* as being "caused by" some specific event or situation such as a drunk in a bar, a misinformed electorate, or a disengaged student in the classroom.

The Role of "Symbolization" in Intensifying Value Feelings

Some of our actions aren't motivated by the desire to attain what we value at all. Some are geared toward intensifying the experience *of* the sense that those things have value in the first place—to intensify the simple experiencing *of* these values. We can intensify a feeling of the value of cherished people by looking at a photograph or hearing music. Epic poetry or majestic music may "symbolize" and thus intensify the excitement of a historic event larger than ourselves or enthusiasm in training for an athletic event.

I use "symbolization" here in Gendlin's sense. Since conscious processes such as emotions and value feelings aren't supernatural things, they need to be acted out in the physical realm of our bodies (often including speech acts) in order to be fully felt.[1] Embodied symbolizations—words, phrases, images, metaphors, or even musical ideas—resonate with the felt sense, bringing it more fully alive.

Certain utterances or images that we actively execute (even if only with our brains) can enact the way we feel in an embodied way, and therefore they can more fully activate the concrete feeling of its uniqueness and specificity. A symbolization that resonates specifically enough can "pull up" the felt sense—pull it fully into our conscious emotional awareness. A phrase like "I feel like a battle-tired soldier, vigilant against attack but too tired to resist" may allow the *distinctiveness* of the feeling to come sharply and accurately into focus ("I feel a tightness when I think those words"). Those specific words speak to the bodily felt sense in a more specific way than generic words like "angry" or "insulted."

Most people can relate to poetry or music as examples of the way this part of the symbolization process works. When Robert Frost repeats the line "And miles to go before I sleep. And miles to go before I sleep," the words enable us to feel more than they actually denote—especially if we speak them aloud. The difference between focusing and poetry is that with focusing we need to find our *own* symbolizations that speak specifically to the unique feeling.

The words in this case aren't functioning as representations, but as fuller embodiments of the way we feel. The body can answer the resonating symbolization in a way that helps redirect the "about" question away from stock category assumptions and toward the specificity of the symbolic imagery or allegorical symbol. The symbolization isn't "in" the word or image, but it is rather in our embodied enactment of it.

A colorful example occurs in the film *White Palace*—named after the fast-food restaurant with whose waitress the wealthy protagonist finds himself in love. The well-to-do protagonist attends a soiree with one of his rich friends and happens across his hostess's "dust buster." He notices that "she doesn't have any dust in her dust-buster!" Exclaiming this phrase over and over, he rushes out of the party to go to his working-class true love (who probably would have dust in her dustbuster, both literally and figuratively). "She doesn't have any dust in her dust-buster!" is the most accurate descriptor he can find of the unique felt sense he has of his situation at that moment. For someone else, the descriptor might have been something completely different.

In the same way, by enacting symbolizations for values, we appreciate their value more intensely. This is why we say eulogies to a departed loved one, sing troubadour songs to a romantic lover, or genuflect before the image of a saint.

B. F. Skinner (1968) is correct that the odds of one vote deciding an election are smaller than the odds of getting hit by a car on the way to the polls, but he misses the emotional significance of voting. By voting, we symbolize the importance of the values involved and therefore literally feel their value more intensely. During the peak of the Covid-19 epidemic in 2020, before vaccines were available, the Wisconsin legislature refused to allow voting by mail in a local special election. In response, a larger than usual surge of voters risked Covid-19 to stand in long lines—symbolizing, for themselves as well as others, their feeling of the value of being treated fairly in the political process.

Oddly, the more *specifically* we symbolize the unique felt sense, the more *broadly* contextualized it seems to become. Maybe the motorist who cut in front of me "treated me as if I don't exist!"—but it would be silly to expect some specific motorist to care whether I'm treated "as if I don't exist"—or for me to care what the motorist thinks or doesn't think about me. To have such an intense feeling of "He treated me as if I don't exist!" must involve more than just that one trivial incident. In what other contexts am I treated as if I don't exist? Some of those must be what the feeling is about. And even beyond those, the *general fact* that the world is such that we necessarily depend on others not to treat us that way is an inescapable existential issue about which I also feel—and those feelings are also rolled into the more specific instance.

There is little point in achieving anything if we can't at least minimally intensify the feeling of the value of what we value. And symbolization plays a key role there. Depression results not from an inability to achieve whatever it is that we value (as in Bradshaw's four Super Bowl victories); instead, it results from deintensification of motivating values, reflected in imbalance of the SEEKING system. We have trouble feeling inspired or "enthusiastic" about imagined actions or even experiencing their value when achieved. In that case, there is little point in trying to achieve anything.

The magic trick of symbolization in good tragedy is that, by helping us feel the tragedy of a character's existence, the tragedy itself intensifies our feeling of the *value* of being a conscious, sentient being capable of valuing things. The thwarting of the values makes us feel them intensely. We appreciate the value of Homer's Hector not in spite of, but because of his tragic failure to win in combat and subsequent dragging of his body through the streets. In this way Homer drives home the value *of* Hector—and by extension the universal "as such" that the fictitious character symbolizes.

The tragic paradox in literature—that we "enjoy" the sadness—raises a crucial question for our purposes: If we intensely feel the value of helping the poor, does this mean we are strongly motivated to do something about it? Or does the sadness *de*-motivate us so that we don't have much enthusiasm to mobilize toward doing something? A badly written tragedy only depresses us. Bertolt Brecht was specifically focused on this distinction; he wanted his audiences to leave the theatre with their fists held in the air. The difference hinges on whether we intensely value something but regret that it isn't achieved or, on the contrary, fail to intensify our valuation of taking action in the first place.

For the depressed person, sadness may be the only way left for this symbolizing-intensifying purpose. But the sadness doesn't serve as a good motivator for action. A minimal baseline of inspiration needs to be felt intensely enough to compensate for inevitable existential challenges—including but not limited to challenges to the normal narcissistic needs presented by the structure of finite reality as such (even in the absence of a narcissistic disturbance). Death, powerlessness, personal insignificance, and potential alienation are all insults to the normal narcissistic need to feel competent and somewhat in control of our lives (as emphasized by Heinz Kohut 1985).

The need to feel that we are competent agents of actions with meaningful consequences adds to the motivation to pursue chains of instrumentalities. Those chains then form an "extended" value system like Rachmaninoff's, where the value of activities involves complex edifices of skills and competencies, and traces only indirectly and implicitly to the value of valuing creatures as such. The valuing creatures in question may just as well be only imaginary or hypothetical, as in the imaginary audience for music or the hypothetical patient to be cured by the medicine that is being developed. Even with music or a scientific endeavor, there is an underlying connection to the most basic intrinsic value that allows the enactive meaning of such activities to be "real," as opposed to an idle whim.

Enactive Meaning and Basic Emotion in Social and Political Contexts

In waves that rise and fall through history, people losing confidence in the underlying meaning of their life activities offer fertile ground for monstrous social ideologies, as well as various and sundry self-appointed gurus and cult leaders. ISIL's explicit doctrine is straight-forwardly nihilistic: As we approach the "End Time," their mission is to drop the scripturally prophesied final curtain by literally fighting the ultimate battle of Armageddon. Similarly, the Q-Anon conspiracy theorists continually hope for a final "Storm." They believed the January 2021 attack on the US Capitol would bring this nebulous Storm, which was to include assassination of the vice president and congressional leaders, leading to some sort of triumphant banishment of all enemies of the movement. For both ISIL and Q-Anon, the cult offers a Grand Scheme value meant to obliterate the problem of enactive meaning in one fell swoop.

In terms of the intrinsic-instrumental conflict, there is a dangerous tendency to substitute the instrumentality toward the objectives of the cult or the authoritarian Grand Scheme in place of the intrinsic value needed to inspire a minimally necessary sense of enactive meaning. In the extreme case, those who get in the way of the instrumentalities become "useless," "good for nothing," or in Nazi terms, "useless eaters."

Standard fascist and authoritarian political movements might initially seem less related to the problem of meaning than Picciolini's assessment of white nationalist terrorism. But I want to suggest that even traditional fascist movements feed off the same frustration of the sense of enactive meaning—the capacity for meaningful action.

I freely grant that many other contributing factors also help account for fascist and terrorist movements. Economic hardship and rapid industrial change can exacerbate emotional problems, including those involving PANIC. Also, the cults' propagandists develop ingenious techniques for bombarding people with the same internet meme from multiple sources, or planting "claques" within crowds to grow a mob of shouting acolytes. Such techniques make people feel that everyone else is drinking the same Kool-Aid.

But the insatiable thirst to which the Kool-Aid appeals reflects something more private: a struggle with the individual's own attempt to define enactive meaning, not only with a sense of community or connection, but also to find actions that can have meaning despite feelings of powerlessness, smallness, and insignificance in the big scheme of things.

In some cases, an implicit frustration with our existentially inevitable smallness and relative insignificance can create an overwhelming resentment against even the most trivial violation of our own "freedom." This perceived lack of freedom triggers rage over the existential issue of personal powerlessness in the larger picture, reflecting Panksepp's observation that the easiest way to evoke an infant's RAGE is to bind its arms (1998, chapter 4). Fundamentally, lack of freedom means that our ability to act feels blocked—the most obvious threat to enactive meaning. We might then become absurdly obsessed and enraged over this issue of freedom. We insist that no one has a right to regulate our carrying of assault weapons or even tell us to wear a mask during a pandemic. "Freedom" then becomes an absolute priority over all other values, leading to a "zero sum" ethos that conflicts with any collective political or institutional attempt to benefit others, as over against my own "freedom." Ironically, the zero-sum calculus then leads us to feel that we can be freer by taking away the freedom of others, and vice versa. The political realm then becomes a Hobbesian "war of all against all."

To a greater or lesser extent, this issue of personal freedom, which is related to the feeling of smallness and powerlessness (the binding of the infant's arms), is one of the fundamental existential issues for all of us. But in the extreme case, it can trigger the anger and frustration that make the Grand Schemes of fascism or white supremacist movements seem like tempting expressions. Frustrated with our own powerlessness, we can at least vicariously enjoy the power of the Führer. The resulting illusion promises to address the inevitable problems of smallness, powerlessness, fear of alienation, and to some extent even death.

Enter the Grand Scheme

It may seem contrary to what has been said so far that the goose-stepping Nazi, capable of cynically inflicting such torment on Viktor Frankl and his fellow inmates, doesn't seem clinically depressed at all yet *does* exhibit many attitudes epitomizing *value nihilism*—by completely devaluing whole ethnicities, races, and religions, as well as existing social and moral norms, including the value of many categories of human lives. Even the most norm-smashing Nazi might seem quite energetic and cheerful—at least, on the surface. How could a violently acting SS trooper be suffering from a shortage of enactive meaning?

Yet Hannah Arendt in her classic studies of the authoritarian mindset (for example, Arendt 1968), consistently with Picciolini's view of white supremacist cults, believes that a type of implicit despair and cynicism sets the stage for vulnerability to the authoritarian movement. This aspect of Arendt's thinking is sometimes underappreciated by those who focus more on her analysis of the "banality of evil"—the idea that even the most seemingly normal person might sign on to destructive movements (Arendt 1963; see also Arendt 1959). In *The Origins of Totalitarianism* (1968), she adds a further dimension to that view. Having not only lived through much of the rise of Nazism in Germany, but also having interviewed Nazi war criminals, she argues that susceptibility to such movements presupposes an underlying feeling of being devalued by the culture and a loss of the meaning previously invested in one's place in the community—a loss of the feeling of one's own instrumentality.

Our next chapter explores the challenge to enactive meaning as it relates to the instrumentalities created by Grand Scheme value systems like authoritarianism, conformism, fascist movements, and various kinds of cult followings. Such Grand Scheme value systems offer to create meaning by making us into *instrumental* values, at the expense of our own and others' *intrinsic* value. These social forces arise out of a desperate need for meaning—the need for our actions to have meaning—and yet they push us away from the actual conscious processes needed to ground a sense of meaning. In these cases, there is a *targeted* or *selective* suppression of the questioning function itself that normally would be subserved by the SEEKING system. These targeted suppressions also involve their own peculiar interplay between PANIC and SEEKING in the necessarily interactive organism. There is a disruption of the normal need to regulate the conflagration of the PANIC system by means of thought processes motivated by the SEEKING system. Let's turn now to this instructive and broadly applicable type of challenge to enactive meaning.

Chapter 5

Hannah Arendt and the Curious Nihilism of Grand Scheme Value Systems

Most actions are instrumental—oriented toward some purpose. Instrumental values like contributing to the excellence of a professional craft, or a humanitarian cause, or the flourishing of an extended family, or the political life of a nation, extend our value system into a more action-motivating realm. Even though the instrumentalities implicitly have their meaning in relation to the valuing creatures they affect, they lead to meaningful action only if we make ourselves into instruments toward achieving results in those more extended arenas.

This need for instrumental purpose can come into conflict with the simple experience of the intrinsic value of ourselves or others. When we make ourselves into instruments, we have to evaluate ourselves and hold ourselves to a standard. How well we serve the instrumentality then becomes part of how we assess the meaning of our life activities. The larger "extended" value—a vocation, a cause, and so on—requires evaluating our own and others' activities according to demanding or even harsh instrumental criteria.

Saxophonist Charlie Parker learned this lesson the hard way. The accomplished jazz drummer Jo Jones was an empathic mentor to the young Parker, but he wasn't "nonjudgmental." After Jones famously threw a cymbal at the young saxophonist, Parker literally "went to the woodshed" and learned to scrutinize the flaws in his own playing (obvious to others but not so much to himself). He constructed practice techniques to address the flaws he now saw, and devoted endless hours to the practice. He learned to evaluate himself ruthlessly according to those instrumental standards (pun intended).

We saw earlier how this instrumentalizing process sometimes threatens to cut into the feeling of the intrinsic value that valuing creatures are felt to have by virtue of simply *being* valuing creatures *per se*. Jo Jones as a mentor couldn't just say "I accept you just as you are." This is an unavoidable tension. The more we focus attention on the intrinsic value of ourselves or others, the more we have to admit that this intrinsic value would be the same *irrespective* of whether we are serving a grand value effectively, or ineffectively, or not at all. This intrinsic value is always in tension with our instrumentality.

From the standpoint of a person's intrinsic value, as Sartre famously puts it at the end of *Being and Nothingness*, "it amounts to the same thing whether one gets drunk alone or is a leader of nations" (627). But this acknowledgement conflicts with the need to value people, including ourselves, in *instrumental* terms as well. From the standpoint of enactive meaning, it isn't enough to just get drunk alone.

The more we define enactive meaning by whether valuing creatures can instrumentally serve some larger, long-term value, the less sufficient their sheer intrinsic value becomes to serve the sense of meaning. Fascist political programs, cult followings, obsession with material achievements, and even certain kinds of religious attitudes erect Grand Scheme value systems that become counterproductive to resolving the inevitable tension between our intrinsic and our instrumental value. Any Grand Scheme value system runs the risk of reducing us to instrumentalities and thus obscuring the experience of the intrinsic value of valuing creatures as such. The presumably instrumental value of the Grand Scheme has then occluded the intrinsic value toward which it was supposed to be instrumental.

This is where Hannah Arendt's analysis comes into play. The intrinsic/instrumental conflict can become especially acute if, having first defined meaning mostly in terms of our own instrumentality, we now find ourselves *unable* to serve effectively because of resistance from others or from the community of others—a feeling of being devalued by our community. When our profession becomes obsolete amidst rapid change, we are carelessly cast aside, no longer useful. We lack instrumental value.

In addition to the threat of simple economic impoverishment, we also now feel both worthless and aggrieved. We have lost our feeling that we are valued by the community we were trying to serve, yet the community itself is *at fault* for devaluing us. We become worthless in our own eyes due to our lack of instrumentality, but we also lose our sense of the value of that which we thought we were instrumentally serving in the first place—the community itself.

In Arendt's (1968) view, just such a crisis of meaning plagued those who were attracted to Nazism and other twentieth-century totalitarian movements. Before being recruited to fascism, they had already developed, without conscious awareness, a cynical and somewhat nihilistic overall view of social and community interaction in general. They felt that the instrumentalities they had once served were now devalued in the rapidly changing economic and cultural climate. There was no hope for the existing social system to restore the instrumental value of their lives. In Arendt's analysis, this cynicism offered fertile ground that the authoritarian movements could exploit with their blatant lies and disparaging of traditional values. The fascist propaganda became like an addictive drug, on which the follower increasingly depended to stave off feelings of meaninglessness and despair.

SEEKING and the Crisis of Meaning in Authoritarianism and Other Totalizing Projects

The fascist followers' internal confusion as to what their already "cynical" feelings were actually *about* is reminiscent of the alexithymia that Picciolini now finds among violent white supremacists. Given the followers' trust in the cult leaders to interpret their feelings as fear or hatred of Jews, of immigrants, or of a fictitious conspiracy of communists and bankers, Arendt writes, "A mixture of gullibility and cynicism . . . became an everyday phenomenon of the masses. In an ever-changing, incomprehensible world the masses . . . would, at the same time, believe everything and nothing, think that everything was possible and that nothing was true" (Arendt 1968, 382).

Arendt is aware that anti-Semitism is as old as Christianity, and older. Similar ethnic and religious divisiveness characterized an entire world epoch dating as far back as the invention of farming and subsequent overshooting of population niches, leading to ultracompetitiveness, frequent warfare, and enforced fealty, as long ago as 15–20,000 B.C. (E.g., see Steve Olson 2003.) Feudalism was its own form of fascist brutality.

But the early twentieth century saw a uniquely different spike in the trajectory of social disintegration and misplaced hatreds, driven by an updated kind of disinformation. People *deliberately chose* to submit themselves and others to a neofeudal monolith, from which they previously had been free, and to believe its absurd lies.

Mass propaganda discovered that its audience was ready at all times to believe the worst, no matter how absurd, and did not particularly object to being deceived because it held every statement to be a lie anyhow. . . . Instead of deserting the leaders who had lied to them, they would protest that they had known all along that the statement was a lie and would admire the leaders for their superior tactical cleverness. (Arendt, 382)

Anne Applebaum (2020) has shown through sheer factual reporting how central the organized spreading of disinformation is for the rise of totalitarian political movements. But even though disinformation is the main weapon of fascist appeal, Arendt emphasizes that *susceptibility* to that particular kind of disinformation is rooted in the *pre-existing* cynicism she describes. The underlying nihilism or seminihilism in such cases can be hidden from view because the devotee to the Grand Scheme professes such unequivocal devotion to the project, thus enthusiastically affirming its supposed value.

The hard core of fascist followers, on average, weren't worse off financially than those who rejected fascism, although everyone was living through an economic depression. Arendt sees the cynicism of the masses in a more nuanced way. Rather than just a scapegoating of their economic problems, let alone a belief in some policy prescription that could solve them, fascism appealed to a dark view of society and human nature in general. The masses had come to believe that in their existing social framework the corruption of the ruling classes would always be rewarded, while honesty and hard work never could. It was a short step to be persuaded that human nature is inherently selfish and corrupt and that only an egoistic and even immoral ruthlessness can thrive. Similar cynicism rose in the United States after the economic crash of 2008, which was perceived as resulting from corrupt profiteering that went unpunished and even rewarded, while the working class lost their houses, jobs, and retirement accounts.

An important aspect of what was lost, in both cases, was hope for the future, not just economic satisfaction with the present. Hope is needed to motivate action. Motivation for action in turn is needed for the meaning of an action trajectory. Without hope, there is no possibility for construction of a sequence of meaningful instrumental values. The resulting dampening of the SEEKING system calls for some artificial replenishment. The fascist propaganda then becomes a spiraling addiction. More and more of it is needed to fuel a fundamentally faltering SEEKING system.

In Arendt's analysis, the fascist followers in all the various totalitarian movements of the twentieth century (not just Germany) initially didn't share any common political agenda that they believed might solve their problems—whether liberal, conservative, socialist, or nationalist. Even the initial hardcore of Nazi and fascist followers were about equally likely to come from any of these disparate camps; they formed a "classless" movement, as Arendt puts it. Their commonality wasn't simply an economic problem, but also and more importantly it was an emotional one. Unlike their nonfascist but equally suffering compatriots, they shared a fundamentally nihilistic value system, combined with a desperate willingness to subordinate truth to the grievance narratives offered by the authoritarian leaders.

Hitler's initial rallying cry already included a decisively dehumanizing element. The central point was to make the Jews and alleged communists pay for the "decadence" and the cultural damage they supposedly had done to the society. The rhetoric played on a tacit assumption that everyone's motives were base and that large categories of humans were without value. It appealed to a cynical belief that any political process other than "might makes right" was hypocrisy. In the absence of any philosophically justifiable intrinsic values, people could have only instrumental value relative to the Grand Scheme.

The destructive expression of the fascist followers' grievances was driven by frustration over loss of context for social belonging and the erosion of their own instrumental value relative to their society. Here again, in the absence of the feeling of the intrinsic value of humanity as such, only instrumental value could remain. To paraphrase John F. Kennedy, the grievance wasn't just that their country didn't serve them, but also that the country no longer allowed them to feel that *they could serve it.*

In short, there was a crisis of instrumental meaning. After first overemphasizing their own and others' instrumental as opposed to intrinsic value, they then felt their instrumental value itself being diminished and dismissed by the culture. Even the vulnerability to grotesque disinformation campaigns stemmed from an already ongoing crisis of meaning.

The amorphous frustration with the lack of enactive meaning, along with brutal lashing out at arbitrary scapegoats, in Arendt's view, correlates with a pronounced degree of value nihilism. When the fascist follower can devalue entire categories of conscious beings (religions, races, ethnicities, etc.), a crucial question arises for those who devalue so many of their fellow valuing creatures. Does such a seminihilism of value undermine the feeling that *being* a conscious or sentient being *per se* has much value or meaning at all—that is, intrinsic value? Even prior to exposure to the fascist ideology, had the potential recruits already lost touch with the intrinsic value of themselves and other valuing creatures, and attempted to substitute instrumental value in its place?

Such a crisis of meaning leads toward an implicit devaluation of conscious creatures as a universal set, in the sense of intrinsic value. If simply being a valuing person, aside from any instrumental usefulness toward industrial production or toward "The Cause," doesn't automatically bestow value upon a valuing creature (and implicitly, all valuing creatures), then what does? All values at that point would seem to become merely instrumental—valuable when and if they serve the Grand Scheme. But then what is the purpose of the Grand Scheme itself, absent the intrinsic value of the people it was presumed to serve? This question implicitly lurks just under the surface of everyday consciousness.

But how do we assess a condition of cynicism and despair that isn't consciously *felt* as such? The fascist followers seem to behave as if altogether enthusiastic and inspired. It certainly can't be that the SEEKING system is entirely suppressed.

On the contrary, authoritarian attitudes involve their own particular kind of *compartmentalized* suppression of the SEEKING system, which includes targeted suppression of the exploratory drive. The fascist follower becomes less and less respectful of the idea of seeking the truth, but only in certain circumscribed contexts. This compartmentalized suppression of truthfulness requires targeted suppressions of the exploratory-drive component of the SEEKING system. The SEEKING suppression in turn points to underlying difficulties with a kind of *selective* alexithymia. The less awareness we have as to what our frustrations and anxieties are about, the more we open the door for others to fill in the blanks. And in our selective disregard of criteria for truth, we can believe whatever we want, but only in those compartmentalized arenas. In other contexts, curiosity, exploration, and even "openness" may remain.

Yet, for the cult follower, even the usefulness of those other endeavors—effectiveness in our work, creativity in math and science, and so on—can have meaning only in relation to the Grand Scheme. We then become increasingly dependent on more and more absurd versions of the fascist propaganda to prop up the underlying sense of minimal, everyday level of tonic inspiration.

"Useless Eaters":
Authoritarianism and the Intrinsic-Instrumental Conflict

In the fascist worldview, certain categories of people can be completely devalued. But if conscious creatures *per se* can't have intrinsic value—simply *by virtue of* being conscious and valuing creatures—then we are left flailing and frantically grasping for something "for the sake of which" anything can have instrumental value. If our Young Stockbroker can't define the meaning of his instrumental actions in relation to things that have enough intrinsic value, if he can't feel the presence of some such intrinsic value strongly enough, even implicitly, to ground the instrumentality of his actions, he will be left desperately flailing in search of something to ground the meaning of his actions.

A person in this position may then be tempted by a Grand Scheme, relative to which we could all have instrumental value, by serving the Grand Scheme. Yet no Grand Scheme by itself can serve this purpose effectively, given its near-complete instrumentalization of the value of humans themselves. Those who don't further the Grand Scheme cause become merely "useless eaters."

The Nazi policy of killing disabled children was therefore closer to the center of its philosophical position than often acknowledged. The children couldn't have value simply by virtue of being valuing creatures. They were "useless," and therefore without instrumental value. Thinking of human value as primarily instrumental reflects an underlying, even if unacknowledged, void of intrinsic value.

As a result of the loss of intrinsic value, ever-more-aggressive insistence on the Grand Scheme and its symbolic enactments escalates as the movement continues to gather steam. The less effectively a movement fills the vacuum of meaning, the more vigorously the follower strives to make it do so. When something doesn't work, just try harder! If an addictive drug fails to deliver its high, increase the dosage!

Increasing denials of reality are needed to maintain logical coherence within a denial of the value of arbitrary categories of people and mutually beneficial norms. The resulting worldview requires more and more convolutions of logic and fantasized ad hoc hypotheses for its justification. Devaluation of those not serving the Grand Scheme is justified through factual misrepresentations of world history, ad hoc genetic hypotheses, conspiracy theories about coalitions between Jewish bankers and communists, and so on. The necessary reinterpretations of reality eventually include selective inattention to moral principles involving respect for many categories of valuing creatures—leaving an even wider void of intrinsic value and resulting challenges to the sense of enactive meaning.

Given the need for ad hoc justifications for devaluation of categories of people, the cult follower becomes locked into a rigid refusal to consider conflicting information. Each denial requires a slightly further suppression of the SEEKING system, to silence the questioning process demanded by the exploratory drive inherent in the SEEKING system.

But it isn't as if the fascist follower no longer has an exploratory drive. Such an integral natural impulse can be suppressed only sporadically, and with some effort. On the contrary, this type of nihilism or seminihilism of value requires a different kind of suppression—a *selective* suppression of the specifically *exploratory* aspect of the SEEKING system. There is a lack of curiosity toward exploring aspects of reality that threaten the Grand Scheme ideology, which because of its tacit negation of the value of valuing creatures as such becomes implicitly nihilistic or seminihilistic. The nihilism is selective and self-imposed.

This compartmentalized dampening of the exploratory drive allows for extreme confirmation bias, ignoring or reinterpreting any disconfirming evidence to prop up the unquestionable belief system. It becomes necessary to deny realities as obvious as a gifted Jewish musical composer, the factual validity or invalidity of vote counts (whichever is needed to prop up the regime), or even logical self-contradictions. There is a sporadic and almost surgically *targeted* inhibition of the exploratory drive.

"Authoritarian personality" in the sense used by Adorno and colleagues (1964) and Altemeyer (2008), almost by definition, requires compartmentalized self-constrictions of the exploratory drive. Anything inconsistent with the accepted authority must be rejected, any reasonable questioning suppressed. As Tim Snyder (2017) emphasizes, removing even the *capability* for distinguishing between truth and falsehood is the strategic first step toward any form of totalitarianism.

Authoritarian movements like fascism, white nationalism, or cults of personality are meant to supply the kind of meaning capable of overshadowing the most crucial frustrations of our existential condition, a condition that we all face: the threat of cultural alienation, relative powerlessness, smallness, and so on. Yet such movements are incapable of serving this purpose because, as we have seen, they implicitly reject the intrinsic value of valuing creatures simply as such. They must therefore constantly one-up themselves with increasingly extreme measures. When the belief system fails us, we just renew our efforts—especially if what we are trying is felt as a desperate last measure.

At some point, it isn't enough for Q-anon followers to persuade themselves that Donald Trump is secretly saving the world from a clandestine cabal of movie stars and liberal politicians selling children into sex slavery. It eventually becomes necessary that the evil-doers are also eating the children and drinking their blood. And soon, even that isn't enough. The absurdities continually multiply because no critical mass of its melodramas can fill the void of meaning. In order to suppress questioning of the elaborate conspiracy theory, the cult follower resorts to even more outlandish ad hoc hypotheses concocted to explain away the questions.

And yet the rest of us can hardly look down our noses at them. As just one of many examples, almost all of our incessant human wars—"terrorist" or otherwise—are senseless, irrational, and without net benefit for humanity or even the specific countries involved (as so eloquently argued, for example, by David Chan 2012). The pointless US invasion of Iraq is a classic example, with the resulting rise of ISIL and flooding of Europe and Eurasia with starving refugees whom the United States then ironically refused to accept. To understand the ubiquity of absurd destructiveness by otherwise-intelligent and compassionate people, it might be good to begin with a source of irrationality that is equally ubiquitous for all of us—the struggle with the most basic emotional meanings that are literally universal for finite intelligent creatures.

In effect, we all have some of the cult follower in us. For better or worse, we necessarily try to interpret new experience to make it fit an overall pre-existing worldview that has built up from a lifetime of thinking, feeling, and sensing. The default is to maintain the previous worldview with as little ongoing revision as possible, while we "hermeneutically" interpret new phenomena that are difficult to fit. For the most part, only when they can't be fitted do we consider revising our understanding of how things work. We are constantly tempted to block out inconsistent information, in a dynamic not entirely dissimilar to the cult follower or fringe conspiracy theorist.

But paradoxically, even the most convoluted reasoner in the service of self-deceptive casuistry is still motivated toward questioning and truth-seeking *in general*, as a natural part of the exploratory drive—despite the tendency to increasingly suppress the questioning function *in certain contexts*. Even while accepting unquestioningly a cult's propaganda, there remains enthusiastic scientific curiosity about the best way to build a bomb or run an internet disinformation operation. There is endless creativity and curiosity to develop, seek out, and consume cognitively sophisticated conspiracy theories.

At the same time, the follower of the authoritarian cult selectively *dampens* this same exploratory drive whenever inconvenient facts or logical implications arise. This dynamic shows up in the authoritarian's measurable lack of "Openness" on the Big Five personality inventory and the resulting extreme confirmation bias. These tendencies are reliably correlated with the Adorno and colleagues "authoritarian personality" and the Altemeyer "Right Wing Authoritarianism" (Adorno et al. 1964; Altemeyer 2008; Duriez and Soenens 2009; Hodson et al. 2009).[1]

The robust correlations already documented in the authoritarianism research can't be ignored. But in my view, we need a more nuanced understanding of the *real-time patterns of emotional feeling* underlying what we often call authoritarian personality. Those patterns involve tendencies to selective inattention, confirmation bias, and targeted suppressions of the exploratory drive. As a disillusioned war veteran told me, every small denial of the truth kills still another small piece of—in his terms—"the soul." In Panksepp's terms, it kills a small piece of the SEEKING system. The more situations call for selective suppression, the more the SEEKING system is dampened. As the value system necessarily becomes increasingly convoluted, occasions for SEEKING suppression multiply exponentially.

This selective dampening of exploration creates periodic gaps in the ongoing need to ask questions about the meaning of our affective processes as well as other aspects of the world. By preferentially allowing and protecting those gaps, the cult follower maintains the cynical and seminihilistic worldview of the authoritarian movement with its reduction of human value to instrumental purposes.

This implicit seminihilism involves its own peculiar interplay of SEEKING and PANIC. The cult follower's compartmentalized suppression of the SEEKING system is targeted specifically to use selective inattention—both to avoid contradictory facts *and* to rationalize rejection of the value of so many categories of people and mutually beneficial norms. Those attitudes, in turn, can be both cause and effect of a disturbance of the social bonding function, especially including the PANIC system. Devaluation of entire categories of people and moral norms must affect the experience of value and meaning in ways we can learn from. Is what it means to be a conscious creature still very much regarded as having intrinsic value in this case? And if not, are one's *own* life processes being implicitly devalued as well?

Authoritarian value systems represent a special case of the more general problem of competition between intrinsic and instrumental value. The Grand Scheme value system erected by the authoritarian group is an attempt to compensate for a deficit of intrinsic valuation and to generate meaning by making ourselves instruments toward the Grand Scheme. The hope then is to define the value of valuing creatures relative to the Grand Scheme—as merely instrumental.

But even for those who are less prone to authoritarian thought systems, there is still a related problem. We still need to "extend" our value system to include commitment to some sort of project that is "larger than ourselves," such as a profession or avocation. Even in this more "normal" case, we still confront the inevitable conflict between instrumental and intrinsic value. To the extent that we veer toward the instrumental, we have a similar basic conundrum to that of the authoritarian cult follower. How are we to define the "for the sake of which" that supports the instrumental value of the project in which we are embarked, while still allowing the meaning of our actions to be contingent on the project itself? As we evaluate ourselves in terms of success toward the project, do we lose the sense that our intrinsic value is *sufficient* for meaning—whether the issue is our own value or that of humanity and other conscious creatures generally? This puzzle creates an internal conflict for all of us.

The Paradox of the "Agreeable" Authoritarian

Counterintuitively, authoritarian personality, despite its documented racism, xenophobia, and vilification of many categories of people, at the same time correlates somewhat *positively* with the "Agreeableness" dimension of the Big Five personality inventory (Hodson et al. 2009—using Altemeyer's "Right Wing Authoritarianism" scale). Authoritarians can be quite friendly in one-to-one interactions with individuals, even those who belong to the wrong ethnicities or political groups.

One might assume that such an "Agreeable" person would have little disturbance of the PANIC system and would be relatively free of hatred and prejudice. But just the reverse is true. In spite of a general "Agreeableness," the same authoritarians largely reject or substantially negate the intrinsic value of entire *categories* of people (for example, their documented scores on "Racism"). They may react by vilifying those who disagree with their social and political views (as reflected in lack of "Openness" on the Big Five personality inventory, religious intolerance, tendencies to violence, including domestic violence, exaggerated militarism, and the many other correlations documented by Adorno et al., Altemeyer, and others).[2]

To add further enigma to the paradox of the Agreeable xenophobe, Hodson and colleagues (2009) find that a certain subset of authoritarian personalities score considerably *lower* than average on the "Agreeableness" scale—namely, those who also score high on "Social Dominance Orientation," which correlates with "Psychopathy" and "Machiavellianism." The correlation between "Machiavellianism" and "Racism" is an astonishing +.60. "Machiavellianism," virtually by definition, means treating others as merely *instrumental values*. But both authoritarianism *and* Social Dominance Orientation correlate with racism, xenophobia, and religious intolerance—all instances of devaluation of categories of people. So, counterintuitively, even though "Social Dominance Orientation" doesn't correlate with "Agreeableness," authoritarian personality per se does.

In experiential terms, for the Agreeable authoritarian, notice that a physically present person's simple visual image evokes direct empathy, regardless of race, religion or ethnicity. Direct perception of a specific elderly lady trying to change a tire evokes immediate empathy. These Agreeable tendencies, for the authoritarian, seem to involve directing empathy primarily toward those who in a sense are "close-at-hand"—friends, relatives, immediate acquaintances, those with whom interaction is most direct. In sum, concretely speaking, the authoritarian empathizes with those for whom *vivid and detailed perceptual imagery* is available. Even those with strong "Social Dominance Orientation" and "Machiavellianism" can empathize with family members, personal acquaintances, and fellow-travelers in an authoritarian movement.

The person with whom we are currently interacting presents physically direct imagery. The imagery is extensive and detailed enough to represent a concrete individual, not just a category. The Agreeable authoritarian tends to sympathize with this direct image. But not all aspects of respect for universalized human rights or well-being lend themselves to such easy imagery.

There is little direct imagery of the suffering of Palestinian refugees or the conditions in which they have lived. Fairness in the distribution of opportunities and resources, or a universalized principle of freedom of religion or the right to vote or to unionize, don't easily present direct images—except, again, where this freedom involves close associates or people who "look like me," whose empathic imagery can be easily conjured.

"Freedom of religion" is then applied to religions with which I am familiar on a daily basis, not so much to others. The people around me in my daily life constantly present direct images.

Correlatively, authoritarianism requires *blocking* certain types of imagery. Since the image of the elderly lady changing a tire evokes empathy, both the authoritarian leader and the follower tacitly cooperate to keep a devalued group in a segregated location, "on the other side of the tracks." The imagery of them must be carefully manipulated in the popular media—the "Welfare Queen," the "Big Healthy Buck Trading Food Stamps"—so as not to pull too much of the "Agreeable" authoritarian's empathy. The homeless are forced into a less conspicuous part of town. The images of Palestinians must be confined to mug shots of terrorists, lest the Agreeable authoritarian's empathy should get in the way of devaluing them as a category. If immigrant children are kept in cages, camera crews must be either forbidden or carefully controlled. The cameras see them from a distance—the vague representation of a category, not the image of an individual.

To be sure, the image of the "Welfare Queen in her Cadillac" may evoke antipathy. But when the authoritarian actually sees such a person close-up, in real life, with detailed facial features—for example, shopping at the local hardware store—the "Agreeable" tendency kicks in. The Welfare Queen is presented verbally in political speeches, not as a fleshed-out, real-life person with direct vivid imagery. Even in the famous George H.W. Bush "revolving door" campaign ad featuring criminals going in and out of jail, the figures are only dim, dark shadows. Extensive imagery of their faces is never offered.

Hence the paradox of the Agreeable racist. In spite of an individually directed Agreeableness, whole *categories* of oppressed people, whose empathy-pulling imagery is less accessible (or is deliberately *kept* less accessible) can be devalued or simply disregarded with indifference. In one sense, this devaluing is a deceptive appearance. When the Agreeable authoritarian sees direct imagery of them, empathy is naturally evoked—while at the same time the authoritarian does manage to devalue or ignore the value of many categories of people.

This failure to universalize the value of conscious creatures simply *as such* threatens an implicit devaluation of what it means to be a human being per se—an obvious problem for the underlying sense of meaning that can ground in turn the long-term instrumentality of our own actions. If any of us have intrinsic value simply by virtue of being human beings, then so do all humans. For the authoritarian, this implication is felt most fully in response to the direct presence of an individual, even one who is a member of the generally hated group. When the Agreeable authoritarian stares into the face and has a direct perceptual image of someone upon whom suffering is to be inflicted, interesting internal conflicts can boil to the surface.

Racism is often called "America's original sin." But devaluation of "the other" could just as well count as the original sin of virtually every other culture—at least since the invention of farming fifteen to twenty thousand years ago, and the resulting overshooting of population niches, leading to scarcity and intense inter-group competition. Far from an accidental personality foible of certain individuals, racism and xenophobia are the most glaring examples throughout history of the implicit devaluation of humanity per se, which Arendt connects to an insidious nihilism of intrinsic value, and which I suggest for the same reason is connected to the most fundamental challenge to the most basic enactive meaning of our ongoing emotional sense of intrinsic-instrumental value structures—the continuous implicit sense of the value of valuing creatures ourselves.

This implicit seminihilism can be both cause and effect of a selective suppression of the exploratory drive. When the exploratory drive wanes, so does curiosity about the truth. This includes truths about internal self-contradictions and the correlative cognitive dissonances. Authoritarianism is obviously buttressed by selective suppression of the exploratory drive, but at the same time it creates a further motivation for the Grand Scheme value systems that call for still further suppression of exploration. This targeted type of SEEKING suppression is reflected in the low scores of authoritarians on the "Openness" dimension.

Authoritarianism, "Openness," and Living at the Edge of Nihilism

It is now a truism that we all struggle with a tendency to ignore counter-evidence against preconceptions (Lakoff 2008; Westin 2008). "Openness" to new evidence and thinking is obviously a matter of degree. Davis and Panksepp (2018) show that the "Openness" dimension correlates quite strongly (+.47) with the robustness of SEEKING system activity, which includes the exploratory drive.[3] For our purposes, this partial failure of the exploratory drive—the interest in searching for the truth—is a crucial factor in thinking about values, threatening in turn to confuse or undermine our sense of the meaning of our actions and their presupposed action trajectories. Perceptions of reality not only are affected by, but they also affect our feelings and motivations.

But far from a complete lack of Openness, the *partial and selective* shutting down of the exploratory drive in authoritarianism can be targeted to specific occasions on which specific topics arise, such as race, religion, or politics. Building better bombs and weapon systems and even the technical mechanics of everyday work can still elicit a quite robust exploratory drive.

Authoritarians don't always just mindlessly accept the worldview of their parents. Contrary to popular assumptions about authoritarianism, Picciolini (2020) points out that young violent cultists tend to rebel against their parents, just as they do against society in general. They *choose their own* authority figures. Repeatedly, Picciolini is hired as an investigator by parents horrified by the racism or Nazism of their own children.

Duriel and Soenens (2009) find a similar pattern. Surprisingly, the racism of parents doesn't correlate strongly with the racism of children, unless a substantial degree of *authoritarianism itself* is passed down. That is, the degree of racism of the children doesn't correlate much with that of parents when authoritarian personality is controlled for. Parents with only moderate scores on the "Racism" scale may produce authoritarian children who are extremely racist. And ironically, authoritarianism can lead children to embrace some *other* authority whose beliefs are different from those of the parents, and sometimes more deadly.

Picciolini is observing, consistently with Duriel and Soenens, that people pick and choose their own authorities. Fox News viewers don't just share its philosophy because they listen to Fox; they also listen to Fox because they have already chosen Fox's worldview. Prasad and others (2009) found that almost all of their forty-nine subjects who still falsely believed Saddam Hussein had been connected to 9/11 refused to change their opinions in the face of conclusive contradictory facts, citing President Bush as their authority. However, holding the office of president wasn't what designated Bush as an authority figure—as evidenced by their lack of regard for Bush's successor in the same office. They chose their own authority. But once the authority *has* been chosen, the authority becomes unquestionable, depending on the individual's degree of authoritarian personality. Whatever contradicts the authority is ignored or denied.

In seminihilistic views like Nazism and xenophobia, which negate the value of many categories of people, the problem involves a curious connection between PANIC and SEEKING—between a disturbance of *social bonding* attitudes (reflected in dysfunctions of the PANIC system) and a selective inhibition of curiosity about certain realms of reality—a targeted and situation-specific suppression of the *exploratory drive* (a function of the SEEKING system).

If we take seriously Arendt's analysis, the authoritarian's surgically selective SEEKING-system suppression eventually leads to a general sense of suppressed despair and nihilism and a shortage of the feeling that human life per se has value independently of the Grand Scheme. An implicit threat of clinical depression is then staved off only by means of the fantasy of the Grand Scheme. But here too, the Grand Scheme ideology has to become more and more extreme in order to continue delivering the same high.

The negation of the intrinsic value of so many human beings then inevitably distorts further and further the functioning of the PANIC system, as both cause and result of a selective suppression of the exploratory drive in the interest of the needed casuistry or explaining away of relevant facts. Negating the value of humanity generally enflames the PANIC system, while at the same time requiring suppression of the exploratory drive. The exploratory drive subserves the search for the truth about reality, including moral and social reality.

Psychology is sometimes called the "science of weak correlations." When correlations are weak, the real story must be more complicated than a simple cause-effect relationship between the variables. Exploring this more complicated tableau requires digging to a deeper level of analysis. We need to look at the real-time progressions of thoughts and emotions that are being generically and somewhat inaccurately captured by the personality variables and empirical observations.

Obviously, we are all guilty of selective SEEKING-system suppression regarding inherently anxiety-arousing issues related to inevitable challenges to the underlying meaning of our life activities. To understand how this suppression can interconnect with a nihilism or seminihilism of value, we should begin by acknowledging (as the work of Adorno and Altemeyer implies) that the suppression itself is more an emotional-motivational issue than an intellectual one.

SEEKING Is an Emotion System, Not a Cognitive Skill Set

"Reason *versus* emotion" isn't the issue in selective suppression of the exploratory drive. The problem is the context-specific selectivity of the *motivation* to use the skill of asking questions on particular kinds of occasions—just as a young adolescent, no matter how intelligent, might self-deceive in the interest of desperately needed peer-group acceptance. I remember as a young teenager persuading myself there would be no danger in entertaining my friends by gunning the accelerator to 100, 110, 115 miles per hour on the expressway. The SEEKING system isn't primarily a substrate for cognitive abilities; it is an emotional system that can motivate certain cognitive processes—or not.

Martin Heidegger's superior thinking ability didn't stop him from joining the Nazi Party. After the war, his excuse to Hannah Arendt was that he simply didn't know anything about politics. Her question, of course, was: Why was he not *motivated* to find out? When we speak of "motivated reasoning," we tend to forget that *all* reasoning has to be motivated.

To be sure, part of the prefrontal cortex (which is also associated with cognitive thinking) does play a role in the SEEKING system. But the prefrontal activity is only a small part of the overall system, which involves midbrain, lateral hypothalamic, and the deeper ventral tegmental areas (all emotional/motivational areas), and a unique combination of neurotransmitters. Suppression or imbalance of this system is more extensive than just a disruption of rational thinking ability. The teenager who shows off "irrational" hot-rodding behavior might be an excellent and even creative mathematician.

It would be an oversimplification to just say that hyperactivating the amygdala's *fear* or *anger* response is enough to suppress rational thinking. Granted, the neuroscientist George Bush (2000) showed that hyperactivation of the amygdala through fear or anger does tend to inhibit the prefrontal cortex, which is needed for logical thought. But while this is true, others have also shown that just the reverse can play out as well. The prefrontal cortex can and typically does regulate the functioning of the amygdala in normal adults (for example, see Lungu et al. 2007). This is why combat soldiers and first responders to emergency situations are able to function effectively in spite of their fear. The determination as to which brain area gains control of the other is complicated (Ellis 2005, 2018). We can't just assume that hyperactivation of the amygdala at the expense of prefrontal thinking ability is normal or typical, even in the face of legitimate fears.

Hibbing and colleagues (2013) offer some help with this paradox with their work on the "negativity bias"—a tendency to perceive neutral situations as dangerous or threatening. They find that this negativity bias tends to correlate both with authoritarian attitudes and also with a tendency for the amygdala component of the fear and anger systems to hyperactivate. Hibbing finds wide individual differences with regard to this tendency.

So we shouldn't jump to the conclusion that authoritarianism is simply an amygdala anger/fear shutting down of prefrontal "rational thinking." An extreme negativity bias, a tendency for the amygdala to shut down the prefrontal cortex, can't be regarded as typical or universal. Something has happened in the earlier brain development of these subjects to create the dominance of the amygdala over the prefrontal cortex, while for other people, or in other contexts for the same individual, the relationship can be just the reverse.

To explore this last question, Hibbing and colleagues would have needed to know more about the life histories of their subjects—their history of possible brain damage, childhood psychological trauma, or perhaps genetic constitution (which Hibbing does assume plays a major role in the etiology of the negativity bias). A lifetime of habit formation and environmental influences can exert major influences on the organization of the brain—as shown with the emphasis on neural plasticity in recent neuroscience.

In short, negativity bias doesn't simply suppress *intellectual* function. To be sure, the irrational ideas of totalitarian thought systems (which do correlate with negativity bias) require suppressing aspects of the exploratory drive. But Adorno and Altemeyer document that authoritarianism does *not* correlate significantly with a lack of general intelligence. More extensive areas than just the prefrontal cortex play into whether the amygdala hyperactivates or whether it continues to be prefrontally regulated.

As a child in the southern United States, when I asked why there were separate "White" and "Colored" water fountains, the answer from some adults was that I was "stupid" for asking such questions. Were those adults' lapses of reason *carefully targeted* in the same way as my manic adolescent behavior on the Atlanta expressways—in the same way as Heidegger's Nazism? Were they trying to train me to suppress my own SEEKING system in carefully compartmentalized ways, by humiliating me for asking "stupid" questions?

Not an *inability,* but a lack of *motivation* to explore for the truth enabled intelligent people to accept the wildly pseudoscientific basis for the Nazi theory of Arian superiority. The pseudoscientific evolutionary work of Alfred Rosenberg (which became even more ridiculous in the secondary literature about it), and such pseudosociology as the absurd discussions of the "Protocols of the Elders of Zion" require such ludicrous convolutions of reasoning that a contemporary scientific reader could hardly take them seriously—not because of subsequent new scientific discoveries, but because of sheer illogic. Yet well-educated and accomplished people, including scientists, managed to believe them.

Similar embarrassing theories were used by otherwise intelligent people to justify American imperialism in the Philippines, discrimination against various kinds of immigrants, virtual genocide against Native Americans, and of course the terrorizing trauma of slavery and Jim Crow. In fact, the Nazis directly picked up some of their eugenics ideas wholesale from US racial theories (Wilkerson 2020).

We can't just blame the belief in such absurdities on social conformism. It is true that authoritarians tend to agree with those who surround them socially, but they also choose with whom to surround themselves. Authoritarianism involves a classic instance of the hermeneutic circle:

I believe XYZ.
I don't socialize with people who believe the wrong things.
Therefore, most of the people in my social grouping believe XYZ.
What most people believe can't be wrong.
Therefore, I believe XYZ. . . .
(Repeat ad infinitum.)

The authoritarian has chosen the group who believe XYZ as the preferred social grouping in the first place. So mere conformism can't explain why XYZ is the chosen belief system. If most people believe XYZ, they can't believe it just because most people believe it. Prior to the conformity effect, why did anyone believe it in the first place?

Enter the Realm of Emotional Conflict

How can we reconcile the self-deception and irrationality of authoritarian tendencies with the idea that the exploratory drive is innate, ostensibly designed to motivate us toward *effective* truth-seeking? Isn't the aim of this emotion to explore *reality*—as faithfully as possible under the circumstances?

Remember that the basic emotions can come into internal conflict with each other. When we deliberately turn away from reality, we selectively suppress a natural *emotional* drive, in favor of equally powerful motivations in conflict against it. In the case of authoritarian belief systems, those emotions include a desire to maintain certain beliefs by shutting down the questioning process whenever necessary.

In the same way, we all tend more or less to shut down key elements of self-questioning needed to work through our own internal problems with our particular version of the human condition. Many of those processes are only incrementally different from those of the fascist cult follower—our need to deny our own relative powerlessness, insignificance, and the continual threat of alienation from others and devaluation by the culture as a whole.

The Nazis' hatred and resentment of Jews required increasingly absurd disinformation and illogic to sustain the blanket devaluation. Every ad hoc hypothesis, illogical inference, or contradiction of fact required still another small suppression of, as we now call it, the SEEKING system—not a thinking system, but an emotional one. More and more far-fetched ad hoc hypotheses were needed. Not only Jews, but also Africans, Slavs, homosexuals, political liberals, and numerous other categories of people had to be devalued.

But could the nihilation of the value of so many humans both lead to and be symptomatic of an underlying struggle with the question whether human life *per se* really is worth all that much? If so, the question of meaning and meaningful trajectory of potential actions must lie just under the surface.

The issue of universalization becomes especially acute when we begin to think about the role of symbolic imagery in motivating value feelings. The universal isn't a visual image. If the devaluing of specific categories of conscious creatures—confining value to a limited group—leads to erosion of the intrinsic value of conscious creatures simply *as such*, then failure to universalize this value undercuts its intrinsicness, its ability to serve as a "for the sake of which."

Universalized valuing calls for a further vehicle of symbolization than the direct visual image of the specific creature. If empathy is pulled only by the close-at-hand person, who easily presents specific visual imagery, then valuation will tend to be less universalized. The next chapter explores the role of the symbolization process for the need for intrinsic and not just instrumental value—a "that for the sake of which" that can either effectively or ineffectively ground the instrumentalities around which we structure our daily lives. This in turn affects how we deal with the problem of defining meaning in terms of both instrumental and intrinsic value, in spite of the inevitable conflict between them.

Chapter 6

The Symbolic Dimension

Gendlin's Embodied Symbolization and the Limits of the Static Image

Before acting, we form imagery of the action we intend to perform. This means that the experienced meaning of an action depends on the ability to create the corresponding action imagery. But forming the imagery in turn requires motivation, which already depends on the value of the planned action.

Experiencing the value of something can mean two different things. Sometimes it just means that we, personally, happen to value X; other times, it can mean we feel X to *be* valuable, in a less subjective sense: "Even if I were to die tomorrow, X would still have value." "Any intelligent creature with a capacity for empathy would value X if attention were directed to X."

In either case, we mean it would be worthwhile to *act* in the interest of the value. To value the well-being of starving children, in either sense, implicitly means that the action of feeding them would be worth some effort, if the effort were feasible.

Sometimes the unfeasibility involves our own inability to gear ourselves up for the motivation to act, for any of a variety of reasons. But paradoxically, even a deliberate *effort* in this direction often seems to strengthen our feeling that the action is worth doing because the fuller enactment offered by a bodily action allows a physical elaboration to the underlying emotion. This is where Gendlin's "symbolizing" function of action (including speech acts and artistic expressions) comes into play. By enacting a motivation, by giving it a physical expression, we often strengthen and sharpen it.

Even with something as seemingly passive as listening to music, we don't just hear the sounds; we also *use* them to enact certain meaningful conscious processes, different for each user of the music and different for the same person at different times. Even conscious acts are en-acted. This enactment in turn is worth the trouble of more overt actions—procuring tickets and getting transportation to the concert hall. We can't value anything without being acting creatures, or at least wishing to be. And strictly speaking, we can't be living creatures without being valuing (and thus acting) creatures.

In order even to contemplate something as a possible action, we first *imagine* what it would be like to perform the action. We can see a cat imagining an action as it plans a jump to a high table before taking the leap. In the case of an overt action such as working toward feeding hungry children, we begin by imagining what it would be like to write a check or help at a local food bank. This process of forming "sensorimotor imagery" of ourselves-taking-the-action is entirely different from the sensory (e.g., visual) imaging process that we tend to think of as the paradigm for "imagery." Action imagery is necessary both in order to plan and execute actions and also to symbolize them in Gendlin's sense. This chapter explores the differences between action imagery and sensory imagery in their role in motivating and symbolizing enactively meaningful action.

Action Imagery

Sensory imagery is different from action imagery. Vision is a modality in which we *receive* information from our senses (afferent signals) as much as we *send* information to our arms or legs commanding them to move (efferent signals). The difference is between passively receiving and voluntarily initiating something.

Granted, even vision is subliminally enactive. We have to pay attention in order to see, and we understand what we see by imagining multiple possible actions—as with the Held and Hein kittens discussed earlier. The kittens passively pulled in the carts were "functionally blind" until they were able to move around and develop imaginable action schemas in terms of which they understood what they were seeing. But even though vision is enactive in this sense, the two types of imagery—sensory and action imagery—can be distinguished, and they involve very different activities, including different brain processes.

As we contemplate an action, the preliminary imagining of the action—action imagery—requires more than just sensory imagery. Jeannerod's brain studies (1994, 1997) show that when we imagine engaging in an action (using "motor imagery"), we are engaging most of the same brain activities as when we actually go through with the action. The cerebellar-parietal-motor circuits execute the substrates of *actually performing* the action, but then the frontal areas inhibit the transmittal of that action command to the rest of the body. This is what the cat's brain is doing prior to the moment of the actual leap. It then ceases the frontal inhibitory process and goes through with the actual leap.

Let me reiterate that this doesn't mean that the cat's brain "causes" it to leap. The self-organizing system that is the cat is using the various brain components to execute first the imagining of and then the execution of the leap. The self-organizing system at that point has already appropriated and rearranged its own components in a flexible, "plastic," and intricate way. The motivation to leap, which grounds even the imagining of the leap (because the imagining is itself an action), is an aspect of the entire self-organizing creature, functioning as a whole. The self-organizational process affects the microlevel constituents at least as much as vice versa.

When we become so dependent on visual imagery that action imagery gets marginalized, we are trying, to a certain extent, to make ourselves into passive rather than active creatures. We look at a photo of a loved one, and it fails to come to life for us, until we remember actions—things we did with the person, or the person's own actions with which we can empathize. If we can't imagine the past actions, the photo seems frustratingly static, or "dead." We need action imagery to make it come alive.

The arts try to prevent images from becoming "dead" in this sense. It is true that visual art, music, and literary art forms do work largely from sensory imagery. But the arts require more active involvement than simple perception. Rather than just receiving the input, we use it to engage in our own imaginative acts. The image in a painting means more than just what something looks like. Homer's Hector isn't just a specific guy, but a symbolization of what it means for any of us to face certain kinds of struggles with a rendezvous with destiny. In effect, we imagine ourselves enacting what Hector does—or even potential actions we can imagine him as contemplating, even beyond the written text. The sensory imagery in the artwork evokes many more subjective processes than just entertaining the image. Part of what is at play, in addition to the sensory imagery, is our own action imagery.

Negative value experiences like sadness, lethargy, or hopelessness tempt us to dampen action imagery and thus flirt with over-dependence on perceptual imagery, as with the "dead" photo, or the static image of the hungry child on the TV screen. Positive value experience would require positively valanced action imagery—including the vicarious action imagery that we form when we empathize with others' actions, using the "mirror neuron system" (which, as we saw earlier, centers in our *motor and premotor* cortex). Valuing in the positive sense refers to the value of acting in some way. Conversely, engaging in a voluntary action presupposes that we already positively value doing the action, at least in a proximal sense. Pressing the car's accelerator presupposes at least valuing the act of pressing it, even if we don't know where we are going.

A corollary is that when we value valuing creatures as such, we are valuing their active nature, since action is what defines them (us) as what they are (what we are). To empathize with another valuing creature doesn't necessarily require valuing their specific actions—the murders of a serial killer, for example. But it does require empathizing with their general valuing nature, their capacity for valuing and suffering.

This empathy in turn requires re-enacting what some of their potential actions might be like (using our own motor and premotor cortex). We imagine the condemned man trying to muster an appetite for his last meal, and we put ourselves in his place as he digs in his heels to resist the guards forcing him to the death chamber. To experience either our own or others' active nature as having value, we need to form our own action imagery—imagining not what it would look like, but what it would feel like to execute the action.

Action imagery enables us not only to experience the value of our own potential actions, but also to experience other valuing creatures as attempting to act; in this way we experience them as valuing creatures per se. Our mirroring of their action imagery reveals their valuing dimension as such, not just their specific desires, aims, or concerns. I understand the drunk at the bar not just in terms of his specific goals (to attract attention, prove his machismo, etc.), but more importantly in terms of his general goal of trying to define the enactive meaning of his life in the face of the finiteness and relative powerlessness confronting any human existence.

Imagery of specific actions can also symbolize broader *categories* of action. Part of the attraction of "action movies" is that they symbolize other actions we would like to accomplish. "Wouldn't it be wonderful if

I could solve major problems in my work as quickly as the TV detectives solve a crime!"

The oversimplified idea that consciousness of an object begins with a perceptual "input"—a sensory image—not only reflects a scientific trend in Western thought; the same kind of facile assumption is also a natural human tendency. Imagery that results mainly from "input" seems automatic, and thus deceptively appears as the beginning point of a causal chain ending in a "response." Even though a thousand self-organizational processes (including SEEKING and motivated selective attention) must already be ongoing prior to the perception, all this presupposed "enaction" usually remains unconscious, and, in the case of simple perception, it seems effortless.

But when we decide we want to do something, perceptual imagery isn't the main way we imagine the acting. Action imagery requires having the *subjective feel* of the potential action. It isn't just a matter of proprioceptively "sensing" our own bodies; that too would be comparatively passive, as when someone else grabs our arm and moves it. Action imagery involves a sensorimotor gearing ourselves up, a feeling of "what it would be like" to actually perform the action.

What would our motivational structure be like if we became overly dependent on perceptual imagery to the exclusion of action imagery? Such a condition surely must have ramifications for the experience of enactive meaning.

Perceptual Image Dependence

If there is any truth to Otto Rank's idea that psychological "entropy" (in his sense) leads to a kind of stasis, then this kind of entropy would also reduce our capacity for action imagery and tempt us to depend more and more exclusively on sensory imagery. Rather than feeling enthusiasm for an imagined activity like playing football or music or working at a soup kitchen, Rank's entropy would drive us to depend on perceptual TV images, passive reaction to internet manipulation of our attention, or even the taste of food and drink to entertain us. Even the imagery that comes with "action movies" is a weak copy of what it would be to imagine our own actions, flowing from our own motivations.

To the extent that there is a shortage of action imagery, sensory imagery will be required to inspire action. The kind of sensory imagery that makes us feel the intrinsic value of valuing creatures comes in a facile way with regard to family members, close friends, everyday associates, or an elderly lady trying to change a tire—people whose imagery can present itself with a certain degree of vividness.

The tendency to rely heavily on such easily available sensory imagery to trigger the action imagery needed for empathy helps with one of the paradoxes of authoritarian value systems that we discussed earlier—that the racism and xenophobia of authoritarian followers still allows them to score as "Agreeable" on the Big Five personality inventory (Hodson et al. 2009). We form vivid imagery of friends, family, comrades in arms, or the specific person with whom we are interacting at the moment. Empathy for those who "look like us" reflects reliance on the way things "look"—that is, perceptual imagery.

The out-of-work ditch digger "on the other side of the tracks" isn't familiar enough to offer very attention-pulling sensory imagery, especially if of a different race, ethnicity, or religion. As a result, for the person overly dependent on perceptual imagery, the imagery is too weak to inspire much attention to the ditch digger's intrinsic value, or action on behalf of the relevant values. Even if we do form *visual* imagery of the distant or estranged person's suffering, this imagery is still different from action imagery—the imaging of what the other's attempted actions would "be like," what it would be like if we were to perform their actions. The visual image of starving children's emaciated faces is different from the action image of writing a check or working at a soup kitchen.

Totalizing value systems like totalitarianism and religious extremism encourage us to mirror the action imagery of valuing creatures only to the extent that we have a certain amount of *perceptual* imagery of them as "like us." There is more familiar imagery of the "us" than of the "them." By minimizing our focus on the intrinsic value of the distant or different person, which would need to be symbolized not by specific visual imagery, but rather by our own *action* imagery, we miss one of the important vehicles for positive valuation.

This implicit void of intrinsic value in turn might be expected to dampen Panksepp's "enthusiasm"—a rudimentary level of inspiration. The more voluntary and self-initiated an action is, the more it is tied in with the SEEKING system's dopamine circuits, which are needed for the imaging as well as the execution of action.

When we restrict value to a subset of humanity, the resulting constriction of the feeling of the intrinsic value of conscious creatures per se (simply by virtue of their status as conscious creatures) can lead us to define our own and others' value in terms of instrumentalities that aren't well enough grounded in intrinsic value. Because the instrumentalities are implicitly felt as unsupported by enough intrinsic value, we eventually begin to feel "useless" or "superfluous"—Sartre's *"de trop."* Motivation for action then diminishes, and we become even more dependent on perceptual imagery to call us to any action at all.

The idea that authoritarians depend on perceptual by preference over action imagery may seem at odds with the observation that Hodson's "Agreeable" authoritarians can also gear up for quite *vigorous action*, in spite of their reliance on sensory imagery of the "us" to evoke empathy. The January 6, 2021, storming of the US Capitol in the attempt to install the preferred authoritarian leader as head of the government was a quite enthusiastic action.

But remember that the authoritarian follower's SEEKING system is only *partially and selectively* suppressed. There can be robust action imagery, but only when triggered by just the right perceptual imagery. The key is that any actions that come into conflict with the authoritarian imagery have now lost their motivational effect, because of the selective suppression of the SEEKING system. In fact, the authoritarian's dependence on perceptual imagery allows easy manipulation (by cult leaders, propagandists, etc.) of both empathy *and* antipathy.

Notice also that the action of storming the Capitol depended on vivid *perceptual* imagery to trigger the relevant action imagery. The insurrectionists dressed in elaborate costumes, carried flags with portraits of Donald Trump on them, and fantasized the Q-Anon images of government officials drinking the blood of kidnapped children, and the gallows on which the vice president was ostensibly to be hanged. They exchanged videos of each other vandalizing congressional offices, dressed in their finest Trump "swag," and many sported Nazi or Q-Anon slogans emblazoned on their T-shirts and motorcycle jackets. The insurrection was a remarkably colorful visual spectacle. Even the devotion to Trump from the beginning depended on the perceptual images projected in his popular TV show, *The Apprentice*.

TV and social media somewhat exacerbate an overemphasis on direct sensory perception by offering imagery selected for its ability to manipulate feelings of empathy and antipathy. At the same time, TV and internet media also have a beneficial power, to present socially constructive imagery of *far-away* suffering that would have been unavailable to the Vikings or to the medieval supporters of the Crusades. People of those untelevised times consequently may have been in some ways quicker to support their own age's aggressive wars and unnecessary suffering.

It now seems obvious that the US civil rights movement would have been far less successful if not for the invention of television. But to fully appreciate the values involved, it was also necessary to take overt actions. Going into the street or working for a political campaign symbolized and thus intensified the value feelings.

In sum, in order to motivate action, the perceptual imagery also needed to be accompanied by action imagery. Action imagery in turn has to be motivated by more than simply receiving perceptual inputs.

Direct visual or auditory imagery comes without much effort, especially when presented in actual perception rather than generated by our own imagination. Righteous political indignation is easily triggered by a video image of an innocent man being murdered by a racist police officer. For most of us, even when we do *voluntarily* call up a perceptual image in our imagination, it still comes with less effort than action imagery since it is more or less derivative from some combination of visual inputs received in the past. Action imagery is less facile and less automatic.

Even in depression, a late-night TV ad featuring images of starving children or mistreated animals easily triggers a negatively valanced appreciation for the intrinsic value of those valuing creatures, but not so much the inspiration to take action. To feel enthusiasm for action, we need to form imagery of actions that we ourselves could take. If we feel hopeless or deflated, such action imagery is difficult to sustain.

If perceptual imagery isn't the most important kind for planning and getting motivated for action, then this problem of perceptual-image dependence can help toward understanding the importance of the action-value connection at the level of the ongoing and always-presupposed enactive meaning of a long-term action trajectory as it motivates specific emotions and actions along the way. Let's move directly into this question of the role of perceptual versus action imagery in the positive *versus* negative valence of motivating emotions.

Imagery of Suffering and the Negative Value Experience

While positive value experience requires action imagery, the negative value experience can be easily facilitated by perceptual imagery. If we already suffer from either clinical or normal depression, the needs of starving children, neglected animals, war refugees, and generally the suffering of living creatures can call to us *more urgently* than the positive values that might be achievable in our own lives. The value experience in response to the TV ad can be intense, but always with a negative valence. We intensely lament all the suffering of the world, sometimes to the point where we feel immobilized.

The irony is that, if we suffer from the de-inspiration of depression and lethargy, we can sense the subjective valuations of creatures *other than ourselves,* whose images are vivid to us (the neglected animal in the TV ads), while at the same time we can't intensify the feeling that *our own actions* have value. It is as if our own feeling of inability to take much action dampens our feeling of the value of ourselves and our own actions, yet the vivid image of *others'* suffering continues to call to us, seemingly involuntarily. The sensory imagery comes to us without much effort. The more depressed we feel, the more it seems as if only images of *suffering* can call us to any action at all.

Getting inspired to *act* on these values would require experiencing the value of the corresponding actions in a more "positive" way—which in turn would require generating imagery of our own motivated actions. Partly *because* the depressed person (with depressed SEEKING system dopamine circuits) can't get motivated to take action, there is a temptation to relieve internal conflict by taking the attitude, or at least flirting with the attitude, that "nothing really matters in the Ultimate Scheme of Things."

So, again paradoxically, in depression we might experience more intensely than ever the (negative) value of *others'* suffering, even while devaluing our own actions, and thus implicitly ourselves. A well-done TV ad depicting neglected animals can trigger just enough action imagery to enable us to get out our checkbook. The depressed person requires the vivid perceptual image of the suffering to inspire even that much action—yet even then, there is a feeling that the action isn't worth much "in the Big Picture."

A further paradox here is that, in depression, even though only imagery of suffering can inspire action, we can't be inspired to action by the image of our *own* suffering. Such imagery only inspires further lethargy. Imagery of our own suffering dampens the incentive to form action imagery. If it weren't for the vivid imagery of the suffering of others, we would fail to be inspired to any action at all. To be sure, the depression itself might be partly attributable to the "blockages" to action described by Ann Weiser Cornell (2005)—the internal conflict between wanting to act and concerns over the risks of action. But regardless of causation, if we are depressed, the result is that it is difficult to feel inspired other than by vivid perceptual imagery.

Even as we lament the suffering of the hungry person whose imagery is so vivid, we don't automatically feel inspired to go out and work at the soup kitchen. This impediment involves the depressed person's suppression of Panksepp's SEEKING system (which normally would gear us up for action) more than it does the social bonding systems. The latter systems (for example, NURTURANCE and PANIC) still allow us to empathize with specific individuals.

Both in depression and in the clannishness of the "Agreeable" authoritarian, although for very different reasons, valuation tends to be limited primarily to those whose *perceptual images* are ready-to-hand, at least in the vague outlines offered by mental imagery. Those who are closest or most present (as on the TV screen) usually present the easiest imagery. In authoritarianism, the universalization of the valuation of others can be blocked by dependence on the needed imagery of those specific individuals or "look-alike" categories of individuals for whom the authoritarian is able to form easy imagery and thus feel valuation. But absent the intrinsic value of humans *as such,* there is now too little grounding for the instrumental value of actions. In depression, universalization itself isn't blocked so much as the needed *inspiration to act* on the generally acknowledged value of valuing creatures.

Depression allows intense feeling of the intrinsic value of the suffering creature depicted in the visual imagery of the late-night TV ad, yet not so much feeling of the value of the depressed person's own life activities. For the authoritarian as well, different in so many other respects from the depressed person, everything also seems dependent on sensory imagery. "Agreeable" feelings extend to the person who is immediately present—the lady changing a tire or the one who "looks like us"—the familiar countryman. They present easy perceptual imagery.

We can flesh out still further the difference this perceptual-image dependence makes by considering it in the context of a controlled experimental situation: the Milgram electric-shock studies.

Milgram and the Prison of Perceptual-Image Dependence

Even the famous Stanley Milgram (1974) experiments illustrate the problem of perceptual-image dependence. Milgram *assumes* that authoritarian personality is the explanation for why up to 60 percent of his subjects are willing to deliver presumably extremely painful electric shocks to other subjects. But subsequent researchers don't always find a very strong if any correlation to measures of authoritarian personality (for example, Bègue et al. 2015). Stein Bräten (2013) goes further, evaluating the actual conversations between the experimenters and their subjects. He shows evidence that what is really happening is that the subject *empathizes* more with the researcher than with the subject receiving the shock, simply because the researcher is in the same room, conversing directly with the subject, whereas the other subject is in a separate room.

Those who *refuse* to deliver the shock, in Bräten's analysis, tend to be less dependent on the imagery of the close-at-hand person to elicit their empathy—in this case, the experimenter. They therefore empathize with the suffering of the subject in the other room more than with the researcher, and thus refuse to deliver the shock.

On the enactivist analysis, hearing the screams of the other subject doesn't just elicit *perceptual* imagery. The primary subject in this case imagines what it would *be* like to enact those screams—action imagery.

The image dependence in this context would be expected to correlate only slightly with the "Agreeableness" of the authoritarian personality (as Bègue et al. 2015 show, consistently with Bräten's analysis). Even many nonauthoritarians also have a similar problem with image-dependence. It makes sense that the image-dependence would tend to be a little more prominent in authoritarian personalities, and thus would mildly correlate with it in some of the studies.

In the Milgram setup, studies show that depressed people are somewhat less inclined to deliver the shock (see Virgil Zeigler-Hill 2013). This is consistent with our observation that the depressed person's empathy tends to extend toward the image of *suffering*. It is the other subject, not the experimenter, who is suffering. The function of the image-dependence in this case is that the image facilitates feeling the other subject's value with a negative valance, which is available to the depressed person.

All these findings are consistent with the surprising positive correlation we noted earlier between "Agreeableness" and "Right Wing Authoritarianism" (a mild correlation of +.21 in the Hodson study). There is no contradiction in hating Muslims in general, while honestly affirming "Some of my best friends are Muslims." Even if the elderly lady trying to change a tire doesn't "look like" the authoritarian, the image still evokes empathy, but the empathy doesn't extend to her entire ethnic or religious group, who still don't present the direct imagery.

If action presupposes motivation, which implies value, then there must be an important role for action imagery in the baseline level of minimal "enthusiasm" needed for the underlying trajectory of enactive meaning. If empathy (directed at the intrinsic value of valuing creatures) supplies a good part of the feeling of the intrinsic value that implicitly underlies our instrumental actions, we need to consider how both perceptual and action imagery play their role here.

The Role of Enacted Attention in Value Feelings

Experiencing someone's intrinsic value is a function of directing attention. This attentional focus isn't simply caused by blood relationship, clan membership, or other such facts. An adopted child or stepchild can pull empathy just as much as a blood child. A comrade in combat might pull empathy as much as a lifelong friend. Even a fictional character in a novel can pull it. The crucial determinant is not some objective fact of blood relation or community membership, but rather the way we direct our attention.

As I gradually get to know a friend, why is it that this person gradually comes to be included in the category of people whose intrinsic value I can strongly feel? The crucial change is that now I direct more *attention* to the person's valuing dimension. This attention sometimes might be focused because of blood relationship, friendship, the person's similarity to myself, or some other reason. But whatever the cause might be, the *criterion* is whether we focus attention in this way. In the case of the loud drunk at the bar, we might be less likely to focus this attention, but we could learn to do so.[1]

In the feeling that someone has intrinsic value, we acknowledge that this person would have value for anyone who would pay attention to them qua valuing creature. Those who are close at hand (family and friends) offer easy imagery that pulls the needed attention. To the extent that we are dependent on concrete perceptual imagery, the scope of our experience of the intrinsic value of various people and categories of people is correspondingly limited.

But we don't have to be currently paying attention to someone to feel their value implicitly. There is an implied *affordance* of potential empathy in the case of *any* valuing creature, at least prima facie, whether we happen to be paying attention to that specific individual at the moment or not. We know preconsciously that in principle we could. Even the "Agreeable" authoritarian can't feel, without internal conflict, that the meaning of "X has value" could be reduced simply to "I value X."[2] That would preclude the feeling that X will still have value after I die.

The exploratory drive (in conflict with other emotions) pushes us to ask ourselves questions. If the fact that my child's being hungry entails that the child's getting something to eat is a worthy outcome, can I then feel that it would *not* have been a worthy outcome for that same child if I had died the day before and therefore was unable to ground its value by subjectively "valuing" it? If I discover that individual A rather than B is my child, accidentally switched with B at birth, would A's values *not* have been worthy of pursuit until I discovered that A is my child? And correlatively, would B's achieving it then *not* be worthy of pursuit after all? The choice of whom we intrinsically value, and how strongly, is not genetically hardwired.[3]

It would be easy enough to simply explain away this fact. To be sure, natural selection would attribute survival value to step-parenting. The survival of the gene pool *of the group* requires that a child whose father or mother has died must be nurtured by someone. But this is just another way of saying that there is almost infinite flexibility in our ability to intrinsically value others; the valuation here again depends only on our *directing attention* to the valuing dimension of the creature in question. We tend to direct more attention to a child with whom we continually interact; but this doesn't mean that we don't implicitly understand that hungry children in the Sudan also have the same kind of intrinsic value, given that we *could have* directed the same amount of attention to their valuing dimension.

In concrete terms, the *presence of* and *interaction with* a person, rather than genetic relatedness, easily increases our attention to the person's valuing dimension. In less typical cases, we *suddenly* feel inspired to risk our life to save an unknown person (as in the remarkable Bråten 2013 studies of incidents showing heroic altruism on the part of ordinary people). In cases of "falling in love," we very quickly and intensely appreciate the intrinsic value of another person. We direct attention to the person's valuing dimension in all its detail and vulnerability.

Generally, the more a given individual qua valuing creature is in my field of attention (whether gradually or suddenly), the more likely I am to include that person in the sphere of those with whom I strongly empathize. The "mirror neuron system," needed for empathy, subserves the capability for action imagery as opposed to mere sensory imagery (Stamenov and Gallese 2002). So there obviously must be a connection between the ability to form action imagery and the ability to empathize with the other's motivations for action, thus the person's valuing dimension.

When we entertain the generalized value of valuing creatures, the imagery of an individual functions as a "symbolization" in Gendlin's sense, a symbolization not just for present imagery, but rather for our valuation of valuing creatures as such—not in the subjective sense of "I like ice cream," but in the less subjective sense defined at the outset of this chapter: "X would still have value even if I were to die tomorrow." "X affords being valued." We can use the way an individual symbolizes valuing creatures in general to intensify our own valuation of valuing creatures per se. This feeling of the intrinsic value of others expands the amount of intrinsic value in our value system, which is needed in turn for the everyday baseline of inspiration toward long-term action trajectories.

The image of the neglected animal in the TV ad can inspire us not only to help neglected animals, but also to work toward *any* endeavor that directly or indirectly favors the well-being of *any* conscious creatures—to be a more effective teacher for our students, to work toward political solutions to problems, to work at a soup kitchen, or simply to be friendly to the check-out clerk at the store. The meaning offered is more expansive than simply whether I can help the specific neglected animals represented in the TV ad.

But the universalization of the empathy requires action imagery, in the sense that we imagine actions that could be taken in the service of the extended value system, including the complicated instrumentalizations of our lengthy "supply chains" of instrumental values that serve other instrumental values, and still others in turn, and so on as instrumental values by their very nature serve other values beyond themselves.

The Importance of Inspirational Needs

In everyday life, attributing intrinsic value to others doesn't necessarily mean just "benefitting" them, in the sense of helping them obtain the things they value. We can also benefit anyone we meet simply by being "nice"—by helping to enhance the conditions needed for their own valuational feelings in general, their everyday inspirational feelings, their feelings that life is worth living, and that things are worth doing. This can include a wide range of everyday friendly and group activities, as well as working toward a feeling that there is a "community" of valuational interrelationships. It can include creating artworks and political movements and family and friendship relationships that enable the intensification of the other's feeling that achieving whatever it is they value actually *has* a significant amount of value. It can include being friendly to the local convenience store clerk.

Such activities may not instrumentally serve the concrete, easily measurable needs of people, but they do contribute to enhancing others' sense of enactive meaning. In this sense, not all values are instrumental.

The inspirational need itself is also an important value, for others as well as ourselves.

Even if parents give their children all the measurable benefits—everything they want or need toward *fulfilling* whatever aspirations they may have in life—the child's feeling of inspiration can still be dampened by feeling that whatever they may ever ultimately achieve, it will never be quite enough. It will never amount to anything significant in the "Ultimate Scheme of Things." Art or music lessons are provided, yet real "success" would be counted as becoming a "world-class" saxophonist or oil painter. The value of the achievement is thus defined instrumentally. But since the value is only instrumental, a further implication is that if we "fail" in this quest to be "the best," that's fine too. There are already so many accomplished saxophonists and oil painters that it really doesn't matter whether we add one more.

By extension, nothing the child does really matters. Even the *instrumental* value of the achievement is implicitly diminished, based on an unacknowledged assumption that something very "grandiose" is needed, while the same logic implies that no amount of grandiosity will ever *really* be enough to be worth striving for.

The resulting semiapathy can exacerbate the difficult balance between intrinsic and instrumental value. A saxophonist must strive for excellence if meaning is to be defined through the music, yet the value of the saxophonist can't be completely instrumental toward that purpose. At the same time, the feeling of everyday inspiration requires that the saxophonist's enactive meaning trajectory does depend extensively on trying to achieve excellence.

The result may be that the resources are completely available to fulfill the child's aspirations, but the child is unable to feel that those very aspirations can be *experienced* as having much value in the first place, since the meaning of the activity is only instrumental toward the relevant "Grand Scheme" value. The parents are fulfilling the child's consummatory needs, but suppressing their inspirational needs. Achieving what we value and experiencing the value of what we value are two different things.

Action versus Reaction: Why Enactive Symbolizations Are Needed

Damasio (1999) shows that consciousness is a function of emotional rather than cognitive brain activity. Again, the "consciousness" Damasio means to refer to in this sense is simply the kind of subjective experience that we don't seem to have when in a dreamless sleep. When subcortical emotional areas are subdued, the subject loses not only certain cognitive functions, but consciousness itself. These deeper subcortical processes are the purpose-creating and action-generating centers of the brain. They initiate larger patterns of self-organizing activity that then extend throughout much wider areas of the brain, and then have the power to move the body.

To be purpose directed in this way, a system has to be self-organizing—structured with a tendency to reorganize its own parts when needed to maintain the overall pattern of activity that defines the system. While the microcomponents obey laws of cause and effect, the system is constantly rearranging the background conditions that are presupposed by those cause-effect mechanisms.

Flipping a switch "causes" a light to come on, but only if we assume background conditions such as a good bulb and certain patterns of wiring in the circuit. In a self-organizing system such as a living body or brain, some of those background conditions can be rearranged *by the system itself* on an as-needed basis. For example, alternate sets of cells can be adapted to cause similar outcomes to the ones that previously were caused by cells that are now destroyed, as in certain methods of stroke recovery.[4]

The more sophisticated acting creatures not only act in this sense, but they also understand the environment in terms of *imagining* possible actions relative to environmental affordances. Think of the cat tentatively exploring a table top—trying to imagine whether its leap is likely to succeed.

Gendlin (2018) emphasizes that this understanding of action affordances can be "implicit." It doesn't have to be conscious. We see how conscious imagining of action can become *subliminal* in the case of Donoghue's monkeys, who learn to play computer games by moving a joy stick "with their minds" (Donoghue 2002). They first move the joystick with their hands to make the computer game work, but then Donoghue's implanted electrodes pick up their action-imaging brain activity and send the corresponding signals to the computer because the neural substrates of a given *action* are similar to those of a *merely imagined* action (as Jeannerod 1997 had earlier established). As a result of the electrodes picking up the action imagery, the monkeys can now play the computer game by merely imagining the movement. This process is now being used to develop more and more sophisticated prosthetic limbs and even communication devices that subjects can operate mentally, by implicitly forming the corresponding action imagery.

The imagination of an action means that the brain initiates the action command, but the signal is inhibited later in its circuit (at the level of the motor-parietal circuits). Donoghue's electrodes pick up on the neural substrates of the monkey's action of moving its hand, and ipso facto on the very similar brain activity of merely *imagining* moving the hand. Eventually, the monkeys may be consciously thinking only of playing the computer game, without any hand movement whatever, but the neurophysiological picture shows that, subliminally, they are still activating the movement commands that constitute the inhibited motor imagery of their hand movements. The change from conscious to unconscious motor imagery is gradual. In Merleau-Ponty's (1945) sense, it becomes "sedimented." In Gendlin's sense, it now occurs "implicitly."

In the same way, musicians can memorize music by imagining moving their fingers as if fingering an instrument; then gradually the imagined movements drop to a subliminal level. The efferent motor representations of the finger movements gradually become less pronounced and less conscious.

We can normally tell the difference between the subjective feel of deliberately moving ourselves, and on the other hand the feel of an involuntary movement by an external force. The feeling of deliberate movement involves both proprioceptive and "sensorimotor" imagery, which subserves our own intention to act. The feeling of involuntary movement is *only* proprioceptive—a sensing *that* our own parts are moving, but without necessarily having the sense that we ourselves are moving them. With externally forced movement, we subjectively read the afferent "input" from the moving limb, but not the efferent *effort* of moving it ourselves. The efferent and afferent nerves usually run to and from the extremities in separate but parallel pathways.

A composer wakes up in the morning and decides to write a piano concerto, without any presently occurring external stimulus "causing" this action. Damasio (1999), Panksepp (1998), and other neuropsychologists show that self-initiated actions begin with the activation of motivational processes rooted deep in the subcortex, processes involved in orchestrating the organism's motivations. The lower brain stem is especially important in activating the SEEKING system. But as a precursor to any action, we need to first *imagine* the action to be performed—Jeannerod's action imagery.

The same action-generating processes are needed, whether in actual movement or just action imagery. And they in turn require embodied emotion systems to motivate them. These emotion systems are precisely the thing that nuts-and-bolts computers lack since they aren't self-organizing biological systems. The computers can *imitate* emotional behaviors, as in the friendly vocal inflection of the GPS system's helpful voice; but that is different from actually feeling the emotions.

Action Imagery as Symbolizing Values in Gendlin's Sense

Action presupposes valuing. A murderer may not know what the motivation for the murder is, but what is clear is that the murderer *wants to pull the trigger*. The idea of pulling the trigger is a value that drives an action. The action imagery has to occur first, in order for the possibility of pulling the trigger to be considered as a possibly valued outcome. Given the way beings like humans are organized, we can't avoid acting in certain patterns that involve placing a value on the outcome of completing an action.

The strongest candidate for an outcome that is intrinsically (not just instrumentally) valuable involves aspects of the well-being of valuing creatures (including ourselves). This may *initially*, in our early years, include only those others who are the objects of CARE, PANIC, and other social bonding systems. Later in childhood, the SEEKING system, with its exploratory drive, then motivates us to explore further and notice that those same value sentiments can apply to any valuing creature, to the extent that the creature is capable of consciousness, simply because we experience the value as intrinsic rather than instrumental (that is, instrumental relative to our own or someone else's purposes). The exploratory drive invites us to compare and contrast the way we feel toward different people in different situations.

But initially, even prior to this universalizing process, the social bonding emotions are unavoidably already extended to at least *some* other subjectivities. The exploratory drive then eventually prompts universalization of this valuing, as well as the resulting extended value system, as in our earlier example of Rachmaninoff.

Another composer, Richard Wagner, was sometimes specifically accused of *not* caring about others' feelings (their valuing dimension). This would be an exaggerated caricature of Wagner's attitudes, but suppose it were true at least to some extent. In the final analysis, if asked to justify *why* his music is more valuable than other kinds of music—or why it is valuable—he would have to refer, just like Rachmaninoff, to the subjective responses of potential users of the music. In fact, in his published essays, this is just the way Wagner did discuss the subjective responses of listeners to music (for an interesting discussion of some philosophical implications of Wagner's essays, see Eli Kramer 2021).

In modern thought, there is a tendency to reduce morality to a social or cultural "veneer" lain over the top of an essentially reinforcement-driven "brute nature." There is often an underlying assumption—tracing back to Thomas Hobbes's primitive theories about chemical reactions in the brain—that people always act out of direct or indirect self-interest, trying ultimately to maximize their happiness or "positive reinforcements," including "social reinforcements." This leads many people informally to embrace a kind of egoistic view of human nature, with an attempt to limit the value of subjectively valued outcomes to just one particular conscious subject—myself. All our behavior, including social behavior, then seems to function merely as a means toward this end. Hard economic times, as descried by Hannah Arendt, can also exacerbate this way of looking at human nature. But the more we approach this radically egoistic attitude, the more we find ourselves living just on the verge of nihilism since the realm of intrinsic values would then be so limited.

As we have seen, only a literal psychopath could really take this attitude. Such a limitation of intrinsic value to a desire for our own "happiness" or "positive reinforcement" would be difficult to reconcile with the intrinsic value of others that is required by the normally endogenous social-bonding emotion systems such as the CARE and PANIC systems.

This concern for others isn't just perched atop a Maslow-like "pyramid" of values. Poor people are often the most charitable, and moral sentiments aren't lost to oppressed or suffering people. The intrinsic value of valuing creatures as such is still appreciated. And the SEEKING system, which motivates curiosity and moral development, is just as active in impoverished settings as otherwise. Even the "Wild Boy of Aveyron," after he was retrieved from the wild, acted according to moral principles (Bettleheim 1959). The value of others was already acknowledged, as a result of natural human development, without the "moral indoctrination" of civilization.

Egoism or even the expanded egoism of "clannism" doesn't refrain from taking a position that something has value or is worthy of action. Instead, it limits the class of things that are held to be worthy of pursuit to the valuations of a *small subset* of people. If we also then compensate for this limitation of intrinsic value by resorting to a "Grand Scheme" or "ultimate" value to be powerful enough to motivate action, it will consequently seem even more hopeless that any action could do enough good to be worthwhile in terms of that Grand Scheme, given our own smallness as finite creatures.

But to be motivated to action on the basis of empathy also requires action imagery. Action imagery is always necessary for planning and executing any action. If we suffer from a depressed psychological state, the problem is that we find ourselves unable to intensify the valuation of *our own actions* in any other way than by demanding easy or vivid *perceptual* imagery on the part of a valuing (and suffering) creature. We can't feel inspired with a positive valence by the imagery of actions that we might take.

There is another way, besides either perceptual or action imagery, to symbolize and thus intensify feelings of value. We can intensify them by actually taking action. Action serves to give concrete embodiment to the feeling being symbolized—in this case, the feeling of valuing, the sense that something "makes a difference," although not in the "totalizing" way of a Grand Scheme value system. Value feelings in daily life are routinely intensified by acting in some concrete way to "symbolize" them—whether by working at a soup kitchen, or creating artworks that celebrate the importance of subjective values, or even just by working to make our fellow employees' lives easier.

While social work is grueling and often thankless work, and hardly makes the worker "happy," it can be meaningful even in its difficulty. Being considerate toward our fellow employees may not win us a promotion or pay raise or any outcome that increases our own well-being, other than enhancing our ability to feel the intrinsic value of other valuing creatures, thus expanding our feeling that action is worthwhile. Political action in the service of human rights or universal dimensions of human well-being can be similarly meaningful, aside from any happiness or unhappiness that might result from success or failure. By acting in such ways, we amplify action imagery and thus avoid becoming overly dependent on vivid perceptual imagery to enhance feelings of value.

∼

The nihilistic shortage of enactive meaning, grounded in failure to intrinsically value valuing creatures as such, can be seen clearly in the most extreme cases—the "sudden murderer," the "family annihilator," and to a slightly lesser extent, the "hate crime" murderer. Studying these extreme examples can help understand the more normal case. Our next chapter considers these particular extreme forms of value nihilism and their relationship to the shortage of enactive meaning.

Chapter 7

Total Failure of Inspiration

Lessons from the Sudden Murderer and the Family Annihilator

Criminologists tell us that 70 percent of murders are "sudden murders"—eruptions of anger or hatred, with nothing to gain from the crime, no premeditation, and no attempt to avoid detection and prosecution (Schlesinger 2004; see also Cartwright 2014; McCaghy 1980; Weiss et al. 1960). Sudden murder in this sense represents the ultimate sacrifice, not only of the other, but of oneself as well. The lack of precautions to avoid detection and the absence of any gain from the crime reflect unconcern with the perpetrator's *own* well-being, at least for that instant.

In a typical instance, a man shot another over a one-dollar gambling debt—and as a result not only served a life sentence, but also never recovered the one dollar. In another case, a man riding a bus shot the driver, in front of many witnesses, simply because "he was in my face." In all such cases, arrest and imprisonment are obvious consequences, with literally nothing to gain from the crime. Just as neurologists learn about normal function by studying its absence in extreme dysfunction, we can learn about the valuing and devaluing that drive action from this most extreme negative case.

As Gendlin emphasizes, it would be a mistake to count a feeling-category like "hatred" or "anger" as referring to a specific affective quality. Stock category words like "hatred" are inadequate and even misleading when used to name or describe a specific, unique experience. I use "hatred" here to indicate a *wide range* of emotional feelings that have the effect of totalistically, or almost totalistically, negating the value of another subjectivity's valuational dimension.

Sudden murder isn't just an expression of anger or hatred. We can easily feel emotions within the broad "anger" category while still *more or less* respecting the value of someone's existence. Most people don't kill their spouse or co-workers, even when angry. We don't have to constantly remind ourselves, "I know I'm angry, but let's remember not to kill this person."

Beyond even an intense feeling within the "anger" category, sudden murder involves a much more unique frame of mind. In the specific instant of sudden murder, the value of *either* person's being literally counts for nothing as far as the killer's own motivation is concerned. If it did count for anything (in that specific instant), then destroying the other person wouldn't seem important enough to justify a crime for which nothing is gained, and with certainty of punishment. This "nothing" that is gained is more important (in that instant) than *the existence* of the other. Furthermore, the murderer's *own* well-being counts as having less value than this same "nothing to gain." The value of either person's existence is literally less than this "nothing."

In short, for the sudden murderer, both self and other are devalued in the same devaluation of what it means to be a valuing creature per se. The fact that most murders are sudden murders reflects this underlying principle; absolute devaluation of the self and of the other go hand in hand, because both negate the intrinsic value of humanity per se.

This negation of the intrinsic value of subjective beings per se entails an implicit value nihilism. With no intrinsic value of either oneself or the other that is worth affecting action, the very bedrock of the entire edifice of intrinsic and instrumental values collapses. The result is that literally nothing matters. Complete devaluation of the other implies devaluation the self, in the sense of intrinsic value.

The Existential Despair of Sudden Murder

Even in the case of killing an enemy in combat, we might be gripped by anger or hatred, but we still count the enemy's being as *one of* the values on the table, even if not the one that takes priority. As soon as the enemy waves a white flag, extensive effort and resources are expended to get them into a prison, where a basic level of care is expected.

Similarly, when someone hates other ethnic or religious groups strongly enough to motivate doing some amount of direct or indirect harm, the perpetrator of the harm is somewhat devaluing those others' existence, but again to a lesser extent than in sudden murder. The hatred in these cases usually isn't the *absolute* devaluation of sudden murder.

What distinguishes the emotions of the sudden murderer isn't what *is* felt, but rather what *isn't*. While many kinds of feelings can play a role in sudden murder—anger, jealousy, contempt, frustration, fear, or even justified rage—the one feeling that is *not* taken into account in that instant is any regard for the intrinsic value of either person's existence, simply by virtue of being conscious and valuing creatures.

Ordinary hatred, in the sense of *some degree* of disregard for the intrinsic value of someone's being, might involve a similar dynamic, but not as extreme. In the instant when we cut someone off in traffic or retaliate against an insult, telling ourselves something like "The sonofabitch deserved it!" we somewhat decrease the extent of our valuing of the other person's existence—but not completely. We often speak of "hating" someone in a loose sense of the word. But hatred in the sense needed for sudden murder tries to absolutely negate even the prima facie intrinsic value of at least one or some subset of subjective beings per se, in spite of the capacity of those beings to establish value simply by virtue of being creatures who value things.

Even when we refer to a murder as an "act of passion" (which usually falls under the heading of sudden murder—no premeditation, nothing to gain, etc.), what distinguishes this type of murder isn't passion per se, but rather that the value of the other's being effectually drops out of the emotional picture. Even despite protestations that the murder was motivated by jealousy and perhaps therefore even by "love," the value of the other's being literally plays no role in the instant when options are weighed and the decision is made to wield the knife or gun. At least for that moment, nothing matters. Given that an act leading to no valued result (nothing to gain) is worth sacrificing everything, including one's own entire future, we can think of the sudden murderer as coming as close as imaginable to a complete nihilism of value.

I freely grant that neurological issues may play a role. Impulsive murder can involve a shortage or imbalance of serotonin, and correlative loss of "impulse control" (Davidson et al. 2007; Retz et al. 2004). But for our purposes, this only means that in the instant of the murder a shortage of serotonin correlates, in the subjective dimension, with a failure to take the intrinsic value of the other's being (or one's own) as counting for anything.[1] As Panksepp (1998, 2011) shows, RAGE, PANIC, and SEEKING are widely distributed brain processes. Full enactment of the RAGE system usually doesn't result in murder, partly because RAGE is in balance and in conflict with other equally important emotion systems, including very routine prefrontal regulation of the amygdala in normal functioning,[2] as well as the CARE and PANIC systems, however suppressed those might be at a given moment. The relevant thing for us is that the ultimate expression of value nihilation in sudden murder goes hand in hand with an ultimate surrender of all concern either for the other's well-being or for one's own.[3]

To hate in this absolute sense of completely devaluing someone—as currently illustrated in the United States by at least fifteen thousand cases of "sudden murder" per year (out of the twenty-thousand-plus cases of murder overall)—entails a totalistic failure, even if only momentarily, to acknowledge even the most basic intrinsic value, whether instantiated in victim or perpetrator. Nothing matters, and no one matters. Obviously, no deterrence effect of the criminal justice system can stop these types of murders because no consequences of action are relevant from the standpoint of the sudden murderer's almost completely nihilistic mindset.

The sudden murderer's unconcern with the murderer's own well-being is reminiscent of the way Arendt's totalitarian followers initially aren't motivated by rational self-interest and are even willing to sacrifice their own interests to the movement. We read of cases where the totalitarian followers willingly succumb to obviously unfair "trials" in which they themselves are falsely declared traitors to the cause (Arendt 1968, 318). It isn't simply that the totalitarian cause is felt to be so worthy as to warrant the sacrifice. Succumbing to such unjust treatment *doesn't* particularly further the cause. The willingness to be unjustly accused and punished reflects the fact that the follower's nihilism is so extensive that no one's well-being, not even the follower's own, is counted as having much intrinsic value.

The hatred on the part of a narrowly ethnocentric person, as with the sudden murderer but to a lesser extent, eliminates the intrinsicness of the value of valuing creatures since now no value can flow from simply being a valuing creature *as such*. This means that the ethnocentrist's own value is implicitly negated as well, simply qua valuing creature per se. This negation then undermines the coherence of the sense of enactive meaning, leaving the person open to the Grand Scheme offered by the authoritarian cult leader.

Like the totalitarian follower, sudden murderers might hide their nihilism under a facade of moral talk about "ultimate" values such as "the Will of God" or even "the Teachings of Jesus," until the void of intrinsic value breaks through in the utter nihilation of the other's value. The progressively nihilistic condition eventually prevents the sudden murderer from valuing anything whatever: "Let's just burn the whole house down!" Conversely, devaluing one's own existence implies devaluing the other. The entire project of being a conscious or valuing creature becomes a relatively worthless project. The "very idea" of valuing per se has no value.

This implicit seminihilism, with its correlative dampening of the SEEKING system, could also lead to a suppressed form of depression, although the depression may not be manifested on the surface or subjectively acknowledged as such. Europeans of the 1930s had good reason to be depressed, given the economic depression, the economic damage from recent wars, hopelessness of the future, atomization and *anomie* of individuals in a mass economic structure, and in the case of Germany, the humiliation of paying war reparations.

The resulting value nihilism, whether in Stalin's Russia, Hitler's Germany, Franco's Spain, or Mussolini's Italy, allowed the value of everyone and everything except for the authoritarian follower's own select group to be totalistically devalued. As with the sudden murderer, negation of the intrinsic value of others implies a nihilism or seminihilism of value as such, and thus to some extent a deflation of all the self's instrumental projects. The nihilism of the sudden murderer is the extreme example of this dynamic.

When psychopaths commit murder, they don't completely devalue themselves and their own objectives. Unlike sudden murderers, psychopaths typically do try to gain from the crime and avoid detection. Yet even psychopaths eventually become at least seminihilistic and often end by disregarding their own well-being as part of this general nihilism. Here too, complete devaluing of valuing creatures leads to an effectual nihilism of enactive intrinsic-instrumental value structures. Psychopaths are notorious for "disregarding the consequences of their actions."

Other than the complete psychopath (about 1 percent of the world population, according to Stout 2005), even someone who *claims* to be purely self-interested really isn't. Given the social bonding emotion systems, such a person still has to decide whose value to acknowledge—whether only one's own family, friends, political allies, or in general how wide a sphere of people are to be included, in what patterns, and by what criteria.

This last point leads us to still another type of murder—the "family annihilator"—which illustrates in extreme form what happens for those who try, not to completely nihilate the value of valuing creatures per se, but rather to maintain a sense of enactive meaning while severely *constricting* the realm of those whose intrinsic value is respected. The family annihilator contracts the realm of those who are intrinsically valuable even further than does the ethnocentrist or the cult follower. The result here too is a form of nihilism and eventually a total failure of enactive meaning.

The Family Annihilator and the Infinitely Diminishing Circle of Inspiration

Superficially, the family annihilator values the nuclear family to such an extent that the family has to be saved from some presumably horrible fate—for example, from the humiliation of financial failure or from some fantasized threat (for example, see Yardley et al. 2013). But such overdependence on the nuclear family for a sense of meaning, when the family fails to shoulder this monumental burden, leaves the potential family annihilator with virtually no sense of enactive meaning whatever. The set of intrinsically valued individuals has become so narrow that they are doomed in their attempt to supply the last gasp of intrinsic value. The annihilator demands that the family serve to provide the entire meaning of the annihilator's action trajectory—and therefore ironically turns against them when they fail the virtually impossible task.

Even more obviously than with the sudden murderer, the result here is in effect a murder-suicide. According to Yardley and colleagues, more than 80 percent of family annihilators commit suicide quickly after killing their family, and still others commit "suicide by cop." As with sudden murder, total devaluation of the other's existence implies total devaluation of the self's own existence.

As in sudden murder, here too, the annihilator's life project is straightforwardly and self-admittedly not felt to have intrinsic value. Prior to the murder, the only value that can be appreciated pertains to a severely restricted few individuals; and even their value takes a back seat to the instrumental purposes they serve—respectability, the appearance of financial success, and so on. By attributing more importance to the family's financial success, or to their social respectability or their "correct" religious practice, than to their actual *existence,* the annihilator is also attempting to define their value in instrumental rather than intrinsic terms. By undermining their intrinsic value in this way—relegating them to merely instrumental status—the annihilator has even further scripted them for failure to provide the needed amount of *intrinsic* value. Subordinating them to the annihilator's own desperate need for enactive meaning defeats the purpose. Their only value is to give purpose to *the annihilator's* existence. Their purpose is only instrumental.

It is difficult for a being with a brain like ours (with the primary empathic as well as SEEKING systems plus prefrontal reflective capacity and voluntary control of attention and imagery) to literally deny the intrinsic value of others, unless we also implicitly feel that we ourselves have little or no value. This failure to intrinsically value even our own life activity has nothing to do with whether others *affirm* our value. If my only value is value to others, then I make myself into an instrumental value. The only purpose of my existence then is to be judged by others in a certain way.

In sum, the negation of the intrinsic value of ourselves or of another hinges on the question whether we are capable of being inspired by the value of valuing creatures per se, including ourselves. But one of the main ways we intensify our own inspirational dimension—and probably the most important way, since it is foundational for the others—*is*, at least implicitly, by valuing the valuing dimension of valuing creatures per se, that is, "what it means" to be a valuing creature in general. Like sudden murderers, family annihilators too absolutely nihilate their own value in the instant when they nihilate the previously enshrined value of the family.

Hate Crimes, Selective Inattention, and the Sedimentation of the Implicit

"Hate-crime" murderers superficially seem less nihilistic than the sudden murderer or the family annihilator. For the hate-crime perpetrator, some people are valued (members of the in-group), but not people per se. If such a seminihilist also has an authoritarian bent, the result is an ability to empathize only with a severely selected subclass of others, such as an ethnicity or religion—although the selectivity is less extreme than with the family annihilator, who chooses only the nuclear family.

Since this type of seminihilism selectively suppresses the exploratory drive, there is a lack of incentive to observe the simple fact that the same property by virtue of which some are intrinsically valued is also possessed by all others. Nonuniversalized empathy then becomes a supposedly viable and deceptively attractive possibility. While the family annihilator narrows valuation to a few close-at-hand individuals, the ethnocentrist narrows it to an in-group. The extreme example is the "hate-crime" murder. Such a seminihilistic stance by itself isn't sufficient by itself to motivate a hate-crime murder, but it is a necessary precondition for it.

As we saw earlier, this tendency to narrow the realm of those who are valued is further exacerbated by image dependence. Those who are ready to hand (the clan or the nuclear family) present easy imagery. Universalizing our valuation of others requires more sophisticated brain activity than valuing an in-group, which requires only visual imagery. Action imagery is more effortful, but a certain amount of it is required for a more complete feeling of inspiration toward positive values.

Like the sudden murderer, the "hate-crime" murderer—that is, the politically or ethnically motivated terrorist—also tries with some degree of success to ignore the intrinsic value of selected individuals, especially in the instant when the murder occurs. The nihilism in this case isn't quite as complete as with the sudden murderer or the family annihilator. But we have already seen why the attempt to value nonuniversally leads to a seminihilism of value. Even the nonviolent authoritarian recruit suffers from a similar seminihilism, although not as extreme. Since whole categories of humans can be devalued, the intrinsic value of humans per se has been removed; so what remains even for those who are still valued is, implicitly, only instrumental value. There is then need for a Grand Scheme to provide the purpose to be served by the instrumentality of those who are to be valued.

We should carefully examine the role of attention and inattention in this process. For all of us—not just for the authoritarian or ethnocentrist—the demand to literally empathize with the suffering of *all* valuing creatures in the world would be difficult if not impossible. It would become depressing and debilitating. We all need to direct attention away from the value of the subjective valuations of many others in many contexts. In fact, we normally deflect attention from *most* of the suffering in the world, in order to preserve our own sanity. We can't literally be constantly directing our attention toward the difficult circumstances of every starving child or wild animal.

But we can still know from previous experience combined with a minimal amount of curiosity that the intrinsic value of these creatures is *always capable* of having attention directed to it, just as we know that the other side of the world exists even when we are not thinking about it. Our consciousness of their valuations is always available to us for conscious reflection. It is "preconscious" rather than conscious, in the same way that we know our phone number without constantly thinking about it. And we can form action imagery of some of the kinds of things that could be done to save at least some of the endangered species and limit the environmental destruction that makes their lives unnecessarily miserable.

Mirror Neurons and the Phenomenology of Devaluation at the Edge of Nihilism

For the 30 percent of murders that are *not* sudden murders, there is something to gain from the crime, however trivial. The decision to kill is a weighing of competing values not unlike the weighing of a combat soldier. Yes, it is too bad that the victim has to be sacrificed, but whatever is to be gained is judged to be more important. There is no *absolute* devaluation as in the case of the sudden murderer, the family annihilator, or the hate-crime murderer.

But even in this case, to a greater or lesser extent, the murderer momentarily refrains from empathizing with the valuing dimension of the other person. The mirror neuron system, as noted earlier, is needed to understand a person as a valuing creature. But the mirror neuron system centers in the brain's motor areas. We understand a person as a conscious and valuing being by imagining what it would be like to enact that person's actions or potential actions ourselves. Newton (1996) elaborates this point in detail, especially in the chapter on "Understanding Persons." We activate the same processes that we would activate if we ourselves were to do what the other is doing, but then we use frontal inhibition processes to modify the action circuits so as only to *imagine* ourselves in the other's place (the brain mechanism for motor imagery described by Jeannerod 1994, 1997). We see vast amounts of scientific evidence for this action-imaging process in the mirror neuron literature.[4]

The sudden murderer most clearly of all, in the instant of the murder, doesn't mirror—doesn't empathize with any goal, action, or purpose of the victim. Since values are experienced in terms of the actions they motivate, the failure of mirroring corresponds to an absence of a feeling of intrinsic value, which implicitly applies to the self as well as the other.

In the case of the sudden murderer, and also the family annihilator, and to a slightly lesser extent the hate-crime murderer, the perpetrator virtually cares about nothing in that instant and typically shows no emotional affect in the ensuing police interrogation. In this absence of a sense of intrinsic value, there is a corresponding absence of a minimal baseline level of inspiration—a giving up to existential despair.

Baseline inspiration itself requires that there be intrinsic values in a person's value system, at least implicitly. Mirroring is a necessary component of the ability to feel intrinsic value as instanced by the value of valuing creatures. The same brain processes that enact the value and purpose of our own actions is also used when we understand the other as a valuing creature. This act of empathy is related to the way we establish an overall relatively coherent view of the valuational realm—that someone's value doesn't depend on my act of "feeling" that they have value.

The sudden murderer, the family annihilator, and the hate-crime murderer are extreme examples of this failure of the implicit baseline of intrinsic value needed to avoid the "nothing-matters" attitude. For the sudden murderer, this failure happens absolutely, but only for the moment of the crime. For the hate-crime murderer, the devaluation is less than absolute, and the hater unsuccessfully attempts to feel that some but not all human beings can have intrinsic value. Most clearly of all, the family annihilator reduces the pool of intrinsically valuable creatures to only the immediate family, while simultaneously reducing even them to instrumental values. As a result, in all three cases, the feeling of the meaning of the killer's own life is either absolutely eliminated or grossly minimized.

Inspiration, "Paying Attention," and Value Nihilism

For a person with a human brain with even minimal functioning of primary drive systems (including the SEEKING system and some prefrontal activity), a literally *absolute* value nihilism would entail an inability to act. But all conscious beings *are* able to act. Even a completely paralyzed person can *imagine* engaging in actions; and an imaginary act itself is also an action, although the only thing that moves is the chemistry of the brain. Since action presupposes value, to imagine the other's actions also implies that we re-enact the other person's valuational consciousness, at least to some extent.

Consider the opposite extreme from the attitude of the murderer. In an important respect, we often affirm the value of another person's subjectivity *more* intensely than we can affirm the value of our own. In the "Phenomenology of Eros" chapter of *Totality and Infinity* (1969), Levinas describes the way we can intensify our valuation of a subjective being when we empathize with the "finitude" or "frailty" of that being.[5] Levinas's "frailty" implies that the person's ability to exist as a conscious being is limited not only in time (by death), but also by the limitations of the person's relative power in the ultimate scheme of things and, paradoxically, the comparative *insignificance* of any particular individual in the grand scheme. If we focus on these issues in our *own* case, the result tends to be despair or self-pity, not an intense affirmation of the value of our own being. But when another person is the focus of such feelings, our empathy is intensified by virtue of considering these daunting aspects of the other's finiteness, and this in turn intensifies our experience of the person's extreme *value* as a conscious being, often described as an intensified form of "admiration." Levinas calls this paradoxical asymmetry of relationships the "infinite curvature of intersubjective space."

This phenomenon is reflected in the tendency to eulogize the dead and to hold back our hatred or ill-regard for people who are ill or who have just experienced a severe misfortune such as the death of a loved one. When we exaggerate the good qualities of the deceased, it may seem as if we are extolling their *instrumental* value—that they serve some instrumental purpose with great virtuosity. "He was such a great scientist!" and so on. But actually, we are also and more importantly using those exaggerated praises to symbolize our own appreciation for the person's *intrinsic* value, qua valuing creature. We use the instrumental values to which they devoted their actions to activate our own mirror neuron system in order to intensely empathize with the deceased person, to experience not their instrumental, but their intrinsic value.

The tendency to feel inspired by late-night TV ads featuring images of mistreated animals or starving children shows how focusing attention on the "finiteness" and "vulnerability" of a creature counter-intuitively increases the intensity with which we feel their positive value. For these reasons, various kinds of feelings of love can be experienced more intensely than "self-love" or love of one's own self-interest. Hence the familiar phenomenon that many forms of love can play an inspirational role in intensifying the sense that not only are there values, but that these values are pronounced enough to make action worthwhile.

The flip side is the phenomenology of the hate-crime murderer. The capacity to empathize with others can be *selectively* shut down (as with the "Agreeable" racists in the Hodson et al. study). The empathy is shut down, not by an *inability* to experience others as valuable, but rather by the manipulation and self-manipulation of attention and inattention.

Living at the Edge of Nihilism

Criminologists often marvel at how "normal" the sudden murderer can seem, right up to the point when the conflagration erupts. The "normal" prospective murderer speaks in everyday, mundane terms about the value of various people and outcomes. They often obsessively tout ultrareligious values and cite religious texts as sources of their supposed inspiration. Yet this normal talk is deceptive. Under the surface is a serious and prolonged flirtation with value nihilism. Similarly, as Arendt describes, fascists, racists, and other believers in extremely irrational and harmful value systems think that they attribute tremendous importance to certain values, even while living at the edge of nihilism.

Even the "normal" structure of enactive value differs from that of the family annihilator and sudden murderer only in the degree of separation from the experience of intrinsic value—whether we experience it directly or, as in Rachmaninoff's case, indirectly through our instrumentalizations of it. Racism and xenophobia substantially nihilate the value of all but the ethnic "in-group." In that respect they can be understood by comparison to the value nihilism of the family annihilator, who is able to value only the nuclear family. Whereas the family annihilator's inspiration can be triggered only by vivid imagery (imagery of the nuclear family), the ethnocentrist is motivated to *deflect attention away* from any possible imagery of the valuing dimension of many categories of others.

For both the family annihilator and the ethnocentric hate-crime murderer, only vivid imagery of the close-at-hand person can relieve a tendency toward value nihilism. For the family annihilator, the image of the nuclear family is the failing last bastion of hope for any intrinsic value. The close-at-hand for the ethnocentrist includes the family member, but also the friend, the clan member, the one who is "like us." The family annihilator and hate-crime murderer both are image-dependent in this respect. Yet the availability of the imagery itself is manipulated in the service of selective attention.

For the family annihilator, image dependence becomes so important that the image outweighs the value of those of whom it is the image. When the family no longer lives up to the image of "the perfect family," "the religiously correct family," or whatever other image the annihilator is trying to maintain, at that point the family's ability to sustain any feeling of inspiration fails. The family has become an instrumental value, in the service of propping up the desperately needed image.

To a lesser extent, similar dynamics obtain for the authoritarian. The image of the "patriot" or "Good American" must be lived up to, on pain of devaluation or self-devaluation from the standpoint of intrinsic value. As in the case of narcissism—which in the Hodson study also correlates with racism and xenophobia—images have then become more important than reality.

It isn't paradoxical that a terrorist organization like ISIL can use religious doctrines to mobilize criminals, psychopaths, and other nihilists and seminihilists with a claim that the Will of God can be promoted without consideration to the well-being of valuing creatures. In all these examples, the person is tempted to compensate for the lack of inspiration by positing suprapersonal, "Grand Scheme" values.

It is noteworthy for our purposes that a *vast majority* of murders fall into the "sudden murder" category, where all value is nihilated, including the value of the self. Such a nihilation of the value of subjectivity implies a nihilation of the value of ourselves in the same act that destroys the other.

Whether in sudden murder, hate crimes, family annihilation, merely xenophobic hatred, the emotional incoherence of trying to limit intrinsic value to one or a few people, the attempt to define value only instrumentally—all these various degrees of negation of an underlying intrinsic value feeling owe in part to the problem of careless interpretation of our own consciousness. Reading the meaning of our own motivating emotions is difficult for all of us. The next chapter uses the extreme case of "alexithymia" to focus more specifically on this problem.

Chapter 8

Lessons from Alexithymia

The Role of Phenomenological Reflection in Understanding Enactive Motivation

How is it possible that there could be such a persistent gap between what our emotional-motivational feelings are about and what they superficially appear to be about? We have seen repeatedly that emotions are largely about enactive intrinsic-instrumental value trajectories. But on the surface, they seem to be predominantly *re*-actions to specific situations—for example, the aggressive drunk at the bar. On a casual reading, emotions seem to come to us involuntarily, as if "caused" by some sort of perceptual input. Yet we have seen that they are more enactive than reactive. If one trigger hadn't afforded them, another eventually would have.

It may seem strange that knowing how we feel is an epistemological problem, but failure to interpret what we feel carefully enough is one of the main contributors to the incoherence of any thought process. As we have seen, even science and philosophy are affected by the selective attention motivated by implicit value trajectories.

Of all the facts that tend to get distorted to make a viewpoint or the value of a course of action seem more coherent than it is, our own feelings are the *easiest* to misconstrue. Others can't correct our assertions about our own feelings, so it is tempting to think that such assertions are "incorrigible" simply because we seem to have direct access to our own consciousness, and others don't. For this reason, one of the important dimensions for understanding the construction of systems of enactive value and meaning is to realize that some degree of emotional unawareness is always present in all of us.

In effect, we all suffer from some degree of alexithymia—the inability to read our own emotions. The meaning of a gut feeling doesn't come with a label attached to it. Interpreting what a feeling is about requires a difficult hermeneutical process, even though we are always tempted by some simplistic way of categorizing the emotion—usually by associating it with whatever stimulus event happened to trigger it.

Inner conflicts make it harder still to interpret the meaning of feelings. An overall pre-existing worldview demands looking away from the guilt or anxiety of starting a deadly war, or even choosing a ruthless business practice. It misrepresents why we say hurtful things to a friend or co-worker. In politics and social relationships generally, the SEEKING system makes us want to know the truth, while PANIC often motivates self-deception.

Each person's individual existential a priori includes stubborn preconceptions that demand constant suppression or misrepresentation of certain emotions—especially the ones that interact with the exploratory drive. The more we deceive ourselves to prop up a convoluted worldview or value system, the less we can direct attention to increasing numbers of our own emotions.

But as hinted earlier, it is also possible that some of these hermeneutical obstacles can be overcome. We can read stories of people who went *against* their own preconceptions to ask themselves questions about what they really felt. A case in point was Supreme Court Chief Justice Earl Warren, appointed by Dwight Eisenhower. Eisenhower thought he was appointing a conservative justice, but Warren surprisingly pushed for aggressive reforms of long-festering racial injustices. Once appointed, Warren tells us in his autobiography (1977), he had to think hard and long about his values and beliefs, because Supreme Court decisions need to set a coherent standard—even in those cases where the traditional majority opinion goes against the claims of justice, and in fact especially in those cases.

Warren quickly evolved into one of the most progressive justices in history—so progressive that almost every southern US highway was dotted with billboards reading "Impeach Earl Warren!" and "Earl Warren = Communist!" I know because I saw the billboards myself as a child. One of the most poignant passages in Warren's autobiography describes the way he finally feels about his much earlier decision, as governor of California, to set up concentration camps for Japanese Americans throughout the course of World War II. He describes the way he later couldn't get to sleep at night because of his obsessive guilt over that decision.

This kind of soul-searching would seem to call for some ability not to *completely* misread one's own emotions and to overcome the prejudices of our childhood. The temptation toward reliance on "moral intuitions" risks drowning in those prejudices. But an equally facile temptation is in the opposite direction, with an A. J. Ayer–style "emotivist theory of ethics." If we think value feelings are grounded in nothing more than "likes and dislikes," they become only idle whims and cease to inspire. We can't really believe something, let alone feel very energized by it, while at the same time cheerfully admitting that it has no more basis than a prejudice or idle whim.

"Moral sentiments" are often treated in academic discussions as if they were arbitrary, self-transparent, and not further analyzable. A. J. Ayer (1946, 1965) referred to the meaning of ethical statements as mere "preferences," as "expressions of emotion"—as if there were nothing further to say about them. But this too is a way of "looking away" from the inner facts of our enactive value structures. If emotions are arbitrary whims, we can justify looking away from the hermeneutic distortions of the motivated worldview that gave rise to them.

And yet part of what *is* true in emotivism is that we need to look at the role of emotions in driving our patterns of valuing and disvaluing. The coherence criteria for anyone's overall outlook (including our own) are shaped by an inevitably emotion-permeated hermeneutical process of selective attention and inattention.

It isn't just that emotions distort thinking. Thinking also distorts emotions. We may even espouse emotions *that we otherwise wouldn't even feel,* except that we want to kick up enough dust to cover an otherwise incoherent value system. For instance, those who engage in terrorism would be the first to express moral outrage if someone were to perpetrate the same kind of act against their own people. They pretend to feel that such actions are morally outrageous, yet this isn't really an honest description of what they feel. We often believe ourselves to feel outraged by the behavior of a political opponent, but not at all by the same behavior from a member of our own political party. This isn't an instance of "emotion clouding thinking"—just the opposite. It is an instance of a thought system clouding the reading of our own emotions.

Thoughts and emotions drive each other in a circular process. Not only are beliefs affected by emotions; how we feel is necessarily influenced by beliefs, even when the feelings are genuine. If I *believe* the dignity of tenant farmers and sharecroppers ought to be promoted, then I will be genuinely *glad* if it is, and *sorry* if it isn't.

So we need to examine a little more carefully what is involved in the interpretation of the meaning of our own emotional feelings. As a starting point, it might help to think about what happens in the most extreme case of *in*-ability to read one's own feelings or their meaning: the extreme example of literal alexithymia.

The Paradox of Alexithymia

Alexithymia is often defined as an inability to feel one's own emotions or, as John Lambie (2008) puts it, to feel them *"as* emotions" (see also Ellis 2008a, b). There can be little debating whether this paradoxical condition is a reality. I mentioned earlier Sundararajan's case in which a man killed his father out of anger, without being aware that he was angry. There was no motivation for the killing other than the apparently unconscious anger. The man fully realized intellectually that the evidence showed he "must have been" angry—but he was unable to *feel* the anger or any such feeling.

Alexithymia can shed light on the crucial interconnections between feeling, valuing, and acting. We have seen that acting creatures like us can't coherently claim that we don't value anything. Acting requires valuing something. Even if I only "feel like running," with no particular destination, I still value the opportunity to perform the act of running. The feeling values doing something.

Yet in an important sense, the alexithymic is largely unable to feel such affective states "as" emotional feelings. They may be felt only as bodily aches and pains; or alternatively, the proprioceptive visceral sensations may not even be "received" from the viscera into the circuitry of the brain at all. In a milder case, they are available, but little or no attention is paid to them.

The paradox is that the person *does have* emotional processes and is motivated by them and acts on them, but the feelings aren't felt *as* feelings or can't be felt in consciousness at all. One acts, and thus implicitly values one's ability to act in certain ways but doesn't know why. "I killed my father, but I don't know why."

The alexithymic also has trouble reading "intuitive" feelings about social and moral situations. Normally, we grasp what we value in the same way that a baseball player grasps whether a pitch is a curve ball—not analyzing all the details, but simply intuitively. But notice that there is no mysterious, innate "intuitive knowledge" about curve balls. We have picked up the knowledge through a *lifetime of experiencing,* and we refer to our "felt sense" of those "implicitly" (Gendlin 1978, 2018.)

In the case of valuational "intuitions," the intuition isn't the *basis* for the judgment, but it is rather the *culmination* of a lifetime of judgments. Every instance of sexual exploitation or violence calls up a lifetime of experiences about sexual injustice. We unconsciously refer to all those feelings and relevant circumstances. The alexithymic, however, is unable to do so in a way that meaningfully connects the feelings with their circumstances. Thus, we say that they can kill someone "for no reason." That is, they are unaware of the reason.

What can it mean to have an emotion, which presumably is a mental state that is "about" something (not just a physical event with no intentional meaning) and yet not be mentally *aware* that one is in that particular mental state?

Lambie's definition of alexithymia implies that not only the feeling, but also the intentional content—the "aboutness" of feelings—seems unavailable to the alexithymic. "Aboutness" doesn't consist merely in a combination of proprioceptions of internal body states ("enteroceptions") coupled with associated external perceptions or perceptual images. In many cases, the alexithymic *does* have a quite vivid enteroception (ability to feel one's own bodily feelings), and normal access to perceptual events and images (e.g., the trigger stimulus), yet still can't "interpret" the enteroception *as* an affective feeling (Bagby et al. 2009). A feeling that most people would recognize as fear may be interpreted as a stomach ache. This "somaticizing" type of alexithymic does have the proprioception/enteroception (or as Damasio 2003 puts it, the "perception" of a visceral state of the body) yet can't know what the feeling is *about*—that is, can't understand its intentionality, or even recognize that it is an emotion. It gets read as merely a physical sensation.

What is the alexithymic missing? A philosopher once explained how he knew that he loved his wife by saying he observed a consistent correlation between her presence and certain pleasant feelings. Thus, he made the inductive inference that his wife must be "the cause" of those feelings. If this description were accurate, we would still be missing the same ingredient that the alexithymic is missing. Sundararajan's patient understood intellectually that his visceral feelings "must have" been associated with his father and could logically infer that his father "must have" been associated with those feelings, but he didn't know what the feelings meant or what the anger was about. The intellectual inference of a cause-effect relationship isn't the same as understanding the *intentional meaning* of a feeling.

We can't equate "aboutness" with a presumed "cause" of an emotion. A locked gate disturbs us only because it interfered with an action that we already wanted to take—moving in a certain direction. A vast amount of what the feeling is about has to do with the destination we were trying to reach—not merely the locked gate. Listening to Tchaikovsky's Fourth Symphony (a powerful trigger stimulus) may either inspire or depress us, or simply have no effect whatever, depending on the mood and other emotional factors in our lives. High blood pressure can lead to anger over the most trivial things. The external event is a trigger for an "action readiness" (in Frijda's sense) that was looking for an opportunity to express itself. The person with high blood pressure would have found something else to react to in the same vitriolic way.

Knowing how I feel requires more than knowing that listening to Tchaikovsky's Fourth Symphony is what "caused" the feeling. The same music could have triggered a number of different possible feeling tones under different life circumstances. Knowing the "cause" wouldn't distinguish those feeling qualities from each other.

Alexithymia and Action Imagery

If not the intellectual understanding of a cause-effect relationship, then what *is* the alexithymic missing? Bermond (1997) suggests that there are actually two different types of alexithymia, corresponding to two separate problems. One is the "somaticizer," who does feel the enteroceptive feelings from the viscera but interprets them simply as bodily feelings, not emotions. This person feels something but doesn't know what it is.

Bermond's other type is the person who simply doesn't feel the visceral sensations in the first place or feels them very weakly. The feeling might be accurately identified as something like anger or fear, but misinterpreted as being much *weaker* than it actually is. This second type usually appears to have a very bland affect. "My father only slightly irritated me, yet I killed him. How strange!"

Bagby and colleagues (2009) offer a more subtle analysis. They find that these two kinds of alexithymia fail to cluster as separate "types" (in a statistical factor-analysis), and instead they should be considered as two *dimensions* of the same process. In other words, someone may be high in one dimension and low in the other or low or high in both. The same person may suffer from both "types" to various degrees.

Whether we think of the two problems of alexithymia as different *types* or only as two *dimensions* of the overall condition, it seems clear that there are two separate issues at stake. On the one hand, there can be a simple *lack of attention to visceral feelings*—the dimension emphasized by Damasio (2003). This kind of alexithymic lacks "proprioception"—the ability to "receive information" from internal states.

The other dimension is inability to know what a feeling is "about"—its intentionality. Understanding the "aboutness" of a feeling involves ideas, images, and also, importantly, *sensorimotor* imagery indicating what the feeling *wants us to do*, what kind of action it wants to motivate. This follows from our previous point that action requires feeling the value of something, even if unconsciously as in the case of the alexithymic. Remember, it isn't that the alexithymic lacks emotions and feelings but, paradoxically, only that the emotions remain unable to enter into consciousness.

And yet, we can't say that unconscious emotions are "only physical events in the body." On the contrary, they do have *meaning* and are usually somewhat available to reflection. Moreover, when we do manage to identify some of their meaning, it turns out to have been shaped by earlier conscious experiences, at least in part.

Awareness of the *meaning* of affective feelings requires not just sensory and proprioceptive imagery, but also *sensorimotor* imagery about what the emotion wants us to do, which is entirely different from sensory, proprioceptive, or "enteroceptive" imagery. As Damasio emphasizes, enteroception—the physical sensing of our own viscera—results from signals received from the body's interior through afferent nerve pathways, just as any perception of an *external* event is received through afferent pathways. "Afferent" in this context means nerve signals that move toward the brain from the extremities or from the viscera. *Sensorimotor* imagery, on the other hand, means imagining "what it would be like" to perform some action, but without actually performing the action. It becomes conscious through the action of *efferent* rather than merely afferent pathways. "Efferent" in this context refers to signals that travel "away from" the brain toward the body's extremities in order to command overt actions.

Remember also that action commands have first been instigated through the brain before they are inhibited to form *action imagery*. In that context, those action commands can also be thought of as "efferent" because they are on a trajectory that would lead to bodily movements unless inhibited.

This efferent-afferent distinction can be helpful for our purposes. Besides proprioception and enteroception, which are *afferent*, the action-imagery component of emotion also requires an *efferent* system, which begins with an impulse toward action and then inhibits the action command to form action imagery, needed for understanding of the intentionality of an affective feeling. Even the "interneurons" in the brain, which form a bridge between afferent and efferent nerve pathways, facilitate this "efferent" system by enabling action imagery.[1]

We know that alexithymia correlates with a deficit of mental imaging ability (Alfredo Campos et al. 2000). What is less appreciated is that "mental imagery," by contrast to actual perception, is a largely efferent rather than afferent process (Ellis 2005). That is, it requires a "looking for" process, as opposed to "looking at."

Try a simple experiment. Look at a white wall and see if there is any hint of pinkness in the white. You are doing the same thing you would do if you were to *imagine* that segment of wall *as* a pink wall. Forming a mental image (for example, the pink wall) is a more active, self-initiated brain process than simply receiving a perceptual input. It is something we *do,* not something we receive. It is more similar to "looking for" than "looking at."

In terms of action imagery, we also know that an alexithymic can quickly initiate *actual* motor movements, but has trouble *inhibiting* the motor movement to form what Jeannerod would call a "motor image" (Kano and Fukudo 2013). This inability becomes crucial in understanding the connection between action imagery and interpreting the meaning of emotions. The alexithymic's inability to inhibit actions to form action imagery is an important clue as to why there is a kind of blindness to the meaning of emotions.

Enteroceptive signals from the viscera are somewhat *passively received*, like perceptual inputs (Damasio 2003), whereas action imagery is more *actively generated*. As Newton (2000) emphasizes, knowing what I feel requires "knowing what I want to do." I know that a traffic light "makes me angry" because I know I already wanted to get somewhere. Without understanding where I wanted to get, I wouldn't understand the anger at the traffic light. Newton's idea here is consistent with Panksepp's view (1998, esp. chapter 8) that emotion begins with activation of the brain's action circuits (rooted in the deep subcortex—the midbrain and PAG areas) and only then begins to involve other brain areas.

Why would it be wrong to just explain the split between conscious and unconscious emotions simply by positing that an emotion is merely a bodily state, whereas a feeling is the "consciousness *of*" the corresponding emotion (bodily state)—the registering of it in a higher place in the brain?

Of the many problems with this analysis, one glaring shortcoming is that it forgets that even though enteroception is necessary for feeling the *physical quality* of the feeling, how we register the *intentional meaning* of the experience is a more difficult question. The "somaticizing" alexithymic, who interprets emotions as merely physical sensations like "a stomach ache," may well sense the enteroceptive sensations coming from the body but doesn't know what they mean—their intentional meaning or what they are "about."

Here again, we can't simply define what the feeling is "about" by reference to what might have "caused" it. A bar-room drunk's aggressiveness may cause me to feel angry, but the anger may actually be about something else entirely, without which I would have paid no attention to the drunk.

We are often confused about what a feeling is about, even if we do feel it quite intensely. When someone wants to bully me in some trivial way, how much is my feeling about this specific bully, and how much is about everyone who has ever bullied me? "*This* time," I tell myself, "I'm not going to let the sonofabitch get away with it!" This means that all the "*other* times" are also referents of what I feel.

It is never easy to understand what our emotions are telling us we want to do. Is what I feel about the aggressive drunk at the bar telling me that I want to punch him in the face? Certainly not. I can easily realize that he doesn't really *instantiate* any real impediment to me, but rather *symbolizes* one. He isn't the important thing; what he symbolizes is. At most, he represents the general theme of bullying.

Further focusing on this "bullying" theme might reveal that the felt sense contains a dark, brooding element. It doesn't want to lash out, but it feels powerless in the face of so much of life that bullies. But wait. "Bullying" also doesn't very well describe those general facts of life—for example, my profession's recalcitrance against allowing any meaningful advancement of my interests. Less than bullying, it is more like a "backhanded dismissal." My efforts are casually dismissed without even a hearing.

And come to think of it, it isn't just my "profession" that does the "dismissing"; it is an entire socioeconomic system, of which my profession is only an aspect or example. There is no *person* who does the "dismissing." There is no one "at" whom someone might be angry, but rather a general fact of life. The brooding quality now comes to seem unlike anger and has nothing to do with drunks, or even with bullying in general. It is an instance of the way I feel toward the overall fact that, in the life situation I am in, and given my status as a finite and inescapably interdependent creature, my power to do what I plan is more limited than I wish it were.

When Dostoyevsky's *Notes from Underground* (1864) describes intellectuals' ruminations about what they "really" feel as an aberration, while assuming that the "natural man" would simply punch the offending party in the face, he is actually *reversing* the normal case with the atypical one. In everyday terms, most of us would be quite shocked to see a fully grown adult punch someone in the face at a bar over a verbal insult. If this happened in real life (not the movies), we would sense that there is something a little "off" about such a person. The person who simply punches the other is the one whose brain is wired strangely.[2]

Action, Value, and Value Feelings

Gendlin sometimes suggests that, when focusing on a felt sense, we ask ourselves, "What does it want to happen?" The aims of feelings involve motivation to act. Yet sometimes we say, "He made me angry," as if the affective feeling meant receiving a causal input. We may completely ignore the fact that, before we could be angry, we had to first have some aims. The other person thwarted these aims or symbolized something that thwarted them or something that we might fear could thwart them.

We can't understand the intentional meaning of an emotional feeling without reference to its action component. In order to feel even the instrumental *aim* in terms of motivated action, we need to gear up Jeannerod's "action-imagery" system. For example, the easiest way to evoke an infant's "RAGE" is to bind its arms and inhibit its freedom of movement (Panksepp 1998, chapter 4). The "RAGE" is as much about the desire to move as it is about the external pressure applied to the infant's arms. Every emotion involves an implicit action component.

The intentionality of emotions isn't as simple as that of perception. There is never a one-to-one correspondence between "object" and "feeling," as might occur in a cause-effect relationship.[3] We often don't even know, and in some instances can never know, what symbolic referent is symbolized by what we take to be the intentional object of an emotion or affect. Someone hearing an old song might be overwhelmed with feeling, yet the feeling isn't about the song. It could be about something that happened long ago, when the song was popular. My own feelings about being drafted for the Viet Nam War in 1970 are inevitably evoked by songs that were popular at the time. If a different song had been popular at the time, that other song would have symbolized the feeling. In either case, the feeling isn't about the song, but about what the song symbolizes. Similarly, the person who cuts in front of me in traffic "as if I didn't exist" can symbolize everyone who treats me as if I don't exist.

We are often tempted to think of consciousness (and mind) as a sort of display screen for information received from the senses or from our bodies. In the attempt to "explain" consciousness, we try to think of it as a passive receiver of information that somehow causes the consciousness to occur. The inadequacies of this simplistic picture were evident as long ago as Descartes and even earlier. Dualism, long before Descartes, was prompted by the temptation to think of emotion as if it were analogous to perception—to think of the mind as a passive receiver of inputs from the "physical world."

But even if perception itself were only a passive receiving of information (which it isn't), emotional *motivations* can't be passive—as we have seen repeatedly throughout this book. If knowing what a feeling is "about" includes understanding what it wants us to do, then it requires sending efferent action signals, while inhibiting the signals as they move through the motor, premotor, and sensorimotor areas of the brain, in order to form the "action imagery" of what the feeling wants us to do, as well as which factors facilitate or thwart what we want to do.[4] Because the alexithymic has trouble inhibiting actions, there is an impaired ability to form the needed action imagery.

In the case of symbolization, there are felt similarities between the action affordances of the symbol and of the life issues being symbolized. But identifying the respects in which they are similar requires careful focusing. When I dream that all the tires on my car are flat all at once, what issues in my life make me feel that my actions are similarly stalled out or have gone flat, even to the point that using my one spare tire is useless?

To the extent that alexithymia includes a malfunction of the efferent action-command system, the alexithymic would miss much of the intentional meaning of the action component of motivations. We would know *that* we feel something and could even feel it with considerable intensity, based on the enteroceptive signals from the viscera. But we would still be confused about *what* we feel, and why—what the feeling is actually "about." We would understand that something triggered the feeling, and thus we would be tempted to interpret this trigger stimulus as what the feeling is about.

The alexithymic who killed his father—unable to form action imagery while simultaneously inhibiting the actual going through with the actions—couldn't understand the "action readiness" of his emotion in any other way than by actually going through with the idea of killing his father. He couldn't entertain in imagination the idea that "This really makes me feel like killing him!—by God, I can imagine picking up this knife and stabbing the sonofabitch!"—but without actually doing so.

Like any introspective process, a capacity for proprioception, enteroception, and sensorimotor imagery (not just visual imagery) can be developed through practice. The fact that Gendlin's focusing method (and other methods of emotional awareness) can be taught illustrates this point. "Neural plasticity" allows the brain to subserve the needed processes. Everything we think or feel, including action imagery, involves brain processes, but this doesn't imply that we can't learn to execute new processes.

Alexithymia and the Meaning of Value Feelings: Transition to the Hot-Cold Meter

Even for those who don't rise to the clinical level of alexithymia, either enteroception or action imagery can fail to some degree and thus lead to denial of what we feel or confusion as to what we take our feelings to be "about." This process affects the hermeneutics of value and meaning when our own self-directed pattern of attention leads us to pay *selective* attention or inattention to these feeling processes within ourselves. It isn't just that we can selectively suppress attention to *external facts and logical arguments*. We can also selectively direct our *internal* attention and thus misrepresent our own feelings even to ourselves.[5]

If I ask myself at some random time "how I feel," the initial answer might be something like: It seems to be going pretty well; or, I feel somewhat frustrated because it isn't going so well. But what counts as "going well" depends on what my immediate goals are, and the immediate goals depend on longer term goals. Yet who can specify with any clarity what our ultimate goals in life are (aside from simply *staying* alive) or why we want what we want? In the case of goals that involve simply maintaining the self-organizational balance of the body, it may be impossible in principle ever to describe them or to have much conscious access to them.

The almost-infinite regress in the long-term indirect purposes of everyday actions reflects uncertainty and ambiguity with regard to what we value. The less we know what we value, the less we can balance various instrumental values within an overall value system. Throughout a lifetime, most adults have already built up a set of attitudes about the appropriate balance among different values, both intrinsic and instrumental.

We are constantly in a hermeneutical process of recalibrating the relationship between our current situation at any given time and the long chains of instrumental values that we have so far decided to be driven by. Each new situation presents new ways in which the balance of different values might need to be reorganized. A person who has never given money to a beggar on the street, for example, suddenly has a change of heart and begins doing so quite routinely.

But misreading the meaning of our own feelings can prevent us from noticing how the feelings have already affected our tendency to tweak or distort bits of new information to avoid adjusting the overall valuational existential a priori that has already been formed. As a result, we get stuck in a value system from an immature period of our lives or a system into which we were in effect forcibly indoctrinated as children. In other cases, the inevitable murkiness of emotional meanings presents similar problems. Alexithymia is only the extreme case.

In Gendlin's sense, the more we are unable to "focus" on the unique feelings that affect our hermeneutical interpretations at each subsequent moment, the more resistant we become to critically reconsidering the pre-existing interpretations. Our next chapter will explore the relevance of this focusing process specifically in relation to overall value systems and the process of defining enactive meaning.

In our everyday "semi-alexithymia," the hermeneutical process is normally conducted on an "intuitive" basis. These "intuitions" aren't some special intellectual faculty; they result from past experience and thinking. If we try to focus on *why* we intuitively "feel" that such-and-such is the right way to go, we can notice the way pre-existing feelings have already motivated distortions in the process. This reflection is something that a complete alexithymic can't do, and the rest of us do only incompletely and with difficulty. The continual re-calibration of our value system, within a continual hermeneutical process, is as difficult to understand as it is to execute. Yet we all do execute it, with greater or lesser degrees of success, in our real lives.

Our next chapter makes a special study of this process. How does the hermeneutical process sometimes manage to overcome the inertia of the previously existing value system that may have been grounded in the thoughts of a past, perhaps less mature, period of our lives or as a result of peer pressure, or even authoritarian indoctrination? How do we avoid letting presuppositions determine which new information is accurately assessed, as the example of Chief Justice Earl Warren seems to illustrate? And how much is it tweaked or distorted, as in the case of Arendt's authoritarian followers? How do we get around this aspect of the "hermeneutic circle"? The next chapter takes on this question.

Chapter 9

The Hot-Cold Meter

Unlocking Internal Conflict by Updating Hermeneutical Worldviews

If the enactive meaning of motivations goes beyond a mere trigger stimulus—if instead they are about an underlying desire to act—then the actions themselves are usually in the service of long chains of instrumental values. But if the purpose of the ongoing action plan is traceable to the intrinsic values on which the instrumental ones are based, then how can we ever get to the bottom of what any motivation (and thus any felt emotion) is really about in this regard?

Granted, sometimes the purpose of an action is simply the action itself—for example, the sheer joy of long-distance running, even beyond any utilitarian outcome achieved by it (and even when the running itself becomes more painful than pleasant). But in most cases, where actions are meant for some purpose, a good bit of the enactive meaning of a motivation isn't just to pursue a direct instrumental purpose for its own sake, but rather to further the long-term trajectory of a life plan.

Most of the things we value are merely instrumental values. I want to keep some motor oil in my garage so that I can put oil in my car so that I can drive to the hardware store so that I can get some tools so that I can . . . and so on. By definition, instrumental values are things whose value depends on leading to some other outcome. To be sure, we might intrinsically value the pleasant experience of going to the store, putting the oil in the car, and so on. But the primary value of each of these actions is dependent on something else having value. Even the pleasure of driving to the store makes the driving into an instrumental value in the service of the pleasure it brings, in addition to the other purposes it serves. Sometimes the "reward" of driving isn't pleasure per se, but rather stimulation of the exploratory drive, which may have been allowed to lie dormant for too long.

Is my frustration with the aggressive drunk because he *symbolizes* a larger frustration with my career progress? If so, then what is the meaning of my emotional commitment to the career itself? Is that commitment based on narcissism, or sheer survival, or the need to exercise my exploratory drive, or a need to please my deceased father, or a commitment to "doing something useful," as the Young Stockbroker puts it at the end of the movie?

For the most part, our lives are elaborate edifices of instrumental value that would entirely fall apart if only a few bricks were pulled from the layer of *intrinsic* values on which all the countless numbers of instrumental ones depend. If for no other reason, there will always be great resistance against any change or questioning process that might threaten to disrupt those crucial intrinsic value substructures. Normally, we are so far from questioning our own basic system of intrinsic value priorities that we seldom even become consciously aware of which intrinsic values are being served by the plethora of instrumental values around which our lives revolve.

Instead, we usually focus attention on the *best way to achieve* some short-term goal that in turn is in the service of a slightly less short-term goal, which if we were to reflect, we could notice is in the service of a medium-range and ultimately a long-range purpose deeply embedded in our life project. Yet in spite of this continuous unclarity as to the ultimate purposes that are being served by these long strings of instrumentalities, we always seem to know what we want to do in each instant of each day.

How do we know so automatically what our short-term goals are, even though we would be very much at a loss to identify the long-term values that they are ultimately meant to serve? From the standpoint of Mother Nature designing an action-oriented organism whose actions have to be motivated in real time, it seems unavoidable that some sort of "automatic" mechanism would be needed. It would be impossible for someone to plan all their momentary actions by consciously considering all the short-term, medium-term, and long-term effects of the actions relative to some self-aware intrinsic values to be served. Instead, there would need to be an automatic ability to simply "feel" what the best thing to do is at the moment.

In the moment, is it better to stand up against an overly demanding boss or to just shrug off the incident? There would need to be an automatic and mostly-unconscious "felt" connection between the momentary feeling and the purposes served by whichever action *seems* best at the moment. I may have a murky sense that quitting a job is the best course, with or without the promise of a new job, but articulating the rationale behind this feeling would be difficult and often impossible. Even the choice of a profession depends on still-longer-term values and commitments.

But at the same time, continuing valuational experience requires that we occasionally revise the long-term goals—the intrinsic values served by our actions. Normally we aren't engaged in such a process in real time. Only when forced to it can a long-established hermeneutical value system be shaken from its presumptive roots. Understanding how this hermeneutical process works requires, at a minimum, exploring the phenomenology of the way we normally choose a course of action that in turn *already presupposes an entire valuational structure*.

Phenomenology of the Hot-Cold Meter: How Do I Know What I Should Be Doing?

A musician composing or an artist painting can refer, at any given moment, to what Gendlin (1978, 1992) calls a "felt sense" of the ongoing situation. The felt sense is a bodily feeling that is *available to* consciousness although it typically remains preconscious—"preconscious," in the sense that it is *capable* of becoming conscious, but we normally don't bring it into consciousness, like the knowledge of our own phone number. It includes a sensing of our overall relation to a situation, as when Merelau-Ponty's (1945) football player senses the changing configuration of players on the field.

Gendlin uses the example of trying to remember what I forgot. I may have a vague felt sense yet remain unable to bring the forgotten element to consciousness. I try out several possibilities that seem obviously not to be the one I was trying to remember. When I do find the right one, I recognize the missing element because it matches the felt sense that I already had. Similarly, a musician has a felt sense of the emotional effect that might be produced if some of the notes in a chord were altered or if extensions were added to the chord—and of how those alterations would affect the general "feel" of the music. A teacher has a felt sense that a student needs more challenge or, on the contrary, more reassurance.

For our purposes here, one relevant aspect of the phenomenon of "felt sense" is the one that helps us decide at any given time what we "should" be doing, whether in the "moral" or "non-moral" sense of "should." It tells us, "Yes, what you are doing is getting closer to the right thing to do—you're getting warmer," or, "No, you're getting colder." I use "right" in the broadest possible sense, that is, what would be most desirable on the whole and in the long run, potentially including our feelings about others' interests as well as our own and relative to very long-term as well as short-term purposes. Some of those purposes may be explicitly articulable with some effort, while others are not.

For example, on waking in the morning, we can distinguish between two very different felt senses. On the one hand, there can be a feeling that getting an eighth hour of sleep would be "beneficial on the whole and in the long run," or "the best thing to do, all things considered." Even if I would like to get up, I may decide that I need more sleep. On the other hand, there can be the very different feeling that it simply would be more *pleasant* to sleep longer. We usually can tell the difference without much effort, but sometimes the difference is murky. The alarm goes off, and we say, "I need more sleep," when what is really going on is simply that it would be more pleasant to sleep longer. I may decide that my musical practice session has gone long enough, or I may feel simply that it would be more pleasant to be relieved of the daunting work of practicing longer. Sometimes it can be hard to tell the difference.

The distinction between these two felt senses—on the one hand, the sense of what it seems I should do, and on the other hand what simply would be pleasant to do—is not reducible to the difference between rational calculation and intuitive feeling. It would be neither possible nor desirable to rationally calculate means toward all long-, short-, and medium-term purposes, as well as balancing them all, in every present moment of waking life. Nor is it explained by the "moral" versus "nonmoral" distinction. We aren't moralizing when we feel that we should get more sleep.

When I find myself being stern or indulgent with a student, it would be impractical or even impossible to systematically consider in that moment all the long- and short-term goals I might have for this student and what all the consequences of overindulgence or oversternness might be. Usually, I depend on an internal "hot-cold meter" to guide me in the right direction. How do I respond when a student caught plagiarizing responds with a casual "Oh, sorry—that was my bad." How should I respond? If later I realize that my hot-cold meter was inaccurate and led me in the wrong direction, then this later "regretful" felt-sense reads as a "very cold" reading with respect to the past event in which I feel that I veered in the wrong direction.

In some cases, I feel that I know with some certainty what I virtually "have to do"—get to work on time, for example. In that case, the "cold" reading for sleeping late is so obvious that it perfectly matches what a rational calculation would have yielded. But once I have arrived at work, how well I read the hot-cold meter at each moment during the workday may determine how effectively I can work, how I interact with co-workers, and how I allocate my time.

By contrast to the instances where we feel certain of what we "must" do, there are other cases in which the hot-cold meter may seem to have become somewhat or even completely incapacitated. As I will try to show later, this incapacitation of the meter can be an instructive case from an enactive-meaning point of view.

But in most cases, we refer to the momentary felt sense of our trajectory in the same way that a musician hears the difference between a major and a minor chord without analyzing the specific notes that make the chord sound the way it does. Even when our work demands doing what we "have to do," we are constantly deciding *how* to execute each task—and how to interact with our colleagues, the public, or our managers. In practical contexts, we often or even usually tend to rely on this kind of felt sense to direct us, although we are also aware that it often can painfully misdirect us or can lead us to wander for periods in the wilderness.

The fact that we are continually guided by a hot-cold meter obviously has valuational implications. But the fact that we can also easily discover that hot-cold readings are only the tip of a much larger iceberg should also warn us against a simple "intuitionism" either in value thinking or in merely prudential decision making. The most obvious problem with hot-cold readings is that, even though we can't avoid using them on a daily basis, they can also be ambiguous, uncertain, or even altogether misleading.

Yet there seems to be no escaping the fact that this hot-cold meter is continually available for use during any ongoing experience, whether we are painting, composing music, doing construction work, or even flipping the TV channels. We always have available for reflection a felt sense seeming to indicate that what we are currently doing is what we should or should not be doing at the moment, and to what degree our activity reads as hot or cold on the meter—even if such reflection is difficult. Reading the meter may be more difficult for extreme alexithymics, who have trouble feeling their own emotions. But we all differ from the alexithymic only in degree.

Conscience as a Special Case of the Hot-Cold Meter

I have used "should" here in neither a moral nor a particularly nonmoral sense. What many experience as a pang of conscience can also be interpreted as a special case of this more broadly applicable felt sense that includes nonmoral as well as moral situations. If my baseball error caused my team to lose the game, it is difficult to say whether I feel "morally" responsible (perhaps I shirked my responsibility to practice more diligently), or simply nonmorally humiliated, ashamed, or merely regretful that my unfortunate error was responsible for the team's loss.

Even if the regretful feeling is nonmoral, I still might feel responsible to make it up to my teammates in some way. I feel "sort-of-guilty," but in a vague sense, because I failed to perform or caused the team to lose the game. And the feeling may persist until I decide what the best future course of action should be (practice more effectively, stop playing, etc.). When I focus on these potential responses, the felt sense becomes one of "getting warmer"—it feels closer to an indication of which direction I should be moving in. "Getting colder" would be an indication that what I am now doing, or what I am imagining doing, is moving further away from what I should be doing. For example, if I just try to shift the blame for the mistake to someone else, the felt sense of "getting colder" is preconsciously available, whether I pay attention to it or not.

As important as it is to notice that the hot-cold meter is always perceptibly running (at least *attempting* to indicate how close or how far we are from what we should be doing), it is at least as important to notice that these readings can be ambiguous, murky, or out-and-out mistaken. This applies not only to backward-looking issues, as in "pangs of conscience," but also to present, future, and even imagined actions. Even in backward-looking instances, a similar-feeling felt sense can refer to either moral or nonmoral actions, such as baseball fumbles, missed notes in music, or whether or not a musician should have skipped today's practice session. In forward-looking instances, we feel "hot" or "cold" when imagining a possible course of action that seems to cohere with an overall value system, or not to cohere; but we usually can't spell out all the reasons why the imagined action does or doesn't cohere.

For this reason, whether we are dealing with an ethical situation or any other kind of situation, it is obvious that we often would go far astray if we were merely to accept the hot-cold reading at face value. We therefore often take it only as a starting point for an introspection into the question as to which issues are actually being referred to by the hot-cold reading and then try to refine our understanding of what the felt sense is trying to tell us.

For instance, a demagogue might sway us to feel "cold" toward accepting more immigrants into the country. But on further reflection, the "cold" reading may reflect not a political opinion at all, but rather a free-floating feeling more like a generalized fear or insecurity not related to the immigration issue at all. Instead of leading us further in the direction of following the immigrant-bashing demagogue, the cold feeling may be trying to direct us to redirect our attention to those other issues.

Similarly, the "guilt" that a young man feels for wanting to avoid service in a senseless war such as Vietnam or Iraq might read as cold, but further introspection may reveal that the coldness only reflects social isolation or fear of disapproval, or perhaps shame over a suspicion that one is a "coward" or a "wimp"; the feeling may not actually be a moral pang of conscience at all. A cold reading invites us not merely to take a superficially resonating action, but also to reflect on *why* the felt sense seems cold—and similarly with the hot reading that may seem to attach to the immigrant-bashing demagogue's rhetorical devices.

Use of the Hot-Cold Meter Is Pragmatically Inevitable

Whether we are relying on unreflective or carefully reflected-upon readings, the hot-cold reading is normally, in each given moment, the felt sense that guides the continual sequence of voluntary actions in the same way that the body's complex blood sugar regulation system resolves the incalculably complicated problem of adjusting all the biochemical and behavioral systems of the body to hit a target range of acceptable blood sugar levels. It would be *literally impossible* for a conscious mind to resolve such a complex, interconnected balance by means of a conscious mathematical calculation in every present moment.

In the case of the hot-cold meter, the almost infinite complexity of the problem stems from the fact that there are multiple long-range goals, each depending on a commitment to multiple potentially conflicting prima facie values whose best balance with each other is always in need of resolution. All these prima facie values must balance not only with each other, but also with literally infinite arrays of possible chains of direct and indirect means toward achieving them, as well as ways to facilitate the best balance among those instrumentalities.

Such an intricate calculation would be impossible to consciously complete in every new moment to decide what I should or shouldn't be doing with that moment. But the hot-cold meter usually decides it as quickly as a GPS in a car determines the best way to a location—although, as we shall see, the hot-cold meter is less accurate than a GPS and sometimes *very* inaccurate. At each moment, the hot-cold meter spits out its best solution, which is read phenomenally as "You're getting warmer" or "You're getting colder."

We can refer without words to the direct sense that what we are doing feels as if it is getting closer or further away from what we should be doing. If I am out drinking with my buddies at 3 a.m. and suddenly realize the time, I can refer to a very cold reading on the meter. This is getting to be further and further away from what I should be doing at this moment—not for moral reasons in this case, but for prudential ones.

This by no means rules out the importance of rational deliberation; and it certainly doesn't preclude further phenomenological reflection that probes beyond the mere surface reading in determining what I should be doing. In the case of the 3 a.m. drinking episode, I know many facts from past experience—that I will be worthless for work the next day, for example. And I have already made logical calculations from these facts on many past occasions. Whether those calculations were made in the past, or whether I am just now figuring out (at this late stage of my life) that this is not what I should be doing—in either case, the result of the calculation is a particular felt sense to which I can refer if I choose to do so.

For now, our interest is not in the comparative roles of rational deliberation and hot-cold readings, but rather in exploring the working of the hot-cold meter itself. I freely grant that we are sometimes able to rationally calculate the right action without referring to the felt sense. But even those calculations depend on a larger context in which the value of major *intermediate* actions are presupposed by any calculation—getting to work tomorrow, having that job rather than a different one, devoting my life to this rather than that. Many such larger decisions are presupposed by any specific short-term means toward a short-term end.

What we have observed so far about the hot-cold meter is that it lends itself to modalization on several dimensions. It can refer to past, present, or anticipated actions and to what traditionally would be called both moral and nonmoral considerations. It can be either positive or negative to varying degrees. A cold, backward-looking reading in what we call a moral situation reads as a pang of conscience. A nonmoral backward reading presents as some sort of shame, regret, embarrassment, or wish that we had behaved differently. A positive, forward-looking "moral" reading indicates a sense of commitment to some value for the sake of which some action can be taken (or in some cases an intrinsic valuing of the action itself, such as playing football), which may present itself as a feeling of inspiration, a sense that this project is worth investing some energy into. A feeling of moral guilt, or a pang of conscience, is only one of the many modes in which the hot-cold meter continually spits out its readings.

Degrees of Ambiguity and Uncertainty in Hot-Cold Readings

A directly felt hot-cold reading can also be assessed in terms of its degree of ambiguity or uncertainty. Prospectively, I may feel that it would be worthwhile to write a paper on an interesting topic, but there may be considerable uncertainty as to whether this energy will be well spent or not. On the other hand, when my roof is leaking, the sense that it would be worthwhile to put a bucket under the leak can be read with a greater degree of certainty. As a result, we are often biased toward acting on hot-cold readings regarding the more mundane aspects of life, while we hesitate or procrastinate with regard to more speculative projects, which read with greater uncertainty. The *degree of certainty* of a reading affects how much it influences our action decisions.

When it comes to the more speculative and uncertain hot-cold readings, I may feel intensely inspired, a very hot reading, and then the next day realize that I wasted my time—a cold reading. This retrospective cold reading is useful because it can contribute to further deliberation resulting in a new forward-looking "getting warmer" reading. Hemingway always wrote only in the morning and then deliberately avoided looking at what he had done until the next day so he could see it with a fresh eye. Sometimes what feels hot at the moment seems different the next day, but this difference itself, even without any calculative thought, can already indicate which changes would read as "getting warmer."

The direct reading of the hot-cold meter in many instances can actually be *more* accurate than the results of calculation or deliberation. Many scientists during the age of rigid mind-body dualism believed intellectually that nonhuman animals had no consciousness; yet their hot-cold meter read as cold when they caused avoidable suffering for animals.

Sometimes the correct balance between different values can't be determined by any self-conscious formula, and therefore tends to be felt by direct reference to the hot-cold meter. Suppose we are prosecuting a murder case, or writing laws about criminal justice processes. How many innocent lives of future murder victims is it acceptable to risk in order to give a murderer a reasonably fair trial? And given the financial cost of defense attorneys and the factual uncertainties of any given case, *how* fair is fair enough? Even if we have a well-worked-out moral philosophy, we will often find ourselves deciding such concrete cases by direct reference to the hot-cold meter, which may or may not be explainable by previous calculative thinking.

Uncertainty of Readings Confused with Feelings of Coldness Per Se

Hot-cold readings present themselves as involving a degree of uncertainty, and this degree of uncertainty itself usually can be felt. How inspiring or threatening a course of action seems is distinguishable from the feeling of how much uncertainty attaches to the reading itself. But this distinction between the feeling of coldness per se and the feeling of uncertainty isn't always sensed with clarity in everyday situations. Sometimes a reading superficially seems cold, yet on closer inspection, it can be discerned as "warm, but very uncertain." That is, *uncertainty itself* tends initially to feel simply cold.

When offered an unexpected opportunity that requires change and new commitments—for example, a new job offer—the prospect may seem daunting, and we feel confused as to what values would be served by which course of action. The reading may be "warm, but very uncertain." Yet sometimes we confuse this situation with a simply cold reading because uncertainty itself feels cold.

A crucial corollary: What often appears as a cold reading—seeming to indicate a poor choice as to what I should be doing *as a means* to a long-term end—can actually be the *mis*-reading of a feeling of uncertainty with regard to *the long-term end itself*. For example, in the case of US involvement in the Vietnam War, rather than reaching the conclusion "We shouldn't be fighting this war," the increasingly cold readings were read as "We need to fight harder, with more troops and bombs." The uncertainty of the desirability of the long-term goal itself was confused with a mere coldness reading regarding the effectiveness of the *short-term instrumentalities* toward that long-term goal. The coldness initially tended not to be associated with the underlying intrinsic values affected by the war, but only with the more immediate instrumental ones. The *feeling of uncertainty* resulting from lack of knowledge about long-term ends is an everyday occurrence and normally is taken for granted as part of the inaccuracy of the hot-cold meter.

Lack of tolerance for this feeling of uncertainty leads to "excessive scrupulosity." A classic example occurs in the film *The Nun's Story*. The main character, a nun, is so intolerant of her own doubts as to whether she should forgive the Nazi who murdered her father, that she decides she is unfit to be a nun altogether. Her sense as to whether a good nun "should always forgive, no matter what" is extremely uncertain, and she can't tolerate this uncertainty in herself. Ironically, her excessive scrupulosity is what leads to her feelings of inadequacy. She can't tolerate uncertainty in her own hot-cold readings.

Normally, we avoid excessive scrupulosity and accept that the hot-cold meter is inherently uncertain and that the reading is often even ambiguous as to whether it indicates uncertainty of long-term ends or, on the contrary, a poor choice of means. If I feel uncertain that a given action is the best thing to do, is it because I don't feel confident that the action will contribute effectively to a desired end? Or on the contrary is it because the end itself isn't worthwhile? In many cases, it can be difficult to discern which of these scenarios is the source of the feeling of uncertainty. Do I feel uncertain as to whether I am rehearsing enough with my band, or does the uncertainty involve whether I should invest time and energy into playing with this band in the first place?

Sometimes, to be sure, we *do* easily recognize that what a hot-cold reading is telling us pertains not to whether we are using effective means to an end, but rather that the end itself is wrong. Sometimes we struggle to find an effective means, and as the reading gets colder and colder, we notice that the reading itself refers not just to the immediate action we are taking, but to the entire *sequence* of actions leading to a goal that was ill-chosen to begin with. A musician is rehearsing with a group, getting increasingly cold readings, leading to more concerted efforts followed by even colder readings. At some point, the interpretation of the reading shifts, and it becomes easily detectable that the felt sense is saying, "This whole project isn't worth pursuing."

At other times, however, this discrimination isn't so easily reached—as in the case of US involvement in the Vietnam War. In valuational decisions generally, it is the long-term ends that raise the most serious questions—the value of engaging in an entire series of actions per se.

The Inevitable Persistence of Such Confusions, and the Tendency to Privilege Long-Term Goals

It seems inevitable that there should be *some* confusion and uncertainty as to whether the felt sense pertains to means or ends. Actions are typically parts of sequences of actions leading to short-term ends, which in turn are means toward longer-term ends and so forth. We might have a cold reading for a certain military tactic during a war, and the cold reading may be partly because it is uncertain whether the short-term tactic will lead to a strategic outcome, or whether the strategy can lead to a sustainable victory, or even whether "victory" has even been clearly defined—as in the case of the Vietnam War and the US invasion of Iraq—and if so, whether the war is worth "winning" in the first place.

The more questionable the ultimate goal, the more uncertain and confusing any hot-cold reading will feel with regard to short-term means toward intermediate objectives whose purpose is ultimately defined in terms of that ultimate goal. As long as poorly chosen ultimate goals remain unquestioned, the hot-cold readings feel as if they have great uncertainty, and it is difficult to get a reading on which actions are "the right thing to do" in the given context. Is it all right to kill a few innocent civilians as "collateral damage" in order to dismantle a military enemy that presumably needs to be dismantled? Or is the goal of dismantling the enemy not worth the sacrifices? The "rules of engagement" may seem rationally calculated on paper but then can quickly become useless in the fog of war.

The coldness of a reading could indicate that there is something wrong *at any point along the chain* leading from shorter-term means to longer-term ends. And the longer the chain becomes, the more uncertainty seems attached to the selection of both the means and the end itself, particularly since the *attainability* of an end plays into the choice as to whether it should be pursued. If there was no attainable outcome to be achieved by the Vietnam War other than permanent US military occupation of the country (which would have been practically impossible) then the ultimate goal of "winning" the war itself may be the unrecognized factor causing disturbance in the normal process of choosing actions and valuing short-term ends. As a result, we may become increasingly demotivated and anxious with respect to our most mundane, everyday value feelings as we evaluate day-by-day tactics.

In the next section, we will consider whether more careful reflection can help us determine whether a felt sense is referring to a breakdown somewhere in the means-end chain, or on the contrary whether it is due to a poor choice of end per se. The point for now is that even careful reflection still seems to leave some uncertainty in place, because there are too many variables involved in selecting short-, medium-, and long-term ends for such selection to become as clear as rocket science in each immediate moment of action.

The uncertainty of a hot-cold reading is further complicated by the fact that, as Alistair Norcross (2010) and others have pointed out, there is seldom one uniquely correct thing to be doing or even one uniquely correct goal to be striving toward. I may have a cold reading because I gave to a very good political candidate while I leave unanswered solicitations from several very needy charities on the table. The cold reading, however, may be a mistaken one if I read it to mean that what I did was unworthy, rather than a degree of uncertainty as to which of several approximately similarly worthy goals to pursue. The less difference there is between the value of one alternative and the value of another, the greater the feeling of uncertainty as to whether I have done the right thing, and therefore the greater the danger of "excessive scrupulosity." There are usually multiple "correct" courses of action leading to about equally valuable longer-term values.

In this connection, lawyers often remark that "hard cases make bad law." What they mean is that, when a legal criterion is designed to discriminate between two options that are about equally good or bad, it makes little difference which one is chosen. Yet that criterion then becomes the precedent for deciding cases that do make a great deal of difference. In the same way, philosophers often become obsessed with virtually unresolvable moral cases—for example, is it better to divert a train resulting in killing nine innocent children in order to save ten other children? The resulting decision principle creates the illusion that there is a clear criterion, which then is used where the choice makes much more of a difference. Superficially, we are merely comparing the value of nine children with ten, but other questions are implicitly involved, such as who has the right to decide; or the longer-term consequences of the choice. And many other larger questions come into play but are not immediately prompted by the "intuition pump" of the thought experiment.

In the same way, feeling guilty because I may have given money to the wrong charity may exemplify "excessive scrupulosity" since both charities do about the same amount of good, even though I can't decide which is better. Here again, the uncertainty of the hot-cold reading is being mistaken for a simply cold reading.

As an additional complicating variable, we should acknowledge that not all actions are means to ulterior ends. Sometimes the action is an end in itself, as in playing football or in naturally motivated exploratory behavior (as Panksepp, Frijda, and White emphasize). Other times, the action isn't even meant to serve as a means to *attaining* the value in question, but rather as a *symbolization* whose purpose is to allow us to feel more intensely the value *of* that which we value—as when we eulogize a loved one or use a work of art to intensify our feeling of the value of something, or of the value of being a conscious being per se.

This observation is consistent with Frankl's point that a failure to feel that "life has meaning" sometimes may be attributable not to the fact that we can't *achieve* the aims that we value, but rather that we can't feel intensely enough our own feeling of the value of those ends. We might feel that we "should" value the everyday means toward our ends, while the more crucial problem, unconsciously beneath the surface, is that we can't feel the value of the ends themselves. What is needed in this case isn't more activity *toward attaining* the aims—the instrumental means toward the ends—but rather activity toward intensifying the feeling of the value of the aims that we regard as intrinsically valuable.

For example, Frankl's patient mentioned in our earlier example, when she imagined looking back from age eighty-five, realized that caring for her special needs child was an intrinsic value worthy of investing substantial life energy into. By reflecting from the perspective of herself as an eighty-five-year-old, she was able to feel this value more intensely. We can also intensify value feelings through artistic, literary, or musical activity, or simply symbolic verbal expression.

At the same time, the meaning of a given reading of the hot-cold meter is rendered still further uncertain by this additional possible ambiguity. Is the activity in question a means toward an end, an end in itself, or a symbolization for other values?

It would be counterproductive to go through life continually questioning, at every moment, whether a current cold reading should prompt a reworking of the structure of the entire value system that guides our lives, including the most ultimate intrinsic values as well as the appropriate balance between them and our own fittingness to pursue them. This would be a complicated and earthshaking endeavor impossible to undertake in every waking moment. To do so would immobilize us, as if we were continually reconstructing the foundation of a tall and complicated skyscraper—while also living in it.

The default position therefore is to assume that a cold reading means that we are acting wrongly in our *instrumental* actions toward achieving a long-term goal that we have already decided upon and that we don't in the present moment call into question. The reading of a hot or cold reading with regard to a military tactic usually assumes the legitimacy of the long-term goals of the war itself, even though this assumption isn't always easy to disentangle from the way we feel toward the short-term tactic.

As a result, it sometimes can be hard to know whether a cold reading pertains to the inadequacy of the means we are trying to use or a poor choice of the ends themselves. In either case, as already noted, the reading may simply read as "cold." This is especially true when there are many steps leading from a short-term means through a number of intermediate steps to one or several long-term goals—which is actually the most typical case.

A classic example is the persistence of attempts to make a marriage work, which then gives way to a consideration that the marriage itself should be dissolved. But even that reading may be a misreading of an even longer-term purpose that we think we have set for ourselves and that the marriage doesn't seem to serve—as in the case of the Young Stockbroker mentioned earlier. In the end, the problem wasn't with his marriage at all. His cold reading wasn't about the marriage, yet it seemed to be.

In short, a feeling of coldness may call into question the short-term means, or any one of the numerous medium-term goals, or the selection of an ultimate goal itself. For the reason mentioned above, we therefore tend to err on the side of giving the benefit of the doubt to our commitment to the long-term goal. Instead of questioning it, we try to find "hotter" means of attaining it.

But this default position, in which we take for granted our *longest-term* purposes, can lead to a complete breakdown in the calibration of the meter as it becomes increasingly inescapable that the normally assumed-without-question long-term goals are the real reason for a particularly "cold" reading for an immediate *short-term means*. We now realize that we have interpreted the cold readings as meaning that the short-term instrumental means toward the goal are ineffective, but then suddenly the long-term goal itself comes into question.

At this point, we have no way to measure the hotness or coldness of *any* instrumental action in our daily activities because we now doubt the long-term goals themselves; nor can we discern *how* hot or cold the long-term goal is because of confusion between the quasicoldness of uncertainty on the one hand, and on the other the feeling of coldness per se. We are not yet certain as to whether the long-term or the short-term goals are "cold," and therefore we have no idea *how* hot or cold *any* given short-term action might be.

In this case, *there is no longer a metric* relative to which contemplated short-term actions can read as either hot or cold. The next section explores the dangerousness of this kind of scenario and its potential fruitfulness both for everyday value decisions and for the ongoing sense of enactive meaning in general.

Anomie as Complete Decalibration of the Meter

At certain moments, the misperception of a cold reading, which we mistakenly think indicates merely a poor choice of means, can suddenly transition to an awareness that the entire cold reading is due to a radical uncertainty of the most ultimate long-term goals. Such a situation can therefore precipitate an "existential crisis," in which the hot-cold meter no longer reads as merely cold, but rather as *no longer functioning at all*—as in the case of the Young Stockbroker. The foundational problem here is that for a long time we have been giving the benefit of the doubt to presumed long-range values relative to which moment-to-moment hot-cold readings had their meaning.

At this point, all the criteria for how to decide on a direction have to be reopened. Nothing that we can do or not do in our daily life is able to trigger any reading at all—hot *or* cold. The metrics of the meter have been eradicated. We "drive around aimlessly," figuratively speaking, not only not knowing what we should do, but in fact lacking any criteria as to which way to turn.

When it becomes apparent that the current cold readings refer not to immediate or intermediate goals, but to *that relative to which* these are measured, suddenly it seems that there no longer is any meter at all. This complete malfunction of the hot-cold meter places us in a precarious state where there is no way we can determine what we should be doing or not doing with respect to long-term goals that no longer seem so clearly justified. At this point, we enter a seemingly aimless state in which we can't read off what we should be doing in any given situation.

This condition of complete *anomie,* or "normlessness," can be especially dangerous for people with addictive tendencies. If no long-term goals can get the hot-cold meter to yield a reading one way or another, then it may seem that the only way to get a reading is to do some action that obviously facilitates an immediate value in the exact present moment. Both addicts and psychopaths are notorious for failing to consider the long-range consequences of their behavior, even for themselves and their own future lives.

If the hot-cold meter gets "broken" in this way, the only meaningful action may at first appear to be what provides an unquestionable value "in the now." To an addict, it may appear that the best or only candidate for such an action is to attain immediate *pleasure*. Those whose choice of addictive behavior is to play music, play a sport, or write academic papers may be able to live for years in a state of complete *anomie* without any public visibility of the fact; the sport, music, or academic work may *be* the addictive behavior.[1]

However, if we follow the phenomenology of meter malfunction through in a careful way, it becomes apparent that there are other options even in the immediate "now" than just pleasure. The next section will touch on the effects of these other values on the eventual recalibration of the meter.

Recalibration of the Meter

There is an upside to the *"anomie"* of meter decalibration. We can now notice that the most *inevitable* values inherent in the consciousness of an active and living creature naturally emerge as guides to what can count as trustworthy commitments to a new list of overall goals of action. Some of the values that are literally unavoidable for conscious and inherently interactive creatures include the basic need to feel empathy toward other beings. They also include the innate and independent desire to explore in search of the truth insofar as possible. This exploratory drive seeks to know what actually is true irrespective of our psychological preferences. In these naturally occurring valuational acts, the end isn't necessarily extraneous to the activity itself (Csikszentmihalyi 1990 recapitulates Aristotle on this point). As contemporary emotion neuroscientists like Panksepp and Frijda suggest, these spontaneously occurring values include more than just the immediate pleasure that comes from an addictive behavior.

These immediately felt values re-emerge without any particular effort because as we have already seen, they are unavoidable motivations of very intelligent mammals such as humans, if not manipulated or selectively suppressed. In the case of humans, with our abstract questioning capacities, the innate exploratory drive, if not suppressed, can lead to a search for what actually is the morally *and* "nonmorally" best thing to do. By "morally," I simply mean taking account of the value of others' well-being as assessed independently of our other preferences. We then are also motivated to take the combination of all these values as a roadmap, resulting in a challenging but now more definitely guided repair and overhaul of the again-functioning hot-cold meter.

For instance, the Young Stockbroker that we discussed earlier finally realizes that his life as a stockbroker doesn't serve any intrinsic values by which he can be motivated. The superficial trappings of wealth and manners lose their appeal, and after considerable internal turmoil and questioning of his marriage to a socialite, he finally identifies the real problem—his career. At the very end of the film, when asked what he will do next, he simply responds with confidence, "I'm sure I'll find something useful to do."

Of course, this is only an example. For many, changing careers isn't a realistic option. But we all can find paths toward the furthering of values that we consider to be worthwhile after realizing that we previously were wandering aimlessly without them—whether the values toward which we can work are in our careers, our families, community work, or our general social behavior.

As soon as we observe that more values than just our own pleasure are inevitably felt (although again this is difficult for the extreme psychopath or the alexithymic), we notice that even a previously dismantled hot-cold meter will lead to one of two outcomes, and most likely both. The recalibrating hot-cold meter may respond in a negative way by focusing our attention on the *suffering* of other conscious beings; or it may respond in a positive way to the value we appreciate in conscious, valuing creatures per se. In either case, we naturally feel inspired to begin calculating how to help toward preventing or alleviating suffering, even if in a small way, and to attempt to decipher what the best way to distribute our efforts might be, taking account of our own well-being as well as that of others.

Notice that this kind of analysis of the role of emotion doesn't need to become enmeshed in a confusion between "is" and "ought" statements. When we combine the inevitable human tendencies to value both empathy *and exploration,* what we are motivated toward is an *exploratory process* in which we try to determine what kind of action really is most desirable from the standpoint not only of our own well-being and the well-being of others, but also to resolve questions of fairness and distributive justice in the best way we can. This questioning process is determined by our natural motives of both empathy *and* exploration, but the answers aren't preordained by those emotions since given those emotions the inquiry can still lead in different directions, depending on the outcome of the thought process toward which we are motivated.

The tools that we use to rebuild a value system—a commitment to long-term values which then will spontaneously motivate the short-term means and ends that typically feed into each momentary hot-cold reading—are essentially the same tools that we perhaps could have used to avoid relying on a too superficial reading of the meter at any point prior to its breakdown, if we could have known not to rely so thoroughly on our initial intuitions and preconceptions in the first place (the "prejudices of our childhood").

But such an optimal personal history is more easily fantasized than to actually have occurred, especially since so much of our history was initially beyond our control. As things actually are, rather than take an uncritical interpretation of the hot-cold reading as simply a "datum" that automatically tells us what we should do, as in traditional "moral intuitionism," we can take the felt sense as an invitation to explore *why* we seem to have a hot or cold reading and what the intentional referent (or aboutness) of the reading is.

When we refer to the specificity of what bothered us about the means toward some intermediate end, we may find that the longer-term goal that all these means serve is mostly what the feeling is about. As soon as we identify this more important issue toward which the felt sense is directed, we suddenly feel less intensely toward the immediate situation that served as the trigger. We are no longer so angry with the drunk at the bar.

We can then delve into why the disturbance in the feelings of the value of whatever we value occurred. We inevitably feel motivated at that point to think about what the intrinsic values are that are worth the investment of our efforts. This in turn may tell us not only what needs to be done, but also what can fuel our inspiration. Rather than feeling dissatisfied with my career choice because it isn't as good a way of getting rich as I would have liked, I may question whether getting rich itself should have been such a high priority in the first place. At that point, I may be at a loss to discover what values *are* more important than getting rich. And there will be many more steps involved in such an extensive reflective process.

One part of this introspective process is to explore why the immediately present action lacked the value needed to inspire me in the first place. Was it a short-, medium-, or long-term value that was at issue? If I stay with the felt sense and refrain from arbitrarily categorizing it, I may eventually find myself questioning some of the goals relative to which the event that triggered the cold reading seemed cold in the first place. Such a radical deconstruction of the overall means-ends structure of my action trajectory may precipitate intense emotions, sometimes disturbing ones. The first step, however, is to avoid symbolizing the felt sense of the situation with stock categories and instead to find a more specific descriptor.

Someone might object that, in our present context, to say merely that a felt sense is "hot" or "cold" is literally *one of the most general stock categories imaginable.* In a sense, such a descriptor is as nonspecific and therefore potentially as misleading as "angry" or "the sonofabitch deserved it!" So of course, it is important, even in ordinary daily readings of the meaning of the hot-cold meter, not to just "go with" the surface meaning, but to go through a reflective process to get past the superficial meaning (usually fairly quick and modest, but sometimes more difficult).

Some may think we would be taking the abnormal case as the normal if we say that the surface reading is *usually* not a very good guide to what a feeling or a valuational concept is about. But almost any everyday hot-cold reading will show that a little reflection reveals the intentional meaning of the reading more truthfully than the completely superficial take on it. Superficially, many people might say that gay marriage feels "wrong" to them or "doesn't seem right," or that homosexuality itself seems "wrong." Without going into the specificity of what the felt sense is about, they would end up just endorsing an intuitive, presumably moral principle that is very far removed from any serious take on what the felt sense is actually about. The real meaning of the feeling requires more careful phenomenological reflection that goes further beneath the surface. Ultimately, calling into question a moral judgment against homosexuality will entail questioning a whole host of more broad-ranging presuppositions about religion, society, politics, and the meaning of concepts like "good" and "fairness."

In the case of a complete breakdown of the hot-cold meter, and the resulting need for a complete recalibration in terms of a new set of long-term value commitments, it is difficult to carry out the needed reflections—especially given the opacity of the hermeneutical process that gets in the way. And even then, it may be still more difficult to devise short- and long-term means toward ends to which we ultimately feel to be worth striving.

But the starting point is that, even if we were to completely jettison the entire value system that previously had calibrated the meter, if we are open to what comes next, we can notice that we are *naturally* inclined to intrinsically value certain things and people and to value many more things than just pleasure. Nor are we disinclined to think about value questions in a way that includes more than our mere psychological preferences because one of the important motives we have is the exploratory drive. This "love of truth," as Hume called it, is inevitably present because it is grounded in an exploratory drive that animals can't do without. Humans are different only with regard to the type of equipment used to seek the truth. We are naturally inclined to act in accordance with this love of truth because the actual feeling of it must be concretely "embodied" or "symbolized" through some symbolizing activity in order to be fully felt.

To be sure, the *anomie* of decalibration of the meter can be a dangerous life position. If we are intolerant of ambiguity and uncertainty, the *anomie* and decalibration might result in our simply following a totalitarian leader or movement or committing ourselves to some other cult phenomenon. Nonetheless, the decalibration situation may not be something we have a choice about. It may happen as a result of earlier value commitments that gradually have lost their ability to inspire.

Even if the resulting reconstructions of the hot-cold meter should prove frustratingly difficult and error-prone, we now have at least one criterion for recalibrating the hot-cold meter that isn't so complicated. The meter reads warmer when we *make the attempt* to determine what really is the best course of action and colder when we don't. And we have a meter to guide us in the process.

∽

Even though the spontaneous valuing of others automatically re-emerges in the recalibration process and begins with direct empathy, it also gets extended universally, at least implicitly—and in fact has always already been implicitly universalized, as a result of a lifetime of experience and thinking. That process requires interaction between the empathy-related emotions and the exploratory drive, which motivates us to think about social and moral issues.

We tend in postmodern times to be quite skeptical about "opinions" and "attitudes" about value judgments because even the very criteria for evaluating such judgments have now been radically thrown into question. This skepticism applies as much to popular culture as it does to academia. In the popular imagination, philosophical thinking has become "merely subjective," "a matter of opinion rather than fact" or "highly speculative," and indicative that different worldviews should be considered "equally valid." It now seems preachy and antidemocratic to propose and evaluate universalized judgments about values.

But in the absence of "truth" about universal human values, we are left with authoritarian or otherwise arbitrary reasons for believing in whatever codification of human values we can bring ourselves to commit to, whether universalized or not. These supposedly "culturally relative" or "merely emotional" beliefs, because they are felt to be at bottom essentially arbitrary, can have little inspirational effect. We are then tempted to depend only on the kind of direct empathic imagery that, as we have seen, is in danger of lending itself to manipulation or self-manipulation of our attention toward or away from the "merely subjective" value of this or that particular valuing creature.

The next chapter specifically addresses some of the problems caused by this kind of valuational skepticism in postmodernity.

Chapter 10

A. J. Ayer's Stepchildren

Relativism, Truth, and the Crisis of Postmodernity

For humans, the exploratory drive—the need to ask questions about the world and ourselves—can become more complicated than for other animals. We might wish we could ignore the information and logical inferences that the prefrontal cortex is constantly offering, but to do so would require convoluted selective suppressions of the SEEKING system, which again is an endogenous *emotion* system. We can't stop being thinking creatures—even if we sometimes use the thinking skills to construct elaborate denial mechanisms.

The need for intricate and nuanced thinking and sensing about the realm of values leads to the problem of hermeneutics and the "hermeneutic circle." As we have already seen, the hermeneutic circle is never entirely or even approximately escapable. But I also want to argue that it doesn't need to pull us entirely into a complete "anything goes" relativism either.

Over a century ago, philosophers and sociologists began to suggest that values aren't a function of reality but only social conventions that can vary from culture to culture. Then at middle of the twentieth century, analytic philosophers like A. J. Ayer (1943) argued that only logic and empirical evidence are legitimate epistemological criteria; by that standard, viewpoints about values can be neither true nor false. This followed from the premise that there is no possible way such statements could be confirmed or disconfirmed. This relativist-emotivist view filtered through the subsequent generations of social scientists, writers, and filmmakers, and eventually became a traditional wisdom of those who considered themselves "in the know" in late twentieth-century culture. Value beliefs are merely subjective attitudes, not objective facts or even "literally meaningful" concepts.

Meanwhile, in the Continental tradition, hermeneuticists and deconstructionists were building on a completely different tradition, but with a notable similarity: H. G. Gadamer (1973) emphasized that we use motivated selective attention to interpret reality in such a way as to try to fit it to an already existing preconceived worldview; but essentially the same approach had already been advocated by Heidegger toward the end of *Being and Time* (1927), and it was explicitly elaborated by Heideggerian existential psychotherapists like Ludwig Binswanger (1963), as well as numerous sophisticated followers of the later Husserl, such as Gerd Brand (1967) and Ludwig Landgrebe (1966). I discussed earlier in this book why we inevitably use a hermeneutic process to determine what we think or value.

But the extreme historicists and deconstructionists among the postmoderns took this hermeneutic trend further. Once we have historically and socially deconstructed what counts as "truth," it becomes increasingly difficult to say what is actually left. There are constructions, mostly carried over from historical tradition, as in Foucault and Lyotard, or from the structure of our language, as in Levi-Strauss and Derrida, or from our economic self-interest, as in Althusser and the neo-Marxist postmoderns. Lawrence Schmidt (1995), himself a practitioner of hermeneutic philosophy, warns of the danger to which this trend could lead if pushed too far—a complete erosion of any distinction between truth and falsehood.

When it came to the human sciences and philosophical ideas, postmodernism made especially clear why we can never know the truth and sometimes simply that there is no determinable truth—only historical traditions, socially constructed worldviews, or accidentally occurring "language games." Ultimately, the hermeneutic circle would prevent us from even knowing to what extent science itself distorts reality. Scientists may simply select Kuhnian research "paradigms" that favor various hidden theoretical agendas. As far as social policy and its value assumptions were concerned, by the end of the twentieth century, the idea of an "objective truth" had been dead in both the analytic and Continental traditions for half a century and haunted academia mainly as a quaint ghostly apparition.

In the contemporary scene, films and other artworks that glamorize, normalize, or relativize the criminal lifestyle are so numerous that it would be easier to list the ones that *don't* do so. Similarly in Arendt's day, it became an easy step for intellectuals as well as ordinary people to assume that "political institutions served only as the facade for private interests" (Arendt 1968, 336). They assumed that people who argued about what "the truth" really is were only espousing the sedimented customs and presuppositions of their culture or social class or espousing doctrines meant to serve their self-interest in a disguised way. The mass leaders' propaganda "is marked by its extreme contempt for facts as such, for in their opinion fact depends entirely on the power of the man who can fabricate it" (351).

When Donald Trump in 2016 publicly retracted his famous false claim that President Obama was not born in the United States, polls showed that almost half of his supporters cynically assumed that Trump had always known that Obama was really born in the United States and was claiming otherwise just for rhetorical effect—as merely a way of insulting Obama, as a teenage bully might accuse someone's mother of being a prostitute. But an even larger number assumed that Trump still believed Obama was not born in the United States and was making the new statement merely for political reasons (Huffington Post 2016). Many pundits admonished the media for "taking Trump literally" (e.g., see Zito 2016)—based on the premise that Trump's supporters knew he did not literally mean what he said. Many pundits now speak of a "Post-truth America" with competing sets of "alternative facts."

Arendt stresses that the cultural elite and the intellectuals of her day were at least as receptive as anyone else to the cynical attitude of Nazis and fascists toward what counts as truth. For instance, she cites the widespread reaction to Brecht's *Three-Penny Opera*: It "presented gangsters as respectable businessmen and respectable businessmen as gangsters. . . . Respectable businessmen in the audience considered this a deep insight into the ways of the world. . . . the [masses of people] welcomed it as an artistic *sanction* of gangsterism" (351). As often happens with satire, the audience mistook the critique of a corrupted lifestyle for a glorification of it.

Post-Truth Culture

Some might initially think that what intellectuals are doing in their ivory tower has little effect on the masses and their politics. How could obscure academic notions like deconstructionism or logical empiricism be responsible for teaching people that there is no truth when it comes to human issues—ethics, politics, or the meaning of their lives? Aren't intellectuals, after all, mostly irrelevant?

But popular filmmakers, journalists, novelists, and business leaders took college courses in psychology, literature, and sociology. The teachers in those disciplines in turn, in their own generation, took a smattering of philosophy courses as undergraduates. In that way, the attitudes of philosophers filter out to the real world, if only in simplified form.

A. J. Ayer, already in 1943, was persuading people that there is no truth when it comes to moral or social issues. Ethical statements can't be proven with logic or empirical evidence, therefore moral beliefs are only expressions of emotion.

Consider the effect on the psychology students who took philosophy from teachers who thought social and moral viewpoints can only be expressions of emotion since they can't be empirically verified or falsified. To be sure, psychologists wanted to believe that their own work was objective and scientific. But at the same time, a generation of those students, given their logical-empiricist epistemological presuppositions, conveyed to their own students of the next generation the attitude that morality and sociopolitical cooperation result from social conditioning in the form of conformity, or from natural altruistic or other cooperative sentiments, which in turn were either socially constructed or built into the human gene pool for reasons of natural selection; a cooperative species increases its chances for survival. So if we say we should act morally, it is only because either our socially indoctrinated sentiments or our innate dispositions (take your pick) naturally motivate us to do so. But "Act morally when and if you are naturally motivated to do so" all too quickly morphs into "Do whatever you feel like doing."

Empiricist epistemology had driven psychology inexorably toward behaviorism, since hedonistically reinforced behavior can be objectively observed and measured. In the popular culture, even TV psychologists like Dr. Phil were compelled to insist that people perform only behaviors driven by positive and negative reinforcements (including the rewards of feeling altruistic toward those we are naturally driven to care about). Even "social reinforcement" is ultimately a form of reward—that is, grounded in hedonism. The reason children lack a moral compass, from this neobehaviorist standpoint, is that the parents "reinforce bad behavior."

A century of intellectual tradition has now made it a commonplace, even among the rank and file of people, that the only motivation for moral behavior is either blind instrumental conditioning or innate cooperative or altruistic sentiment—directed toward whomever our "human nature" naturally directs it toward. Humans develop cooperative arrangements because it is in each individual's self-interest to do so or in the interest of whatever altruistic sentiments they may happen to possess. The implication is usually unspoken that there is no point in recommending that people ought to be altruistic toward those who aren't already the objects of such "natural sentiments" because we can't do what we aren't motivated to do. So the only real moral injunction that can be taken seriously is "Do whatever you are naturally motivated to do."

In short, "You should do whatever you want" (beneficial if that is what you want, or if not, not). The resulting value system is left with little that can inspire a feeling that anything "really" matters. Values become little more than idle whims. On the one hand, we are supposed to know that values are arbitrary feelings, but on the other hand, we are supposed to act according to them.

Most of twentieth-century psychology ignored the idea that there could be an entire independent brain system devoted to an exploratory drive, which doesn't need to be reinforced by either hedonistic rewards or altruistic sentiments in order to express itself. The independence of the exploratory drive—the fact that it isn't derivative from any other emotion system or social reinforcement—reopens the possibility that thinking about values, about the entire extended system of instrumental and intrinsic values, might go further than merely behaviors driven by cooperative or benevolent emotions. Our "love of truth," as Hume called it, might then motivate genuine, nonvacuous social and moral thinking, independently of any combination of desires or survival instincts other than the demands of the exploratory drive itself.

Panksepp (1998, 145 ff.) explicitly interprets his research into the exploratory drive to mean that the search for moral meaning, like any other everyday truth-seeking activity, is energized not only by empathic instincts or social conditioning, but also and more importantly, by an aspect of our innate SEEKING system. The exploratory drive therefore operates somewhat independently of whether we happen to feel altruistic or nurturing in a particular instance.

In fact, the new trends in emotion research now call into question the old assumption that moral lapses result simply from a deficit of empathy or "fellow feeling." The problem instead could stem from a selective suppression of the exploratory drive. As we saw earlier, the proponents of Arian superiority, however intelligent or educated they might be, fail to ask themselves some of the most critical questions about the factual and logical basis of their theory—questions that seem obvious to others.

The Ku Klux Klan terrorist who conspires to assassinate civil rights leaders can then also donate generous charitable contributions to a church, and even to charities focused on helping poor African American families.

James R. Venable, a KKK grand wizard of Georgia (see Federal Bureau of Investigation 1964) engaged in extensive charitable activities (*New York Times* 1993). The Klan, the White Citizens Councils, and other racist organizations were led by otherwise honorable and altruistic people. Many of them served on the committees of various charities (Luce 1960, 35 ff.). What was missing wasn't empathy and compassion, but rather the ability to universalize those sentiments when doing so threatened their entire philosophical worldview. The exploratory drive had to be *selectively* suppressed.

Posttruth Culture and the Problem of Value Nihilism

In spite of the recently renewed interest in the exploratory drive in emotion research, the popular culture as well as many intellectuals are still stuck in the twentieth century as far as the social sciences and other human studies are concerned. People on TV talk shows routinely speak of moral views as "Just the way someone feels about it." "Everyone has their opinion," they say, "I just happen to feel that XYZ." The next step is that masses of people scarcely even raise an eyebrow when their chosen president defends his support of an oligarch who murders political opponents with the casual response "Everyone kills people."

Similarly, in the prewar Europe described by Arendt, ordinary people no longer took seriously the idea that ethical or political statements could be true or false: "An atmosphere in which all traditional values and propositions had evaporated . . . made it easier to accept patently absurd propositions than the old truths which had become pious banalities, precisely because nobody could be expected to take the absurdities seriously. Vulgarity with its cynical dismissal of respected standards [was] easily mistaken for courage and a new style of life" (334). In our current version of moral cynicism, the idea that the president of the United States would grab unknown women's crotches or repost a video of someone shouting "White power!" hardly creates a stir.

For the totalitarian leader, the idea that there is no truth in the moral realm leads to an especially useful form of cynicism. All political statements are taken as hypocritical. "Since the bourgeoisie claimed to be the guardian of Western traditions . . . parading publicly virtues which it not only did not possess . . . but actually held in contempt, it seemed revolutionary to admit cruelty, disregard of human values, and general amorality" (Arendt, 334).

When we try to understand why people would believe "gigantic lies and monstrous falsehoods," as Arendt calls them, we naturally turn to the hermeneutical process. From the hermeneutic perspective, all interpretations of reality are filtered through presuppositions that don't arise merely from the immediate situation itself. What one person sees as a lazy bum who refuses to accept responsibility is viewed by another as someone who has had a string of bad luck, perhaps including the bad luck of poor educational opportunities, childhood poverty, mental disability, or other factors that could have led to unfortunate life events and their later consequences. The way we see any situation is based partly on an already-presupposed overall worldview, in terms of which we interpret the situation. As is now widely accepted among philosophers, a person's overall worldview acts as a "filter" through which we view reality, unaware of many of the prejudices and preconceptions that distort what we see.[1]

In short, we work from a lifelong striving to construct a holistically coherent worldview. When the facts don't fit our overall worldview, we err toward protecting what has already been built up from earlier experience and thinking. Like a centipede crossing an impediment, we tend to adjust the pattern of movements as little as possible, while maintaining its overall coherence as much as possible.

But we shouldn't forget that the "exploratory drive" also grounds a contrary tendency, which Hume had already called a natural "love of truth," treated by Hume as an important ingredient for the universalization of moral sentiment. Much of the cultural revolution that occurred in the United States during the late 1960s was motivated by the need to re-evaluate established worldviews because of their incoherence with increasingly acknowledged *facts* about the Vietnam War and racial and sexual inequality. People naturally want to know the truth, independently of other motives, but this natural curiosity comes into conflict with our interest in preserving a preferred already-existing worldview.

Arendt thinks the rejection of the concept of truth in the moral realm is especially crucial in the rise of totalitarian movements. In addition to the usual points about the "authoritarian personality" and other hermeneutical distortions of thinking raised by Adorno, Becker, Gadamer, and Milgram, Arendt sees the particular social irrationality of totalitarian movements as linked to a certain form of implicit value nihilism (318). The masses in this case are no longer driven by either altruistic or self-interested values, regardless of whether those are presumed to be innate or socially constructed.

Consistent with the fact that the movement is pieced together with followers who share no particular political policy interests, the cynicism of the followers transcends any partisan interest or political belief system.

"The whole struggle in Parliament between the socialists and the nationalists . . . appeared as a sham designed to hide ulterior sinister motives" (357). The assumption that one's political opponent is corrupt (whoever the opponent happens to be) needs no support other than the general assumption that all "traditional" politicians are corrupt. The same charge can be made interchangeably against any opponent of any aspiring totalitarian leader.

The totalitarian movement presents its potential followers with an "alternative truth." As Arendt puts it, "The force possessed by totalitarian propaganda . . . lies in its ability to shut the masses off from the real world . . . the unintegrated and disintegrating masses—whom every new stroke of ill luck makes more gullible" (353).

When people in complex industrial societies lose their sense that they are needed parts of a social community—when they are merely replaceable and ever more unimportant cogs in the machinery of production—they feel, as Arendt describes it, superfluous and expendable. A mass movement then offers them a home, a community that seems to need and value their efforts. Membership in this new home also creates a feeling of superiority over the enemies of the movement—a category that eventually includes everyone who is not a member of the group.

But this solution to the problem of the feeling of social isolation, of "being left behind," also comes into sharp inner conflict with the exploratory drive, which is still urging the cultist recruit to critically examine the truth-claims and incoherencies of the worldview that is being offered. The exploratory drive has to be selectively suppressed in favor of relieving the PANIC of social atomism. How this conflict is resolved, and why it is resolved in one way rather than the other, is part of the difficult question that Arendt is trying to address. What Arendt is describing stems not just from a distortion of the hermeneutical process, but also and more fundamentally from an underlying implicit value nihilism or seminihilism.

If the feeling of being "superfluous" and "valueless" is capable of reaching a tipping point beyond which the result is an implicit value nihilism or seminihilism, there would be even greater danger of this outcome at a time of too-rapid change, when the skills and services people have to offer become ever more quickly obsolete as they are supplanted by new technology and the effects of huge corporations with their "economies of scale"—in other words, times like our own.

To be sure, the feeling of "valuelessness" that occurs in this case rests partly on a confusion between instrumental and intrinsic value—the confused attempt to define our own value relative to some outcome toward which we are instrumental. An obsolete working class feels "useless" because people may not feel that they serve some higher value. But this very attempt to define our own value as merely instrumental is a fundamental component of the nihilistic dynamic, as we have already seen.

Contrasting the confabulatory tendency against the implications of Hume's "love of truth" (now we would say "exploratory drive") suggests that susceptibility to authoritarianism and generally irrational social viewpoints can be exacerbated by a basic and inevitable conflict in human motivational systems. Exploring these inner conflicts can help not only with understanding moral and political belief formation, but also the more general phenomena of scapegoating, victim blaming, and attitudes that justify violence and other harmful behaviors. The latter both grow from and further feed an underlying semi-nihilism, reflecting a shortage of enactive meaning.

Arendt (1968) stresses that the appeal of 1930s irrational theories of racial superiority and other far-fetched "conspiracy theories" had just as much appeal to intellectuals as it did for "the masses"—similar to Luce's (1960) study of the highly educated members of the White Citizens Councils. These intelligent people also weren't generally lacking in empathy or compassion. What was missing was a *willingness to ask questions* and to seek new truths that potentially threatened an already established worldview, challenges to which created fears and anxieties of the kind that the Becker/Greenberg "terror management" psychology describes.

A hermeneutic process is an inescapable part of everyone's process of belief formation and shouldn't be regarded merely as an aberration or neurosis. Nor do we always manage the process by blatantly misinterpreting reality. The crucial question is why we *sometimes* succumb to the hermeneutic confabulations that ease the anxieties through denial and repression, yet other times we don't.

What led the twentieth-century fascists to their elaborately confabulatory worldview was neither a lack of empathy and compassion nor a lack of intelligence. It was a targeted suppression of the exploratory motive—Hume's "love of truth"—with respect to any question that touched on threats to an overall worldview, and whose questioning would have rendered insecure an entire philosophical outlook. Above all else, and in spite of the intelligence of the person holding such a worldview, curiosity and exploration had to be held in check when it challenged the chosen dogma. When the exploratory drive is even momentarily and selectively weaker than fear or panic, critical thinking comes more slowly and with more difficulty.

And this leads to a very different question, which I have postponed up until now. Regardless of how we "feel" about something, does anything "really" have value, as opposed to an arbitrary and frivolous "feeling" of value such as A. J. Ayer's "I like ice cream"? Is the depressed person perhaps correct to feel that no possible action is really worth anything? Was Terry Bradshaw perhaps correct to feel that it really makes little difference in the Ultimate Scheme of Things whether the Pittsburgh Steelers win the Super Bowl or not?

But Does Anything "Really" Have Value "in the Final Analysis"? The Problem of Indexicals

A college friend of mine used to sit around playing a solitary game called Casino. The object of the game was to beat the casino. I asked him, "But why do you want to beat the casino, when the casino *isn't there?*" His answer was a clever play on the "Why do you climb Mount Everest?": "Because it isn't there!"

For my part at the time, there would have been great difficulty getting motivated by something like "Because it isn't there!" As an idealistic young man obsessed with political causes, I couldn't feel the outcome of "beating the casino" as important enough to motivate playing the game. Now, however, I have more respect for my friend's position. If my friend's enjoyment of life didn't have *intrinsic* value, then how could any of my political goals have *instrumental* value? Instrumental value toward what end? I was drifting toward the direction that Simone de Beauvoir warns against in *The Ethics of Ambiguity*—allowing instrumental values to supersede intrinsic ones.

What determines the strength of a feeling that an action is worth enough to motivate engaging in the activity? In depression, few possible outcomes can motivate action. For the authoritarian follower in Arendt's analysis, suffering from a ubiquitous *anomie*, the assumption has already been made that there are no reasonable political or economic solutions to the problem of feeling "superfluous" and "left behind." In either case, we might be drawn toward the notion that "merely subjective" values aren't enough to make a difference in some ultimate sense beyond the tiny concerns of daily life.

In such cases, there is an implicit assumption that, beyond what valuing creatures subjectively value, there needs to be value in some more "objective" sense. We begin to feel that whatever we do is ultimately more or less pointless. If there is no good answer to the "ultimate" value of becoming a great saxophonist, then we feel demotivated. The "Grand

Scheme" value itself (becoming a great saxophonist) doesn't seem to serve any instrumental purpose.

This question of "ultimate meaning," or "nonsubjective value" seems superficially to be a philosophical one: Even if I or others *emotionally* value something, does that thing "really" have value? Does anything "really" matter "in the final analysis"?

But notice the oversimplification of the options here—that the value of things is either "subjective" or "objective." Beyond this simple opposition, we should take account of the complexities of the interrelation between the subjective and the objective. Even if there are only "subjective" values in the sense that value is created by subjective creatures, it may remain true that the ability of subjects to engender value by valuing something might lead to values in still another "objective" sense: In some contexts, "X has value" could be taken to mean: "Anyone with the capacity for empathy and an active questioning function (exploratory drive) would value X *if attention were directed* to X." Notice that whether this statement is true or not doesn't depend on how I, personally, happen to feel about it. In that respect, it isn't subjective.

This notion becomes plausible if we think of X as representing a valuing creature. Any rational creature with a capacity for empathy can formulate the question: If I were to direct my attention to the subjective feeling dimension of person X, would I empathize, if not with the person's specific feelings, then at least with that person's subjective valuing dimension as such—for example, with their potential for suffering? In this case, "X has value" would mean more than just "I in particular happen to value X—but that's just me." The statement that "X has value," in the sense we are referring to now, is meant as a description of a reality, which may be either true or false; it isn't meant simply as a subjective emotion.

This strange conundrum—that value can be both subjective and objective at the same time—raises the problem of "indexicals." The problem of indexicals occurs in the context of philosophy of mind discussions when we ask ourselves whether the universe would have been any different if "I" had occupied "your" consciousness and vice versa. As Woody Allen quipped, "My only regret in life is that I'm not someone else." This version of the problem of indexicals assumes that everything could have been exactly the same physically, yet I would simply be inhabiting "your" perspective and you mine. The assumption here is that everything could have been the same in the "objective" realm, yet our "subjective" points of view could be reversed. Why am I "indexed" to this particular person's point of view rather than that other one?

We might doubt whether Woody Allen's premise here is even a logical possibility. But a more serious "problem of indexicals" affects the question of value and meaning. Suppose I affirm that a few specific individuals—for instance, family members—have intrinsic value independently of the fact that I happen to feel certain ways toward them (for example, that they will still have value after I am gone, and thus would have value even if I weren't here to subjectively affirm their value). Does this mean that I would also have affirmed the value of any given other valuing creature to the extent that I *had* directed my attention to their valuing dimension—and thus that I would also affirm that their value goes beyond my specific feelings toward them?

Does it change the intrinsic value of a valuing creature if its valuing dimension happens to be "indexed" to this or that specific creature? Does value attach only to the specific creatures to whom I have directed my own subjective attention? At what point does the adopted child "acquire" intrinsic value—or is it even coherent to imagine that this value could ever have been "acquired"?

In that sense, the only ingredient missing in the *failure* to intrinsically value a valuing creature is the act of *paying attention* to the valuing creature's valuing dimension (for instance, as the literal psychopath fails to do). There is a sense in which it is an *objective* reality that whether the starving children of Sudan get something to eat has value, given that we can't coherently restrict our definition of "value" so as to "index" one or a few subjects as valuable simply because I personally am paying attention to them.

The person who insists that feeding the starving children has no value if it has no "ultimate" value "in the final analysis" is implicitly demanding that there be a Grand Scheme value system. "Ultimately," it makes no difference whether they get fed or not—merely "subjectively for them"—and possibly "subjectively for me." We have already seen that the kind of Grand Scheme system being demanded here is self-defeating.

Moreover, to regard subjective values as "merely" subjective is to ignore the problem of indexicals. It assumes that something can have subjective value only if the indexical "I" happens to value it. This indexing of subjective valuing to myself is the underlying assumption that leads to the demand for a Grand Scheme value system—something that could have value "in the Grand Scheme of things."

Let's suppose, by some "objective" definition of value, that it really makes no difference in the ultimate scheme of things whether I am successful in helping the starving children of Sudan get something to eat. That is, suppose it makes no difference except in the sense that the starving children as conscious beings *subjectively* value a better outcome. Even in the absence of some ultimate or nonsubjective value, there would still be value in a more modest sense—a value that is introduced into being by the fact that conscious or sentient beings engage in the act of valuing.

This objective-qua-subjective meaning of value becomes the raw material for an entire ethical system in Simone De Beauvoir's *The Ethics of Ambiguity*. It isn't necessary to adopt the language of Sartrean existentialism (as De Beauvoir does) to understand this point.

Suppose someone were to propose some Grand Scheme definition of value that does *not* depend on subjective beings valuing things. As De Beauvoir characterizes this type of position (in contrast to her own), it might be argued that only the Will of God or the Revolution has value and that we subjects are important only as instruments to achieve such ends—that we should set aside our petty human concerns as mere distractions.

This view actually hasn't been uncommon among some political extremists of certain eras, including groups like ISIL, who believe it is their job to hasten the End of Times. A surprising number of Christians, including perhaps as many as 30 percent of American "evangelicals," also share this same glorification of the End of Times (see Rosentiel 2010)—which they believe will indeed occur in our current time. Such believers then reduce both their own and others' subjectivity to the status of means toward some "objective" and "ultimate" end. I myself, they tell themselves, have no value unless I am in the service of some "higher" value. This is the attitude to which I came dangerously close by rejecting my friend's game of beating the casino—as if his enjoyment of the game had no value because it had no *instrumental* value. It led to no "ultimate" value.

One major problem with this "ultimatizing" type of attitude (as J. S. Mill 1863 already argued) is that any time someone believes that X has value on such grounds, there is someone who believes the opposite. Religious texts and cultural traditions themselves are hermeneutically interpreted by individuals and groups and thus can no more assert than contradict any given interpretation of the realm of values. If we compare "Thou shalt not kill" with "Kill everyone in the city . . . but save the gold and silver, for they are precious unto the Lord" (Joshua 6: 17–19), no further argument can be given to prefer the former over the latter, or vice versa—except on the grounds that killing is actually harmful to valuing creatures themselves.

In general, to posit that some "absolute" or "Grand Scheme" value is the ultimate value, to the exclusion of the values created by subjective creatures, would require all kinds of ungrounded assumptions and ad hoc hypotheses, involving considerable emotional and cognitive incoherence. Such a believer will always implicitly doubt whether such a value system really enjoys the certainty that one might pretend it does. Underneath the pretense of knowing, there will always be an implicit understanding that the opposite view is just as likely to be true. And this will exacerbate rather than assuage the underlying existential anxiety.

This is why proponents of the Grand Scheme feel that their interlocutors can't just be argued against, but must be *silenced*. The very existence of opposing beliefs puts a spotlight on the arbitrariness of the doctrine and thus exposes that we don't really *believe* it, however much we are emotionally drawn to it. Hence the burning at the stake of thousands of "heretics" during the Middle Ages, and the more recent sending of political dissidents to "October Work Camps" in various authoritarian dictatorships.

A more practical problem facing ultimatizing viewpoints is that, if I am to make *decisions* as to which value to pursue—a "subjective" or a "Grand Scheme" one—then there must at least be a common denominator in the *meaning* of the term "value" in the two cases; otherwise no decisions between them could be made. If I want to decide whether erecting a monument to the Virgin Mary should be counted as having *more* or *less* value than sending the same money to starving children, there needs to be a unitary sense of "value" in terms of which I can make the comparison. The monument may have important "symbolizing" value in Gendlin's sense, but this value also has to be made commensurable with the needs of the starving children. If there is no way to make the "Grand Scheme" values commensurable with subjective values, we will feel that no reasonable decision can be reached, and the ensuing course of action thus seems arbitrary. This too only exacerbates the problem of implicit value nihilism or seminihilism.

Regardless of how we feel about any "Grand Scheme" or "ultimate" values, we can't give up on values that are grounded in the intrinsic value of valuing creatures themselves—and the "objective" fact that anyone would acknowledge this value if they were to pay the relevant attention. In depression, the problem is less a matter of intellectually acknowledging this simple point, and more a problem of feeling inspired to take *action*. As soon as the depressed person tries to initiate action, even if the action is in the service of other conscious creatures, the suppression of the SEEKING system kicks in, resulting in a lack of inspiration to action.

In terms of Gendlin's symbolization function, a charitable value feeling, which takes the value of valuing creatures per se as its object, might be more strongly intensified by overtly going out and working in a soup kitchen than by merely writing a check to the soup kitchen. Although both actions may do the same amount of good, the more overt activity may play a more effective role in symbolizing and therefore intensifying our feeling of the value of conscious creatures—which, again, is one of the most important value feelings in terms of lifting us from the lethargy of nihilism or seminihilism and toward intrinsic value in more than just the sense that "I like ice cream."

Even without depression, when we feel socially rejected, "left behind," or "superfluous," the PANIC system may be firing on all cylinders. To enthusiastically affirm the value of others while feeling socially alienated can create a considerable amount of inner conflict.

The Problem of Existential Meaning

"Existential meaning" doesn't have to be an esoteric concept. Existentialism just designates a discipline that tries to grapple with the meaning of human existence—hence the root term "existence." Implicit also is to understand the potential threats to meaningful existence inevitably built into the structure of our being: not just death, but also the inescapable finiteness of personal power; the feeling of insignificance as a tiny spec in the grand scheme of things; and perhaps most crucial, the ever-challenging potential for alienation from specific others or from the community of others in relation to whom we need to actualize a meaningful existence. Even the thought that our personality might be substantially predetermined by environmental and hereditary factors (Heidegger's *Geworfenheit*, or "thrownness") threatens our sense of power and importance. All these threats are "existential," woven into the core fabric of our existence—facts without which we couldn't exist as finite conscious creatures. Equally important, there is no escaping the need to feel inspired to action despite these negative concerns and to feel the value of our actions strongly enough to justify the struggles resulting from the negative conditions of our existence.

Existential issues don't discriminate in favor of leisured classes or Young Stockbrokers. They reach tenant farmers and steel workers devalued and "left behind" by the constant upheavals of socioeconomic conditions. Shawn Beaty's *Children of Darkness* looks at an alienated auto mechanic struggling not just to survive, but to find a meaningful direction in the aftermath of a worldview-shattering role in the Vietnam War. James Baldwin's *Go Tell It on the Mountain* reflects Baldwin's own struggles, as a teenager in his stepfather's church, with the pressure to be something he couldn't be, on pain of feeling superfluous and useless in his cultural milieu.

These challenges inevitably interfere with the instrumentalities that we use to define meaning. The basement level of the edifice of motivation and value is the ongoing and always presupposed sense of the "existential meaning" of our lives. Some may hope a "solution" to the problem of existential meaning would propose some doctrine that could somehow vanquish the existential challenges we have been discussing or by some clever logic make them not matter. But they do matter. Death may not seem to present a huge obstacle to meaning until we find our own lives or those of our buddies realistically threatened, as in combat. Alienation from others may not be felt as a big deal until we are forced to kill the enemy soldier, who is only doing his assigned job just as we are—a "brother soldier" tragically forced into the gladiatorial arena—and even this feeling may not emerge until the aftermath. Our relative personal insignificance in the big picture of things may not seem problematic until we find ourselves isolated, forgotten, part of a "nameless list of numbers," just another superfluous steel worker from the shuttered Johnstown factory, another small farmer displaced by Big Agribusiness, another kid not chosen for the football team. Any instrumental action will seem dwarfed if our actions are relegated to an insignificant status. For the same reason, the general theme of basic relative powerlessness may not seem important until we find ourselves unemployed, "on the outside looking in," "irrelevant," without a clue as to what comes next. Any values that we affirm presuppose that we have some power to pursue them.

These existential issues mutually surround and interpenetrate each other. The fact that we need others both creates a danger of *alienation* and limits our *power* to achieve goals, yet we need to feel somewhat in control of our destiny and thus that we have the *power* to influence the community of others in various ways—which again exacerbates the threat of *alienation* as well as the feeling of *insignificance*. The impending *death* of needed others underscores our need for them even more, while our own personal *insignificance* makes us feel *powerless* to attract even the attention of needed others, further *alienating* us from the community or from specific others, or at least presenting a ubiquitous threat of alienation. Whatever instrumental projects we set up are threatened by our own impending *death*, our finite *power and significance*, and so forth.

We can't unravel this existential knot by simply resigning ourselves to meaninglessness. There will always be a need for action to be motivated by some sort of value. Even Zen Buddhist philosophers engage in moral action, which assumes the value of the sentient creatures whose consideration grounds the relevant ethical principles. Zen Buddhists might allow this feeling to emerge spontaneously in each specific instance, rather than thinking of it as a general abstract principle. Nonetheless, without motivation, which implies valuation, we literally would do nothing. We can't just take the position that nothing matters.

The issues of death, potential interpersonal alienation, relative powerlessness, and personal insignificance in the big picture are therefore "existential": No ingenious theory can eliminate them because they are basic facts about the existence of any finite and inescapably interactive creature. This is not to denigrate metaphysics and thinking about the infinite, when done in an honest and serious way. But existential meaning, in one way or another, always remains something we have to create by finding it within our own experience and which we all *do* create in some degree, in spite of inner conflicts tempting us to stand in the way of our own meaning-creating process.

At the same time, the meaning we create demands to be "real," not some sort of fantasy, idle whim, or *trompe l'oeil*. Meaning can be real if grounded in values that actually are intrinsically valuable enough to create non-self-deceptive feelings of "enthusiasm"—a zest for life—intense enough to countervail the opposing feelings of disillusionment and frustration with the existential reality of our own and our loved ones' finiteness, including all the various concrete instances of this finiteness, in all the respects just listed.

And crucially, our own endogenous *exploratory drive,* our desire to know what *is* real, demands that we create whatever we create in good faith—trying to avoid denial or self-deception. This is where any metaphysics needs to remain "deadly serious." The necessary degree of everyday inspiration, if it is to be "real," requires feeling values that don't reduce *us* to instrumental values, as if the main purpose of conscious creatures were to serve some Grand Scheme value, whatever it might be. That would impede the most obvious intrinsic value—valuing creatures themselves. We can feel inspired only if the values that motivate us can support the status of the value of valuing creatures as such—as *intrinsic* values, not just instrumental toward some presumably greater end. At the same time, for the unavoidable reasons already mentioned, we can't just ignore the need to treat ourselves and others also as *instrumental* values.

The inability to experience attainable values vividly enough and positively enough to motivate action, whether in depression or in nihilism or seminihilism, may create the illusion that something much flashier is needed to inspire us. A grand, ultimate value, not dependent on the subjective act of valuing, then seems required to provide an earthshaking enough value experience. It is as if a progressively deaf person needs increasingly loud music in order to be moved, and eventually no music is loud enough. But even if there is no overarching, Grand Scheme value such as what the nihilist is demanding, this doesn't entail that nothing has value. What is missing is not value per se, but rather a feeling of being inspired by the values that do exist.

Chapter 11

The Hermeneutic Circle

A Story of Internal Conflict

Intelligence information supporting the US invasion of Iraq was "fitted" to the already-preferred narrative. Similarly, someone with a history of trauma may tend to automatically interpret all new situations in terms of threat assessment, as in the "negativity bias" studied by Hibbing and colleagues (2013). Binswanger (1963) referred to this filtering of experience through preconceived categories as an individual's "existential *a priori*." Philosophers like Paul Ricoeur (1950/1966), H. G. Gadamer (1971/1975), and Cornel West (1979) expand on this same dynamic under the heading of "hermeneutics." Rather than merely perceiving, we "interpret" reality. Hermeneuticists study the various ways that we form the categories through which we interpret things. Only when a new experience can't be fitted to the already existing overall picture of reality do we consider changing the pre-existing view, sometimes while kicking and screaming.

This hermeneutical process is crucially affected by the always-underlying enactive value-and-meaning trajectory. The ghosts of a past trauma inhabit every corner of the traumatized person's worldview, affecting the assessment of the value of any given action. The resulting intrinsic-instrumental value structure always directs selective attention in each instant, affecting how we perceive the world. The resulting perception of the world then feeds back into our appraisals of the value of various actions, in a circular process.

If we operate in each instant from a pre-existing hermeneutical worldview, then we are always looking at not just one situation, but at how to resolve conflicts between newly presented data and our total outlook.

Sometimes we just automatically "privilege" the pre-existing viewpoint. Other times, we revise our presuppositions. As cognitive dissonances present themselves, the exploratory drive motivates us to constantly look for any possible sense that something in our pre-existing assessment of the world and our relation to it might be "off"—inconsistency with acknowledged facts, tension against presumed facts of our life-long experience, or even logical self-contradictions. The resulting assessments of reality continuously affect our enactive value trajectory and vice versa.

To get at the implicit intricacy of the everyday interpretive process, it might be helpful to look in a little more depth at the ways in which people sometimes use the interpretive process to reject or revise a preconceived view or attitude, while at other times we dig in our heels. What makes that difference? The above-mentioned study by Prasad and others (2009) on authoritarian confirmation bias could be a starting point for thinking through this question.

Hermeneutics and the Existential A Priori

At the time of the Prasad and colleagues study (conducted in 2007, published in 2009), the majority of Americans had already changed their thinking about whether Iraq was connected to the 9/11/2001 terrorist attacks. Finally accepting the truth required overcoming cognitive dissonance, yet most people eventually managed to change their view. They were able to give up support for a particular instrumental action (the war), even though changing their view on the war pushed back against a more basic value feeling (patriotic feelings toward the government that erroneously, and maybe with deliberate deception, launched the war). Eventually, most people acknowledged that Iraq wasn't connected to the attacks.

But a smaller percentage—about 25 percent—refused to give up belief in the involvement of Iraq with 9/11, even when presented with decisive evidence. To do so would have thrown into question too much of their pre-existing value system. It would have triggered troubling questions around cherished presuppositions fundamental to an entire outlook on life. How could the "Shining City on the Hill" deliberately launch a completely unjustified war?

Prasad and colleagues deliberately chose a sampling of subjects who still believed Iraq had been involved in 9/11, noting that most of these subjects got their news predominantly from one source: the Fox cable news network. Fox had consistently given their viewers excuses to continue believing that Iraq might have been involved in 9/11. Fox commentators repeatedly suggested that there might have been some clandestine meeting between someone from al Qaeda and an Iraqi intelligence operative—a story that was factually false.

But Prasad and colleagues emphasize that their subjects had also already *chosen* Fox as their news source because it reinforced their preferred beliefs. In fact, more accurate information was presented to the subjects during the study—for example, a statement from President Bush himself admitting that Iraq had nothing to do with 9/11. Yet forty-eight of the forty-nine subjects still refused to change their opinion. Given the lack of "Openness" that Hodson and colleagues (2009) find especially pronounced among authoritarian personalities (using Altemeyer's "Right Wing Authoritarianism" scale), there is always some possibility in the hermeneutical process for explaining away conflicting facts and inferences. Davis and Panksepp (2018) correlate this lack of "Openness" with an underactive SEEKING system. In this case, the suppression of the exploratory drive aspect of the SEEKING system seems more targeted than general.

But the same hermeneutical process can just as well *facilitate* truth-seeking as obstruct it. Many people rejected from the very beginning the suggestion that Iraq was involved in the 9/11 attacks—not because they had any access to classified intelligence refuting the government's claims. On the contrary, those claims simply didn't fit a *previously established* way of thinking. Some remembered previous governments' exaggerated threat assessments to gear up the populace for wars. Others had some general understanding of Mideast geopolitics. The government's claims couldn't cohere with a preexisting general view of reality.

Whether leading to correct or incorrect conclusions, the very fact that our outlook is always "hermeneutic" or "interpretive" in this way calls into question the supposed objectivity of our attitudes, as George Lakoff (2008) and Drew Westin (2008) emphasize. After all, a majority did at the time support going to war. And those who disagreed didn't have tangible evidence against the government's claims—mostly just a gut feeling, which on further reflection might have been tentatively grounded in earlier experiences.

Yet people often do change their attitudes to accommodate new information. For many in the mid-twentieth-century United States, televised civil rights demonstrations forced attention to the contradictions within their value system—between the enshrinement of "democracy" on the one hand and the racially unjust social-political system on the other. Some were disturbed by the incoherence they now found within their own value system. Others posited ad hoc hypotheses designed to explain away the inconsistencies.

The primordiality of the exploratory drive, in conflict with other equally powerful emotions, leads to a difficult question: What determines whether curiosity about the reality of the world (including ourselves) wins out or whether the inner conflict implodes into elaborate denial mechanisms? Both tendencies derive from conflicting motivations built into our constitution. And this inner conflict plays out in our attitudes about intrinsic-instrumental value questions as well as any other aspect of reality.

Even Gendlin's focusing method doesn't remove the need to hermeneutically interpret each new experience. To be sure, the method does facilitate a better perspective on our pre-established attitudes by deliberately avoiding stock assumptions as interpretations of what our feelings and concepts mean. But even so, people still had to *interpret* what was going on with the claims about Iraq during the buildup to the Iraq War. There is normally a tendency (and sometimes with good reason) to privilege a lifetime of learning by preference over some anomalous new bit of information. In effect, there were good reasons, although difficult to articulate, for being suspicious of the government's claims.

The hermeneutical nature of experience means that no one situation is evaluated purely in terms of that one situation. We are always in some way struggling with our own personal "hermeneutic circle." We are faced with this circle because our attempts to reflect on our own existential a priori preconceptions may already be filtered through that very same existential a priori as we try to introspect. We don't see our own preconceptions for what they are.

But does this necessarily mean that our ideas about reality, including the values that drive action, are automatically grounded merely in arbitrary cultural traditions or idle whims—"explaining away" evidence that doesn't fit our prejudices and preconceptions? Do we always just believe whatever we want regardless of reasoning or evidence? If that were true, I personally might prefer to believe that I am Zorro or Spiderman—yet I don't believe those things. The exploratory drive subserved by the SEEKING system motivates me not to do so.

Phlogiston theory did eventually give way to Newtonian physics, which in turn expanded to relativity and quantum theory. Careful introspection can reveal that we already have some credible yet fallible reasons to accept or reject a given tableau of reality, even if grounded in a history of hermeneutic interpretation rather than simply "reading off" some direct perception of an isolated situation.

At the same time, we need to take seriously the inevitably hermeneutical process in people's everyday assessments of reality, especially with regard to the conflicting motivations toward instrumental and intrinsic values. This kind of investigation will be pivotal for the underlying question of motivational meaning that seems to demand a "for the sake of which," yet also has to be fleshed out in terms of seemingly endless chains of instrumentalities. Most of our everyday feelings present themselves as related to one or more of those instrumentalities, yet they would have no meaning without an underlying value system.

Hermeneutics and Value Systems

In the case of personal value systems, which aren't just matters of fact, hermeneutics is more complicated than usual. Even careful introspection offers at best a limited escape from the hermeneutic circle. Numerous generations *felt* that a value system that included racial segregation could be coherent because they evaluated new facts in terms of their overall previously formed value system. Even if careful introspection could have uncovered layer after layer of implicit and internally conflicting emotional meanings, this process would have been slow to reveal why they had already accepted a certain overall worldview.[1] Whichever values we commit to at a given time are the ones we count on to help create an ongoing sense of meaningful action trajectory on an everyday basis, until new thinking and experience motivate us to change. And this process is opposed continuously by the seductions of confabulatory thinking.

This reliance on hermeneutical interpretation doesn't have to catapult us into some form of value nihilism. We are often tempted to throw up our hands. "Aren't values merely cultural conventions or emotional preferences?" "Isn't thinking that some opinions are better than others just arrogant and narrow-minded?" At this point, nihilism itself might appear to be the most *coherent* standpoint. After all, nihilism seems to assert nothing, and therefore might contain the fewest ungrounded assumptions, the least potential for logical contradiction, and for contradiction of facts.

In an age when films evoke our sympathy for bank robbers and Mafiosi, we are offered an attitude that isn't entirely nihilistic but does entice us toward thinking that values are mere social conventions or accidental emotional preferences, as in "I like ice cream." Even if I, personally, happen to value *all* valuing creatures, this would be only a contingent fact about my own emotions, not a belief that those creatures would have value independently of whether I personally happen to value them. It wouldn't commit to the feeling that their intrinsic value is "real."

People who were directly or indirectly influenced by the moral ideas of intellectuals in the days of twentieth-century logical empiricism may have been especially attracted to this view—as in A. J. Ayer's (1946, 1965) equating of "Murder is wrong" with "I don't like murder" or an emotional expression like "Boo murder!" Many social science and literature professors studied philosophy from teachers of that generation, and many TV and film producers as college students were exposed in turn to the second-hand philosophy of those literature and social science professors. Logical empiricism, in this respect, is the intellectual grandfather of today's popular culture—and also of certain aspects of postmodernism in philosophy, which ironically began with a rebellion *against* logical empiricism. We sometimes grant too easily the assumptions of our intellectual predecessors, even while rebelling against them.

The presumptive universality of claims about value (sometimes called "moral realism"—that values exist independently of our personal feelings) tends to arouse the suspicions of our cosmopolitan times.[2] But at the same time, the value of a friend doesn't seem dependent on the fact that I personally happen to value them. We sometimes want to say that the friend's value is an independent reality in the sense that anyone with a capacity for empathy and a coherent thought pattern *would* respect that person's value if the same amount of attention were paid to their valuing dimension. As Simone de Beauvoir implies in *The Ethics of Ambiguity*, this stronger kind of value statement applies not just to specific individuals such as my personal friends, but to any valuing creature (anyone who, in her terms, is a *pour soi* rather than an *en soi*—a "for itself" rather than an "in itself"*)*.

In the same way, we can have "realist" conceptions of *aesthetic* values. For instance, rather than "I appreciate this musical work, but that's just me," someone might assert, *"Anyone* who pays careful attention and sees the potential for certain emotional meanings in this work *would* appreciate and value it." This doesn't imply that a work could have only one "objective" meaning, but rather that it could have *some* meaning for anyone who understands it and pays attention. In this way, we can distinguish between Mozart and Salieri, even though a nuts-and-bolts analysis would reveal them as being very similar to each other in technical terms.

Patrick Howard (2012) suggests that much of the value of an artwork is that it offers possible material for the "symbolization" aspect of a focusing process for a variety of potential users of the art—that a good work offers this focusing possibility somewhat *flexibly*, for a wide diversity of potential users (see also Ellis 1999, 2021). Salieri's absolutely unambiguous chord progressions try to tell us what to feel. Mozart's less predictable progressions offer endless possibilities.

The "Dog Story" in Ann Weiser Cornell's *Radical Acceptance of Everything* is an example of how a literary piece can resonate with the focusing processes of a variety of different users facing different circumstances. The story likens the disowned, disliked, and disclaimed parts of ourselves to a once-beloved dog who wasn't allowed into the house and eventually wandered away and became wild and disheveled and possibly mean or dangerous. But if we can go into the woods and befriend the dog, its true value might be reclaimed, and it might eventually follow us home. To say that this story "has aesthetic value," in the sense that it can resonate with a variety of readers, is a *factual* claim (true or false), not merely a subjective feeling.

Value sentiments too can be statements about "objective reality" in a similar sense—values whose reality is accessible to "anyone." A complete relativism of value—the notion that value statements are only arbitrary emotional preferences—can create as much of a problem for the sense of enactive meaning as the opposite temptation of totalizing or "Grand Scheme" value systems. If the value of my friend is only a whim, similar to "I like ice cream," then the friend's value becomes only an instrumental value, in the service of whichever of *my own emotions* the friend might happen to serve. This would assume that only *my* valuing of him is what endows him with value. The relevance of this problem to the ongoing sense of underlying meaning is that we can't easily feel very inspired by a merely instrumental value, unless there is a real intrinsic value that the instrumental one serves, at least implicitly.

There is no need to worry that acknowledging the value of, say, a serial killer—by virtue of the fact that the serial killer himself is a valuing creature—might undermine the value of protecting future potential victims. The need to balance conflicting values doesn't negate their value, any more than the value of freedom of expression negates the laws against inciting a lynching. Choosing between cake and ice cream doesn't negate the value of the one not chosen. Different *prima facie* values can come into conflict with each other, and choices have to be made.

With the need to balance conflicting values in mind, and also the need for a commensurability of moral and nonmoral values (they both have to be weighed into real-life decisions), one of the central points I want to make about the always-presupposed intrinsic values that ground the sense of enactive meaning is this:

1. Suppose, out of fear, or a political ideology or for some other reason, I ignore or deny the idea that the value of conscious, valuing creatures is *simply by virtue of* the fact that they are conscious and valuing creatures per se (and therefore universal). If I reject this notion, then I must implicitly feel that their value is only by virtue of something else—something other than the sheer fact that they are valuing creatures. People then could have value only if they serve some other purpose beyond the fact that they are valuing creatures.

2. This would mean that rather than having intrinsic value, people would have value only by *serving instrumental ends*—as good workers, good Christians, good athletes or musicians, or even serving the purpose of bringing pleasure and happiness to me personally.

3. By implicitly feeling that people can have value only to the extent that they serve some *other* purpose beyond themselves, I then end up asking myself what other purpose that could be. Is it enough to serve the purpose of being a good worker, a good soldier, a good athlete, etc.? What could have more intrinsic value than conscious and valuing creatures themselves?

4. If the answer is: "Really, nothing!" then there is a problem with treating valuing creatures as having at best only instrumental value. In the absence of any intrinsic value, either for valuing creatures themselves or for any purpose they might instrumentally serve, I am now in danger of becoming ensnared in a partial or complete value nihilism—the attitude that nothing "*really*" matters at all.

5. I want to suggest further that, to the extent that we are deprived of the opportunity to appreciate with a positive emotional valence the intrinsic value of valuing creatures per se—to value them intrinsically rather than instrumentally—we will end up suffering from a shortage of the "inspiration"

dimension of the SEEKING system, either in general, or in selective contexts. We will have trouble feeling "enthusiastic" or "energized" by values that ultimately must connect, indirectly through a chain of instrumentalities, to those very creatures who must be counted as having value if anything does—the most likely candidates for the assertion "X *really does* have value" (not merely in the sense that "I like ice cream").

Someone might insist that our own pleasure is enough to ground enactive meaning, and that no further intrinsic value is needed. But this would ignore the fact that the social bonding systems, CARE, PANIC, and also PLAY, and to some extent even LUST, do create the feeling that certain individuals, at least, do have intrinsic value. CARE and PANIC, for instance, are willing to trade the mother's pleasure for the child's safety. Even in Panksepp's most extensive formulation of the brain's LUST system (1998), there was considerable emphasis on the overlap between the LUST and CARE systems—for example, the emphasis on the care-inducing neurotransmitters oxytocin, prolactin, and vasopressin. The brain is flooded with oxytocin after sexual intercourse, triggering the CARE system for both males and females. The feelings triggered by these social bonding systems don't regard the other as merely instrumental toward my own pleasure. The other's value is felt as intrinsic, not just instrumental. We don't feel that the other's value would cease if we were to die tomorrow.

The SEEKING system, also independently, motivates us to notice that the one property by virtue of which we intrinsically value someone—the sheer fact that they are valuing creatures—applies to everyone. We therefore acknowledge, at least implicitly, that intrinsic value can be found in all valuing creatures, simply *by virtue of* being valuing creatures per se, independently of whether they serve some other interest, including my own well-being or pleasure.

Some may argue that it is *not* simply "by virtue of being a valuing creature" that we take someone to have intrinsic value. Instead, maybe we consider them to have intrinsic value by virtue of being a *virtuous* valuing creature—that the person is smart, noble, talented, or "beautiful" in some sense. But this path can lead down two dangerous rabbit holes.

First, when we ask ourselves what our criteria for "virtue" consist of, we find that we are focusing on the person's *instrumental* value in the service of whatever makes them virtuous—excellent music, excellent scientific achievement, our own and others' enjoyment of their beauty, and so on. To the extent that the valuing depends on some virtue, it depends on the person's instrumental as opposed to intrinsic value. If a promising child decides to drop out of medical school, don't we still intrinsically value the child? If not, we have tacitly given up on the one thing that could be a reasonable candidate for intrinsic as opposed to merely instrumental value. Granted, this acknowledgment of intrinsic value is also in *internal emotional conflict* with the need for instrumentalization, as we already discussed. And experiencing the person's instrumental virtues can also serve as a matrix of *symbolization* for the sense of their intrinsic value.

There is still another reason for the priority of the experience of the other's intrinsic value as such. I described in *Eros in a Narcissistic Culture* the curious way in which the "admiration" dimension of love (the strong intrinsic valuing of another creature, as distinguished from the need to *be* loved) is actually magnified in intensity when combined with the "compassion" dimension. Compassion in this sense includes not just sympathy for suffering, but also concern for both actual and possible threats to the person's ability to exist—to be who they are—including not only the threat of death, of powerlessness, of insignificance in the grand scheme of things, but also the threat of potential for alienation from relationships that are needed in order to be who they are. We empathize not only with threats to the person's physical existence, but also with threats to the possibility of their self-motivated action potential—threats that include the inevitability of death at the end and the inevitable limitations of the person's powers and social relatedness.

This "compassion" dimension, which paradoxically intensifies our feelings of admiration, directs itself not toward the person's specific virtues, but rather to the simple fact that the person is a conscious and finite creature with all the vulnerability that comes with such. But we can't fully empathize with all these threats to the possibility of a person's being if we are in denial that such threats actually *are* significant threats—to *ourselves* as well as to the other person. So a further paradox here is that acknowledging the seriousness of threats to enactive meaning is part of experiencing the meaning of someone's enactive life trajectory per se—a person's project of being who they are.

The Hermeneutic Circle and "Terror Management"

The "terror management theory" of Greenberg et al. (1997) pursues this last point even further. The theory focuses specifically on the way threats to the existential aspect of meaning affect the interpretative process. These theorists connect the stubbornness of hermeneutical presuppositions with the most ontologically necessary challenges for meaningful action—the underlying anxieties about our fundamentally finite and interdependent condition—and the temptation to deny or repress those threats. Their work is largely inspired by Ernest Becker's *The Denial of Death*. Becker had personally witnessed the ultimate instances of gruesome devaluation of what it means to be a human being. Born in the United States to Jewish parents who barely escaped the rise of Nazism in Germany, he served in the U.S. Army unit that liberated many of the death camps.

Becker is concerned not only with denial of death, but also with denial of *all aspects* of our finiteness—including our inevitable smallness and insignificance and the ubiquitous potential for alienation. Avoiding acknowledgment of any of these aspects of our radical finiteness can distort our views about various kinds of life issues, including what we have called enactive values.

In the Becker/Greenberg analysis, if the significance of our actions is taken to depend on a belief system that simply denies the conditions of finiteness, then there will be a need to explain away inconsistent facts. The result, in the Becker/Greenberg analysis, is a systematically distorted approach to all aspects of our lives, like the "red-shift" of a telescope in rapid motion relative to its object. From the "terror management" standpoint, the attempt to deny the problem of finiteness reflects this kind of distortion.

Grand Scheme value systems try to fend off the existential challenge against feeling more important and in control of our destiny than any of us actually can be, as finite and interrelational creatures. Vicariously enjoying the apparent (and mostly illusory) power and importance of a cult leader serves to deflect from our own feelings of smallness and powerlessness—our finiteness on all fronts.

But a little-appreciated part of Becker's analysis is that he also stresses a contrary danger for those who *don't* define value in terms of a Grand Scheme. In that case, we may try to avoid the whole issue of finiteness by insisting that death, interpersonal alienation, or personal powerlessness and insignificance are things that don't concern us to begin with. In Becker's view, this approach is also problematic because those existential issues, as I argued earlier, do matter. We contort our thinking to avoid these disturbing issues, sometimes resorting to the convoluted reasoning exemplified by absurd cults of disinformation.

Becker grants that some forms of religion, even while including some "ultimatizing" values such as the Will of God, may not be totalizing in this sense. In thoughtful theologies, there are more expansive viewpoints that include both subjectively grounded values (especially the value of subjective creatures themselves) *and* "ultimate" or "Grand Scheme" values. For instance, personalist and process theologians (e.g., Edgar Brightman 1933, Thomas Buford 2011, Randall Auxier 1995) present such sophisticated metaphysical theories. These religious systems do *include* the value of valuing creatures as creating value, at least prima facie, because not to do so would lead to incoherence.

Such metaphysical ideas inevitably propose ontological interconnections between the personal and the ultimate. Both process and personalist theology are congruent with Mark Bickhard's "interactivism" (2000)—that a process is what it is only in relation to all other processes. The value of valuing creatures, in sophisticated religious systems, is always made *commensurable* with the proposed "ultimate" values.

Even the simplest, most speculative, and fantasy-driven religions, when guided by their "better angels," do preach universalized altruism, although the practitioners often forget. Those who do forget, here again, may find themselves living implicitly just at the edge of nihilism, without completely crossing over. This implicit seminihilism then leaves us vulnerable to the hucksterism of the authoritarian leader. We see historically that religious fundamentalists are among the first to follow fascist, terrorist, or authoritarian political movements. Adorno and colleagues (1964) demonstrate this pattern empirically, as substantially replicated in many of Altemeyer's studies.

Privileging the Grand Scheme over our own and others' intrinsic value even undermines the feeling of the intrinsic value of deities or saints. Concretely speaking, if Thomas Moore is our favorite saint, rejecting the intrinsic value of valuing creatures *as such* also weakens our admiration through compassion for Moore himself. The compassion dimension of admiration directs itself to the sheer fact that the person is a subjectively conscious and valuing, yet finite creature.

Betting everything on a Grand Scheme value leads to still another complication. Our own finiteness challenges our ability to serve the Grand Scheme effectively and to a significant extent. We therefore tend to exaggerate our own importance. Galileo's telescope must be rejected if it removes us humans from the center of the universe. Similarly, if an exaggerated doctrine of "free will" is needed for a feeling of controlling our destiny (the existential challenge of powerlessness), we might then denigrate the poor for failing to use their free will to "pull themselves up by their bootstraps."

The reified doctrine in this case tends to further undermine the intrinsic value of the valuing creatures themselves. Belief in a "just God" can lead to versions of the "Prosperity Gospel." Being wealthy proves that you deserved the reward; the logical implication, of course, is that the poor and downtrodden deserve their fate. The value system becomes increasingly casuistic and incoherent. The Grand Scheme has obscured the most basic intrinsic value that was needed for the sense of meaning—which in turn is implicitly presupposed to ground the value of the instrumentalities themselves.

Hermeneutics and the Tension between Intrinsic and Instrumental Value

Ironically, the "totalizing" value system—the erection of an "ultimate value," such as the Fatherland or the Will of God, which we all presumably ought to serve—seems superficially as if it could make up for a shortage of enactive meaning. But we have seen that this move threatens to compete against the feeling of our intrinsic value as such, as well as the intrinsic value of others. To the extent that *instrumental* service to some Grand Scheme value is necessary for meaning, the simple *intrinsic* value of a creature's mere existence can't seem sufficient.

Even those who think they eschew Grand Schemes still find themselves with feelings such as "I recorded my music brilliantly, but it doesn't get nearly as many hits on the internet as others, so what's the point?" "I do good academic work, but too few people read my books or articles, so what is my life really worth?" "Oh no! I just learned that my twitter posts have hardly any following!" In each case, we succumb to the temptation to treat our value as if it were to be evaluated primarily in instrumental terms.

We have no choice but to erect "extended" value systems and thus make ourselves into instrumental values in their service, to a greater or lesser extent. As soon as we value anything intrinsically, the need for a baseline level of inspiration requires constructing a complex series of *instrumental* values that delineate our life activities to give them "purpose." But the edifice of instrumental values is still implicitly derivative from the basic intrinsic value of valuing creatures themselves. There is always a delicate balance between these instrumental and intrinsic values. The more we feel our own and others' value in terms of successful service to the instrumental values, the greater the danger that these projects will compete against the simple intrinsic value of valuing creatures a such.

It would be beyond our scope here to go into the various contingent *causes* of this overemphasis on instrumentality. Neglect of the universality of the intrinsic value of valuing creatures can result from many contingent life events. We may have been rejected too many times ourselves, chronically enflaming the PANIC system. Whenever we have committed ourselves to fully experiencing the intrinsic value of someone—for example in family or love relationships—the response all too often may have been a lack of reciprocity. This rejection could throw the PANIC system into a chaotic and eventually oversensitized condition.

Even attempts to *nurture* someone may have been rejected, as in the case of Fitzgerald's Dick Diver in *Tender Is the Night*. Diver is devastated by the fact that his recovering psychoanalytic patient no longer needs his nurturing. The result is a triggering of Diver's PANIC system. Panksepp shows that both PANIC and CARE (sometimes called NURTURANCE) are endogenous emotions that always must be expressed in some way. Underneath PANIC, as we saw earlier, is a deprivation of a more positive experience: the need to experience the intrinsic value of another creature. One of the dangers of this unleashing of PANIC is that we may become afraid to extend our nurturing in the future.

Conversely, but in a similar dynamic, whenever I affirm my *own* intrinsic value, simply by virtue of my existence and not by being a good athlete or good musician, this affirmation may have earned me a pushback from others. Only by instrumentally serving other purposes—music or athletics—could I feel valued. The implication was that I don't have intrinsic value; I can have at best only instrumental value. The meaning of an artist's life may become so entirely invested in the approval of art critics or art buyers that the PANIC system can go into hyperdrive.

But if I can't have intrinsic value simply by virtue of being a valuing creature, *neither can anyone else*. The very idea of being a conscious being then comes to seem intrinsically valueless, even as we try valiantly to invest it with more and more *instrumental* value. The use of an artist's work by other humans for their own emotional purposes then becomes valueless as well—and the same for any other kind of work we might do. The fact that a few art lovers strongly resonated with the artist's work now fails to inspire. Only a *New York Times* headline or a first prize at the Sorbonne can be good enough. Combine this with the problem that to intrinsically value someone (let alone everyone) might involve too much fear of potential hyperactivity for the PANIC system.

Causation might also be circular. Targeted suppression of SEEKING activity (including the exploratory drive), as in authoritarian tendencies, can selectively demotivate normal, everyday curiosity about these complicated value relationships; in some cases, childhood moral development might be impeded. We then diminish our ability to experientially universalize our valuation of others in practice, even while espousing moral platitudes—as evidenced in the correlations between authoritarian personality and racism (Altemeyer 2008; Duriez and Soenens 2009) and also between authoritarianism and religious intolerance (Adorno et al. 1964). In the extreme case, only family members, "fellow travelers," and others who are close at hand or serve some particular instrumental purpose can have value. This seminihilism of value can lead to a lack of everyday inspiration and thus can further inhibit SEEKING activity.

From the Particular to the Universal in Development

Even if we fail to intrinsically value others as a *universal* set, the social bonding emotion systems continue to kick in and prevent an absolute devaluation of at least *some* others. Unless we are literally complete psychopaths (a somewhat rare condition), we *can't avoid* valuing at least some people. This valuing is driven by both the PANIC and CARE systems. In these cases, valuing someone requires little more than paying *attention* to their own valuing dimension. As we come to know an adopted child, we direct more and more attention to the child's valuing dimension, and thus we feel more and more the intrinsic value of the child.

So it isn't rocket science for a developing child to eventually begin to notice that we *would* also recognize the intrinsic value of any other valuing creature *if we were* to direct a similar amount of attention to their valuing dimension. Our human prefrontal capacity makes this kind of realization not only possible, but also crucially motivated by the innate exploratory drive.

I remember noticing as a young child that when my father was injured, he wasn't immune to pain and suffering in the way I had tacitly assumed. He was capable of eliciting the same kind of empathic feeling on my part that had been triggered when my dog was hit by a car. Eventually, I learned, as most children eventually do, that any conscious creature could elicit this same kind of feeling. I understood that any valuing creature could warrant the same kind of action to alleviate pain and suffering, whether I was in a position to do so or not.

In short, I felt that the value of the creature in question wasn't contingent on my ability to act on their behalf, or even on whether I was aware of them. Their value wasn't contingent on the fact of my valuing them. To put the same point in a different way, I noticed that conscious creatures *afford* our act of valuing their well-being simply *by virtue of* being valuing creatures—not just because they might be in a position to serve some other purpose that we also value.

What is difficult is to *avoid* understanding this simple implication of the nature of valuing; we avoid it only through elaborate ideologies and hermeneutical distortions of each new experience. For this reason, Levinas (1969) argues that we can't escape the "ethical" demand we feel when confronting "the face" of another human being. In my view, this is because we can't avoid the fact (try though we may) that taking anyone to have intrinsic value requires taking everyone to have it.

By using the metaphor of "the face," Levinas imagistically connects the valuing of everyone to the value of a single individual. But we have already seen some problems with a tendency to be overly dependent on imagery such as "the face" to trigger empathic feelings. Positive feelings toward offspring or mates or even clan members—or an elderly woman trying to change a tire—can easily be triggered by *imagery* of those individuals. Universalized compassion for valuing creatures *as such* is more difficult. It requires more than direct imagery of someone whose "face" we can see or image.

Feminist philosophers such as Carol Gilligan (1982) and Drucilla Cornell (1995), in a way that is too little appreciated, argue that moral development has to go beyond mere empathy; it moves us toward the ability to "universalize" our empathy. Their thinking on this point is not entirely different from David Hume's in his *Treatise of Human Nature* (1740). Hume, also in a way too often ignored, says that beyond mere "fellow feeling" itself, the *universalization* of fellow feeling is motivated by an innate "love of truth"—in more contemporary terms, an independent exploratory drive. This demand to universalize human concern implicitly occurs to most of us in the everyday process of feeling the underlying meaning of our actions. It enables us to expand the realm of values in the sense Peter Singer uses in the title of his major work, *The Expanding Circle* (1981/2011).

In the absence of such an expansion of the realm of intrinsic value, we might begin to search out some "ultimate" value such as the Fatherland or the Will of God—or even the Image of the Perfect Family or the Ideal of the Cool Rock Band—relative to which we could have instrumental value. But then we implicitly reduce everyone to a merely instrumental value. We overlook the value of those who *fail* to serve the ultimate end—those who don't serve the Dear Leader, the Company's Bottom Line, the Image of the Perfect Family, or the Final Battle.

Worse still, from this seminihilistic standpoint, even those who *do* dutifully serve the Ultimate End can still have at best only instrumental, not intrinsic value. At this point, we have deprived ourselves of the one thing that we could reasonably feel really does have value aside from our own arbitrary whims—valuing creatures themselves. This leads to an impoverishment of valuing and, as a result, a feeling that there is a shortage of the underlying enactive meanings that direct our action trajectories—an implicitly nihilistic or seminihilistic outlook, or a living just at the edge of nihilism. At this point, we might not yet have arrived at complete nihilism, but we have become like trees in water-logged ground, waiting for any wind to push us over.

Like a flashlight that illumines everything except itself, the question of enactive meaning touches every aspect of life. As we have seen, it becomes a major issue in depression, anxiety, and other psychological struggles, both pathological and normal (as in the work of May, Frankl, Yalom, Goleman, and Greenberg.). It works as both cause and symptom of harmful and irrational social movements such as fascism, cults of disinformation, and ethnic or religious animosities of all kinds. The need to avoid a feeling of enactive meaninglessness implicitly undergirds much of our philosophical thinking—whether in an academic or an everyday setting. Often indirectly, but no less importantly, this need determines our decisions about the way we live our lives and the priority of different values in our lives and our work.

Conclusions

The Embodied Mind and the "That for the Sake of Which"

To be what we are is to engage in motivated actions. Whatever either facilitates or blocks or threatens to block the ability to act has meaning. Nico Frijda describes the corresponding emotional meanings as "action readinesses."

Action in turn presupposes value. But instrumental values, often unconsciously, are in the service of other instrumental values, forming a chain that ultimately depends on intrinsic values. Every passing emotion implicitly refers, among other things, to these intrinsic values—or a shortage of them or uncertainty about them.

Action is a feature of self-organizing systems. Any creature making a judgment with regard to the values that can inspire action must be the kind of being that can generate purposes with instrumental connections to values that in turn depend on intrinsic ones. If value means that something warrants taking action, then the problem of nihilism, or living close to the edge of nihilism, can be understood in terms of whether values can inspire action. Under the surface of this problem is the question of the difference between action and mere reaction. Action requires organizing and directing ourselves. Reaction is easier. It requires only that the environment provides a roadmap offering us direct visual images.

Consciousness—that which we subjectively sense while awake or dreaming, but which fades when neither of those conditions is present—can be built only on the platform of the motivational system of an organism. Self-organization, thus the ability to act, is one of the main differences between an emotional (and living) being and a nonemotional information-processing machine, such as a nuts-and-bolts computer, lacking in subjective consciousness. As cognitive theorists often say, there is nothing that "it is like" to be a robot.

For creatures with consciousness of the kind that humans and other mammals experience, the requisite motivational system includes the "emotional brain"—or more accurately, the emotional brain/body systems. Many philosophers and neuroscientists have supported this last point in recent decades (Damasio, Frijda, Gallagher, Gendlin, Newton, Panksepp, Shevrin, Watt, and Zachar, just to name a few). Granted, our organisms do process incredible amounts of information, but the difference between conscious and nonconscious information-processing systems is that non-organismic machines don't process the information in a *self-organizing* and *organismically purpose-directed* way.

Merleau-Ponty, Gibson, and other earlier action theorists showed that we animal creatures don't only possess computer-like signaling pathways such as occur in microcircuits, although our nervous systems can do that too. In addition, we also understand the world by imagining how we could act in relation to it—understanding its "affordances." When I understand the shape of a bowl, I subliminally imagine performing actions relative to it—for example, running my hand over its surface, filling it with liquid, or conducting measurements on it.

A robot with a mechanical hand may move its hand, but only as an extended series of *re*-actions, not as a holistically and self-organizationally motivated action. In recent years, neurologists have exploited this self-organizing dimension of the living brain in terms of "neural plasticity"—leading to new methods of stroke recovery, better learning methods, new treatments for psychiatric disorders, and even ways to help with Alzheimer's and other forms of progressive dementia. Each of these treatment methods requires some effort on the patient's own part to energize and enact the new patterns of "neural plasticity" involved.

Self-organization makes possible action as opposed to mere reaction, and action presupposes value. But getting at the underlying "for the sake of which" of the emotional values of our actions is more complicated than it appears. It may seem simple that our experience of the value of valuing creatures as such could be taken as an enthusiastically motivating intrinsic value and that our social bonding emotions would feel this value strongly enough. But the social bonding emotions aren't sufficiently universalized until the exploratory drive (part of the SEEKING system) motivates development of an overall value system. Already at that point, there are multiple conflicts within our own emotional life—between PANIC and SEEKING, between curiosity and the desire to embrace Grand Scheme fantasies, between honest acceptance of finiteness and narcissistic delusions.

Even then, an additional layer of conflict arises, between the intrinsic and the instrumental—that is, between the need to extend the realm of meaningful values by instrumentalizing ourselves and others on the one hand, and on the other hand, the need to maintain the sufficiency of their intrinsic value and our own. These two types of value, the intrinsic and the instrumental, engage in a constant struggle. The more important the value is that we are trying to instrumentally serve, the more we regard our own and others' instrumental value as *necessary* for the meaning of our actions—and consequently the less important a role is played by our own or others' *intrinsic* value.

This instrumentalization of ourselves is an inexorable necessity, alongside the need to value ourselves and others as intrinsic values—valuable simply for their own sake, regardless of any instrumentality—creating a constant inner conflict. We are always in danger of losing the foundation of the reality of our value system, the locus of intrinsic value, and a resulting loss of enactive meaning, even for the various instrumentalities. The instrumentalities themselves then threaten to become meaningless.

Each passing emotion might seem superficially to be about an immediate instrumentality, such as getting to the hardware store, but in reality, they are about all the instrumentalities implicit in the situation, as well as the intrinsic values that they serve. All of this is already complicated even before *inter*personal conflicts enter into the situation.

All too easily, we think we are "angry" at a colleague, when actually we might be frustrated with some aspect of our overall existential condition. We feel small, powerless, alienated, or fearful of potential alienation. Each little problem embodies these bigger problems. If we misrepresent to ourselves the significance of the little ones, we might think for example that the purpose of our work is to win career acclaim, which we then assess as a somewhat overly narcissistic goal and thus not really important enough to strongly motivate action. We then lapse into a seminihilism. But when we trace the purpose of our actions and the correlative values to the existential dimension, we may find ourselves buoyed up and pushed along by the inspiration they offer. Serving at the local soup kitchen may not eliminate hunger from the Grand Scheme of Things, but the action can offer meaning. Volunteering as a vote counter might achieve nothing beyond receiving death threats from fascist extremists, but the activity still has symbolizing value.

When we decide which values are worth engaging in, the real question is not which words we use and how we define them, but whether we regard some given value as *worthy of action*—action either by ourselves or by others. The nihilist or seminihilist is unable to be moved to action by "merely subjective" valuations and expresses this inability by saying that, "really," it "makes no difference in the ultimate scheme of things" whether anyone achieves what they value. Values are "only subjective."

We saw that such a sentiment can seduce us into an oversimplified dichotomy between "subjective" and "ultimate" values, as if only the "ultimate" ones were "real" in some objective sense. But the seminihilist—the person living just at the edge of nihilism—experiences just enough shortage of inspiration that "merely subjective" concerns can't provide much impetus to action. So the hope, always dashed, is for some Grand Scheme value that might seem more "ultimate."

If the main value of myself or other conscious creatures is to serve some "larger purpose"—as virtuous musicians, athletes, teachers, business people, or soldiers of the Revolution—then I have reduced myself and other valuing creatures to the status of instrumental values, in the service of those other aims. To the extent that we implicitly devalue ourselves for failing to serve the ultimatized aim, the Grand Scheme will tend to undermine the feeling that our own consciousness or anyone else's has *intrinsic* value, simply by virtue of the fact that we are conscious and valuing beings per se. If valuing creatures themselves don't have intrinsic value, we experience an underlying confusion as to what the purpose of any of our actions is, and consequently what the corresponding emotions are about.

This idea of replacing subjective values with an objectified "Grand Scheme" value is the very notion that De Beauvoir warns against in *The Ethics of Ambiguity*. We try to reduce the valuing creature's value to an instrumental value, when in fact they are the very source of value. If we feel that the value of valuing creatures doesn't create "enough" value to make life meaningful enough, it isn't because we lack a Grand Scheme, but because we are experiencing a mild shortage of what the clinically depressed person lacks in the extreme: the ability to feel a minimal baseline level of inspiration.

The feeling of inspiration is a natural part of Panksepp's SEEKING system, which is present in all animals, especially mammals. If inspiration is in short supply, the SEEKING system is being either selectively or generally suppressed. This same emotion system—the SEEKING system—also subserves exploration. The connection between these two functions is illustrated by the ability of sinister social movements to play on feelings of meaninglessness to subvert the otherwise reasonable questioning and truth-seeking process that normally would block the cultists' recruitment attempts, by allowing the potential recruit to recognize the absurdity of the cult's offerings.

Suppression of a sense of meaning and the *selective* suppression of truth seeking share overlapping brain-emotional substrates—here again, involving the SEEKING system. A similarly compartmentalized blocking of the same truth-seeking function could undergird more everyday psychological defenses such as denial, repression, projection, and the grandiose fantasies of narcissistic disturbance.

The exploratory drive, an aspect of the SEEKING system, exists in all mammals, but in humans it operates on a more sophisticated level than simply exploration of the physical environment. The selective and often deliberate suppression of the exploratory aspects of this motivational system can play a crucial role in xenophobic and generally distorted social bonding processes, manifested in PANIC.

In these cases, targeted and selective suppression of the exploratory drive requires intricate patterns of ad hoc hypothesis, selective inattention, exaggerated confirmation bias, and highly specific suppressions of the truth-seeking and exploratory motivations. This is not a cognitive impairment, but a motivational one. Like every other behavior, truth-seeking behavior has to be motivated. Convoluted intellectual casuistry can then be used to deny the intrinsic value of large categories of fellow valuing creatures, as well as beneficial interpersonal norms.

This seminihilistic attitude is by no means confined to fascists or to people who are inclined toward totalitarian, cultist, or terrorist attitudes. A similar flirting with nihilism can manifest itself even in the most "normal" case, in selective suppression of the SEEKING system.

In Arendt's analysis, a fascist follower's cynical negation of value—especially the value of certain religious or ethnic groups or anyone who isn't on board with "the movement"—represents a nihilistic or at best seminihilistic outlook. In Frankl's sense, this degree of nihilism both arises from and exacerbates an underlying struggle with the problem of meaning. The value of many categories of people has been eliminated from the sense of meaning. In the thinking of existential psychologists such as Frankl, Yalom, and Stolorow, much of the sporadic targeting of the suppressed exploration toward truth, via selective attention and inattention, hinges on the need to meet the larger existential challenges to the emotional meanings that have defined the purpose of people's action trajectories, and which for one reason or another have come to seem tenuous. All these underlying issues are reflected in each passing emotion.

In the most extreme example of value nihilism, the sudden murderer, in the instant of the act, attributes literally no value even to the *murderer's own* well-being. The murder yields no gain, and punishment is inevitable. The absolute devaluation of the other implicitly devalues the self, because both self and other are instances of "valuing creature"—that *by virtue of which* valuing creatures could have intrinsic rather than instrumental value, and in relation to which all instrumental actions ultimately are defined. Similarly, the family annihilator type of murderer begins by investing value only in the immediate family, thus attributing no intrinsic value to humanity in general. When the family can no longer instrumentally serve this purpose—because, implicitly, they have lost their intrinsic value along with the rest of humanity—then both family and killer lack value and their annihilation can seem justifiable.

While the family annihilator devalues everyone except for the immediate family, in a less extreme example, the fascist follower implicitly devalues those who don't serve the ultimate purposes of the clan or the cause. In effect, we are all then reduced to instrumental value, but without an adequate basis for a "that for the sake of which"—that toward which we are supposed to be instrumental.

In effect, the xenophobe, like the sudden murderer and the family annihilator, but to a lesser extent and for different reasons, views the world from the standpoint of a partial value nihilism. But in the confabulatory hermeneutical worldview of the authoritarian, the narrowing of valuational focus is intentionally *self*-imposed, while in the despairing nihilism of the sudden murderer and family annihilator the dampening of the SEEKING system is global and unplanned.

Such attitudes represent a narrowing of the person's feeling of the intrinsic value of being a human being as such. Whenever we try to deny the prima facie value of some particular valuing creature, or of some category of valuing creatures, we implicitly deny that *any* valuing creature has intrinsic value, simply by virtue of being a valuing creature. This implicitly diminishes the value of *every* creature (including ourselves and our loved ones), construing them as having merely instrumental value, in the service either of my own interests and emotions, or of some supposedly "Grand Scheme" value.

When former military opponents meet for a battle re-enactment, the soldiers' inspirational feelings often move them to tears as the former enemies hug each other. By reminding themselves that even the enemy has intrinsic value, they intensify the feeling that being a conscious and valuing creature has intrinsic value, no matter what the circumstances and no matter how many grievances they might have against each other.

It is sometimes assumed that some cultures throughout history and prehistory have simply *defined* value as being applicable only to their own tribe or group. It might seem easy to speculate that the apparent tendency to commit genocide during certain periods of history could stem from this impulse. Similarly with the recently resurgent "white nationalism" movements in the United States and Europe. Someone might still wonder why such an "expanded" egoistic hedonism—in the sense of valuing only a limited selection of valued others—couldn't be at least a "natural" position. Couldn't "value" simply be limited to whatever someone in *my family or tribe or nation* values?

But we tend to give earlier versions of humanity too little credit for having the same neuropsychological equipment that we now have in our brains. If feelings of inner conflict are grounded in a natural respect for truth, driven by the exploratory drive, then the ancient Hebrew or Canaanite soldier must have felt the same ambiguities about killing other valuing creatures for purely political reasons that our contemporary soldiers still feel. We saw evidence earlier that there was considerably more fluidity between early human cultures than often is assumed (for example, Bowles and Gintis 2013; Kelly 2000; De Waal 2006, 2008; Olsen 2002).

As we have already seen, it isn't that "clannists" are literally unaware of the sense in which foreigners have value simply qua valuing creatures. The problem is a failure to focus on this dimension of others, resulting in a shortage of a feeling of inspiration to act in congruence with a more coherent value system. The fact that entire nations of people could do this in unison doesn't change the underlying psychodynamic. Harsh circumstances can severely exacerbate inner conflicts and require brutal emotional compromise. Nonetheless, denial of any human's humanity represents a seminihilistic condition, in which there is a shortage of inspiration except as elicited by specific vivid imagery—the image of the close at hand or clan member, the one who is "like us."

Phillip Luce (1960) in his study of the "White Citizens Councils" shows that extremely harmful social attitudes were adopted by medical doctors, lawyers, talented engineers, and mathematicians. Members of the councils were notably charitable church and community leaders who devoted themselves substantially to the well-being of others, even while supporting extremely harmful racist activities. The reasons for their incoherent value system had little to do with either intellectual capacity or ability to feel empathy. On the contrary, people selectively clouded their own thinking mainly because they were *motivated* to do so.

This failure of curiosity reflects a selective shutting down of the exploratory drive with regard to certain specific issues, as motivated in the ways that Becker, Adorno, and others have discussed. Such tendencies are inevitable temptations for the way the human mind works. Yet as we have seen repeatedly, the attempt to reject the intrinsic value of some groups of valuing creatures inexorably leads to the feeling that valuing creatures can't have intrinsic value, in their own right and simply by virtue of being valuing creatures. The attempt to attribute only instrumental value to such creatures leads to an underlying emotional chaos because no other intrinsic value can strongly enough substitute for the "that for the sake of which." The devaluing of some leads implicitly to a devaluing of all and thus to the subsequent challenge to the sense of enactive meaning.

Conversely, the inspirational effect of the perceived intrinsic value of one valuing creature implicitly "spreads" to include an appreciation of the value of all valuing creatures. A new friend's transition from a seemingly value-neutral to a very valuable status may be gradual rather than sudden; this gradual transition highlights the role of voluntary attention in the act of valuing others; and this in turn raises still further coherence questions against the seminihilism and selective nihilisms described by Arendt in totalitarian and ethnocentric movements.

The totalitarian worldview's negating of the intrinsic value of valuing creatures as such will have already led to a partial nihilism, a living just barely out of reach of psychological desperation. Every devaluation of the supposed enemies of the movement strikes another small blow to the sense of the value of valuing creatures per se. And every ad hoc hypothesis or convoluted conspiracy theory shrinks still further the strength of the SEEKING-system desire to know the truth about the world and ourselves. Continual compartmentalized suppressions of the SEEKING system's exploratory drive are needed to prop up the incoherent value system.

We noticed earlier that, for the clinically depressed person, *vivid imagistic input* is needed to trigger even a mild degree of inspiration. This image dependence represents an involuntary "indexing" of attentional focus to those who afford easy imagery. In the case of extreme depression, the person can't get energized to initiate action, so the only imagery powerful enough to inspire action may well attach to *specific* individuals or groups that can deliver vivid imagery and trigger the reaction—for example, the vivid imagery of suffering animals in late-night TV ads. For the authoritarian, a similar image dependence leads to a failure to universalize respect for the needs of valuing creatures generally.

In clinical depression, the need for vivid imagery in order to be inspired by values seems to be a function of the depression itself—which can result from many factors, including an imbalance of neurotransmitters. In the seminihilism of the "expanded egoist" (for example, the racist or clannist) the causation is almost entirely the reverse. The failure to universalize the valuation of others leads to a kind of limited value nihilism, a lack of empathy *except within a narrow circle*—relative to my own close friends, family, clan, or in-group, for whom I can form concrete imagery. At the same time, feeling the value of valuing creatures exacerbates the potential for PANIC, given the threat of alienation from those whose value we have acknowledged—leading to a vicious spiral between PANIC and SEEKING suppression.[1]

Enflaming of basic existential threats around powerlessness, personal insignificance, alienation from needed others, or death can form the subtext for more specific passing feeling episodes, reflecting an underlying dissatisfaction with our ongoing enactive values. In our chapter on the hot-cold meter, we explored the dynamics of this existential problem. The failure of the hot-cold meter is virtually a shock, as when a person lost in the woods, after frantically wandering aimlessly, suddenly stops and thinks "Hey, wait! I have no idea how to find any good direction here!" A natural reaction to such a radical question is simply to stop the frantic wandering—resulting in suppression of SEEKING. As far as the directions already tried are concerned, we then refrain from feeling inspired to pursue them. We have to reformulate not only which direction to try, but the overall strategy for resolving the situation. Instrumental behaviors then seem to have no value until the question of their "for the sake of which" has been considered.

In the case of authoritarianism, we have seen the self-deceptive maneuvers used by cult followers to simulate meaning. When we don't feel that our actions are meaningful, the hope then tends to be held out for some earthshaking "Grand Scheme" value, such as the pronouncements of the authoritarian leader, that could seem important enough to inspire action. In this case, we have allowed the value of subjective valuations to be evaluated as merely means toward the ends we are trying to pursue. When those ends are thwarted, *all* value then seems to be completely eclipsed.

On the surface, the question of how value comes about seems simple: Does something *have* value in itself, which then is objectively acknowledged when we experience its value—as when we simply perceive blue or yellow? Or is the value of the thing merely *invented* by the fact that we value it? We may then feel that subjective valuations are "not enough," and thus feel a need for there to be some "real" or "objective" value aside from what anyone subjectively values. In spite of acknowledging subjective valuations, we might then want there also to be some objective value "in the ultimate scheme of things"—some value that would exist over and above our subjective valuations.

This oversimplified dichotomy would then lurk under the surface of everything we try to do. The only way any given situation could be satisfactory in the "ultimate" sense would be if we personally were immortal and omnipotent. Only then could we achieve the monumental amount of lasting value that the seminihilistic state demands. Only then could we avoid feeling that "Nothing I do will have any real value" or "There is no way I can have enough power to make much difference in the big picture." Even granted a Grand Scheme value, life would still lack meaning, because the reduction of ourselves to merely instrumental value would amount to a devaluation of our own intrinsic value and that of others.[2]

We saw that there is a paradox in the relationship between "subjective" and "objective" values. We don't say that a friend would have had no intrinsic value if we personally had never existed in order to subjectively attribute that value to them. We feel that the friend's value would still exist independently of us. Conversely, if anything is to have "objective" value in this sense, there must also be subjective values that are important since it is qua subjective creature that the friend is the kind of being that can have intrinsic value. But the friend's value, like the value of valuing creatures generally, isn't "merely" subjective—isn't just an arbitrary whim on my own part. This feeling is important for the inspirational effect that can activate the SEEKING system on a daily basis.

To stake everything on the value of valuing creatures sounds simple, until we consider the equally necessary demand to value ourselves *instrumentally* in the context of an extended value system. The necessary instrumentalization of our own and others' value always tends to be in a zero-sum game against the intrinsic valuing of people. The more I intrinsically value anyone, the more I have to value them *whether or not* they serve some instrumental purpose. The same applies to ourselves. We will always be caught in the struggle between these potentially conflicting tendencies—the tension between the intrinsic and the instrumental value of both ourselves and others.

As is well known among musical performers, only when we begin to listen to ourselves with a critical ear do we begin to improve. Without stern self-criticism, we would live our lives in self-deception, thinking that we were already excellent in our endeavors. So the obviously important goal of nonjudgmentalism—that we should entertain each of our emotional feelings sympathetically and non-directively in order to get in touch with them—always has to be balanced with the need to also evaluate ourselves instrumentally, in the cold light of honest perception.

But we can still find underneath any given passing value feeling the implicit universalization of our feeling of the value of valuing creatures, beyond those who happen to pull our empathy in specific relationships. Even the supposed egoist doesn't value certain selected others only instrumentally. They are valued intrinsically, independently of whether they serve the egoist's interests or not—due to the social bonding systems (such as Panksepp's CARE, PANIC, and PLAY systems). I can neither hold that only my own well-being matters, nor can I coherently maintain the view that the well-being of these others whose value is worthy of action is dependent on the fact that I, the indexical Ralph Ellis, happen to value them. Max Scheler (1954) makes essentially this same point from a phenomenological perspective.

For humans, there is always an implicit question: What are the criteria for inclusion or exclusion from the realm of things that are worth pursuing by virtue of the fact that some given subject values them? Even if I limit the realm of creatures whose valuations matter, I am still taking the position that certain things *other than my own happiness or well-being* are worth pursuing (in other words, have value). An intelligent being with an active exploratory drive then senses that there are further implications of this act of valuing.

The great grandfather of modern Western social thought, Thomas Hobbes, claimed to be an egoistic hedonist—that he intrinsically valued only his own well-being. To defend that view, he created the ad hoc hypothesis that giving money to a beggar made *him*, Hobbes, "feel better"—as if we should believe that it would make a genuine egoistic hedonist "feel better" to violate every ethical precept he believes in rather than to do what he believes is the correct thing. For him, the correct thing should be to remain completely unconcerned with the beggar's well-being except insofar as it affected the egoist's own. There would be no "honor" or "glory" in the mind of a true egoistic hedonist, resulting from acting according to *non*-egoistic principles. If Hobbes had really been an egoistic hedonist, there would have been no reason to feel proud of himself, or in any way to feel "better," by giving money to a beggar. On the contrary, he should refuse and then brag to his friends about how correct his action had been. But instead of following the logical implication of his own egoist position, Hobbes admits that he "feels better" when he helps the beggar.

While the social bonding systems alone can't motivate us to universalize our feelings of care (which requires further exploration and maturation), even this much means that my valuation of those other subjectivities must have an overlap or commonality of meaning with my valuing of my own individual interests. I intrinsically value other valuing creatures *in a sense that is commensurable with* my valuing of myself.

Different "types" of value must be capable of being weighed against each other for decision purposes, otherwise they would be incommensurable. And this means that two different kinds of valuations—those of myself and of at least some valued others—must be allowed within the category of things that potentially can "have value," even if someone were also to posit purely suprasubjective values such as "The Will of God" or "The Balance of Nature." The best way to allocate my responsibility for various others' well-being then becomes a complicated project, requiring maturation and thought.[3]

If we try to form a coherent value system while devaluing entire categories of people, the logic of reality pushes back against this attempt, and we end in incoherence. The difficulty of the attempt to form a coherent attitude on this value question continually pushes back against us. When the reality of a situation resists what we are attempting to do, this can be an indication that we are dealing with something real and not with an arbitrary emotional whim or a mere fantasy.

The underlying attitude of the seminihilist—for example, the terrorist recruit or the white supremacist—represents a selective valuation of others at the expense of a targeted suppression of the SEEKING system. African slaves were in fact human (as was manifestly evident in a thousand ways; Jack Daniel even learned to make whiskey from one of his father's slaves, and much of the managerial and financial work of antebellum Baltimore and other southern US cities and plantations was managed by slaves, as documented in Wade 1967). European governments in fact were not controlled by an "international conspiracy of Jews." All these counterfactual ad hoc hypotheses require still further convolutions of thinking and further suppression of the exploratory drive and consequently of the feeling of the intrinsic value of valuing creatures.

For all of us, the hermeneutic circle will always make it difficult to determine the *extent* of the relevant distortions in any underlying value system that ultimately drives each of our actions. The same prejudices and preconceptions that threaten to distort our thinking may just as easily distort our perception of ourselves in the very process of trying to understand our own preconceived categories and assumptions. Those who strongly want to believe a certain idea, such as their own superiority or the superiority of their race, are tempted to concoct elaborate "conspiracy theories" to justify needed otherwise-unfounded assumptions, or even to make claims that are logically contradictory. These overall value systems are integrally interconnected with the way our PANIC systems function, and their manipulation is facilitated by imbalances of the exploratory drive—an aspect of the SEEKING system.[4]

This point is crucial for the sense of enactive meaning because a disinterest in exploring to discover what is true in the social and moral dimensions affects the ability to feel that being a valuing creature itself has intrinsic value, creating a conflagration of the PANIC system. Yet we can't avoid feeling that at least some valuing creatures have intrinsic value. Instrumental values without some suitably important intrinsic value toward which they can lead tend to lack the power to inspire a baseline level of enthusiasm, as reflected in the SEEKING system.[5]

This underlying feeling of everyday inspiration hinges on the ability to orient an entire coherent value system around a sufficiently intensified feeling of the intrinsic value of valuing creatures as such, including others as well as ourselves. The methods available for such intensification are various, including artistic expression, political action, friendly interpersonal behaviors, and even verbal expression to symbolize the way we feel in a given situation, which ultimately relates to our overall ongoing existential condition. This underlying feeling of intrinsic value then leads to instrumentalizations relative to which the sense of "purpose" can be felt. The trajectories of action around these "purposes" reveal how the world responds, as reflected in both perception and emotion. This pattern of affordances and resistances ultimately shapes our interpretation of reality.

Notes

Introduction

1. For example, Francisco Varela et al. (1993); Giavanna Colombetti (2014); Shaun Gallagher (2006, 2020). A similar concept was proposed under the rubric of "ecological psychology" by Ulric Neisser (1976), and as a "sensorimotor theory of cognition" by Natika Newton (1996). The central idea of enactivism can be traced to nineteenth century pragmatists (for example, William James 1884, 1904), who saw knowledge as resulting from attempts to affect the environment, and then noticing whether the manipulations led to the expected results.

2. The word "consciousness" can be used in many different ways. In the sense that concerns us in this volume, consciousness can't be defined except by experiencing it. But what it consists of can be indicated: Consciousness is the kind of experience that we don't seem to have when in a dreamless sleep. Experiencing this difference is enough to indicate the difference between being conscious and not. But the "seem" here also does some work. We can't be sure that there wasn't consciousness while in a supposedly dreamless sleep—only that we don't remember having been conscious during that time. Nonetheless, we still have a sense of *what it is* that we don't remember. We know what we *mean* by the experience that we don't remember having had.

3. We can already find this action-based view in certain works by Edmund Husserl (1936), Martin Heidegger (1927), William James (1904), and Maurice Merleau-Ponty (1942). Husserl, Heidegger, and Merleau-Ponty already suggested that we first understand the world in terms of its resistance against our actions. Husserl's "life-world" in *The Crisis of European Sciences* (1936/1970) distinguishes the world in which we move around (action) from one that would depend on inferences from perceptual responses (reactions); but those bodily movements themselves already have to be motivated. In a similar vein, Merleau-Ponty's emphasis on "psychophysical forms" in *The Structure of Behavior* (from which Ulric Neisser derives his ecological psychology) is basically a concept of self-organization within the mind/body, which

characterizes the human organism as able to act relative to its world rather than only react (Merleau-Ponty 1942/1967, 47ff). Heidegger too prioritizes action-based understanding in *Being and Time:* The transition from "ready-to-hand" to "present-at-hand" is a way of suggesting that the understanding of reality begins with an attempted action; then when there is resistance to what we are trying to do, we know we are in contact with something beyond our pipe dreams. Michael Slote (2014, chapter 2) also argues that cognitive beliefs are action-oriented, but Slote's arguments are more analytic than phenomenological, and the theory of knowledge from which he starts isn't enactive. Instead, he points out that beliefs are directed toward actions, and that we wouldn't be motivated to entertain a belief unless we could use it for some purpose. Husserl, Heidegger and Merleau-Ponty actually go further: Not only do we use beliefs for action-oriented purposes, but the very process of forming the belief is grounded in trying to execute an action and then seeing how the world affords or resists the action.

4. Natika Newton's *Foundations of Understanding* (1996) develops the difference between machine-based knowledge and the understanding that humans have. A machine might perfunctorily yield the translation of a text without actually understanding the text or the language in which it is written. The extra ingredient required for understanding is the emotional motivation for attempted actions, whose success or failure then shapes the conscious understanding that the mechanical device lacks.

5. Stuart Kauffman (2001), Scott Camazine et al. (2001), Ellis (1995, 2005, 2017/2018), Newton (2000, 2017), Giovanna Colombetti (2014), Natalie DePraz et al. (2003) and others are increasingly taking this approach. In non-biological, nuts-and-bolts systems constructed out of piecemeal elements, no matter how complicated they become, no organism's overall purposes guide the machine's reorganization, but only the push-pull cause-effect mechanisms that were set up by the software designer. This distinction will be discussed further in the body of the text.

6. In recent research, neuropsychologists like Jaak Panksepp (1998, 2000, 2011) and Doug Watt (1998, 2000) have developed extensive evidence that there are a larger number than previously thought of these innate emotional/motivational tendencies. See our Chapter 3 for further discussion of that kind of research.

7. James's point therefore needs at least two important caveats: First, it needs to be reconciled with more recent brain research, which shows that emotional brain processes precede the activation of the motor and pre-motor areas. Secondly, and more philosophically important, James's comment implies that the physical dimension causes its conscious correlate. But if the physical realm causes the mental, then how can the physical event (the cause) be the *same thing* as the mental one (the effect)? A cause can't be the same thing as its effect. So to say that one causes the other would entail a metaphysical dualism of physical *versus* mental. Yet one of James's main aims is to refute this very dualism; hence the provocative title of his other popular essay, "Does Consciousness Exist?" (James 1904).

At a time when most English-speaking psychologists and philosophers were ignoring the role of consciousness in cognition and emotion altogether, Thomas Natsoulas (e.g., 1993) was arguing persuasively that we can't treat consciousness as an irrelevant or powerless "appendage" or "epiphenomenon" to a physical process. It makes many differences whether a cognitive process has the capacity for consciousness or not, as we shall see throughout this book.

8. In Merleau-Ponty's sense, "The world is my body's support" (1945, 366). Notice that the reference list of the *Phenomenology of Perception* includes more empirical psychology sources than philosophical ones.

9. There is no need to get bogged down in the technical terminological distinctions of existential philosophy here, but in the way existentialists usually use the terms, "existential" issues affect my ability to exist as who I am in my uniqueness, whereas "ontological" issues affect my ability to exist as the general *kind* of being that I am—conscious, finite, necessarily-interactive, etc. The existential issues include ontological ones, since I can't be what I am without being the kind of being that I am.

Chapter 1

1. For example, some psychologists were already noticing the independence of the exploratory drive as early as Robert White (1959), K. G. Montgomery (1954), and Harry Harlow (1950).

2. Anya Daly (2021) grapples with this tension in her proposal for an "enactivist account which, following phenomenology, advances an ontology of interdependence and reconceives the subject as first and foremost an organism immersed in a meaningful world" (43).

3. Kauffman, a chemist by trade, believes the self-maintaining quality of these systems is facilitated by "auto-catalytic" reactions—reactions whose own end products further catalyze the renewed beginning of the reaction. The system is designed to use reactions whose own by-products serve to catalyze the reaction itself, creating a relatively stable condition that maximizes the probability that certain patterns of organization will occur and be maintained.

4. Twentieth century behaviorists' skepticism about the independence of the exploratory drive (and other nonhedonistic emotions we will be discussing) was driven largely by *the scientists' own* selective attention, motivated by a preference for certain theoretical commitments such as behaviorist learning theories. Here again, motivation drives attention and therefore shapes our interpretation of reality.

Even when we choose an acceptable level of uncertainty for a study, we are tacitly making a value judgment: We want a better level of uncertainty for nuclear power plants than for whether a nutritional supplement will help with allergies; the criterion presupposes a value judgment based on acceptable risk, as well as which experimental operations seem worth trying given current theoretical assumptions and the predominant focus of contemporary research and "research paradigms." It also requires imagination in choosing which control variables to watch out for.

Chapter 2

1. Aaron Blake (2021), writing for the *Washington Post*, documents that this was one of many weird "conspiracy theories" for how the 2020 US presidential election was supposedly stolen.

2. This distinction is presupposed by the contrast between "body image" and "body schema" (for example, see Gallagher 1986; De Preester and Knockaert 2007; Ataria and Tanaka 2020): Body schema is the way the body feels and acts from within; body image is merely the way we imagine our body would look, or could be represented objectively, while performing the action.

Chapter 3

1. See D. Norman (1977); for an update, see also Peter Afford (2012).

2. Robert White was one of the important twentieth-century iconoclasts who advocated the independence of the exploratory drive from direct or indirect hedonistic reinforcement, along with K. G. Montgomery (1954), Harry Harlow (1950), and a few others.

3. In my *Curious Emotions* (2005), I fleshed out this need for newness, complexity, and a higher energy level in more contemporary neurophysiological terms, as a conflict between "homeostasis" and "homeo-exstasis." The neurophysiology involved can be understood in terms of the dynamics of self-organizing systems.

4. A more direct precursor to Panksepp's SEEKING system, as we have already seen, was the work of some twentieth-century psychologists who argued for the independence of an innate exploratory drive (Montgomery 1954; White 1959; Kagan and Berkun 1954).

5. Panksepp deliberately doesn't distinguish between "emotion" and "motivation," except that "emotion" highlights the ability for conscious feeling and also includes the ways motivation can interact with environmental events; see Zachar and Ellis (2012).

6. Actions have to be motivated. So the same emotional/motivational areas of the brain participate in both emotions and action commands delivered to the rest of the brain and body—even in the case of subliminally imagined actions, where the command is first initiated subcortically, then cortically inhibited before reaching

the body's extremities. This inhibition is the crucial difference between *imagining* an action and *actually executing* it (Jeannerod 1994, 1997; Ellis 2005; Ellis and Newton 2010). Our earlier lengthy quote from Gendlin (2018) shows how he refined and extended our understanding of the role of action tendencies in consciousness—Frijda's "action readiness," which Frijda sees as included in every emotion.

7. Davis and Panksepp, in a 2018 book published shortly after Panksepp's death, tried out still another label—"SADNESS"—but this label can be confusing because there are so many different kinds of sadness. The PANIC system specifically correlates with the anguish of *social or interpersonal separation*. And sometimes it feels more frantic than "sad," as in an initial separation between mother and infant.

8. For example, Alexander et al. (2019), Zikopoulus et al. (2017), and others show that, in many cases of clinical depression, *overactivity* in some parts of the SEEKING system (for example, Brodmann's area 25 of the anterior cingulate cortex, which by means of neurotransmitter activity connects the prefrontal cortex with parts of the amygdala and other emotion areas) may in turn *inhibit* other areas of the SEEKING system (for example, area 32 and the relevant areas of the amygdala).

Chapter 4

1. Thomas Aquinas's scholastic arguments always became even more complicated than usual when dealing with "desires" and "passions" because they were neither physical nor mental, but rather both at once. It was impossible to pick a side in the either/or that scholasticism wanted to choose between on that score.

Chapter 5

1. The last thing most psychotherapists would want to do is to question a cult follower's absurd beliefs. The self-reflection process, which requires questioning, would be instantly shut down if the belief system is challenged.

2. To be sure, *conformism* plays a role here; and we might assume that conformism could correlate with "Agreeableness." Even so, there already had to be a critical mass of people who felt or believed a certain way, to provide the conformist with something to conform to. Conformism therefore can't go very far toward explaining racism and xenophobia.

3. This correlation between "Openness" and SEEKING system activation was obtained not by directly measuring physiological aspects of the SEEKING activity, but rather by using a paper-and-pencil questionnaire designed to measure the prominence of subjective feelings and overt behaviors associated with SEEKING activation.

Chapter 6

1. Edith Stein and Max Scheler, and to some extent also Husserl in *Ideas II* and some of his posthumous papers, elaborate the phenomenology of this point in some detail. Everyone's valuing dimension "affords" being valued, and this "affordance" is what we holistically perceive when we feel ourselves being called to action by their suffering, in those instances where we do pay attention.

2. In an earlier volume (2018), I went further to make the following argument: Suppose we ask whether, hypothetically, we necessarily "would have" attributed value to a given valuing creature whose existence we don't even know of, if we *had* known about them and also had directed our attention toward their valuing dimension. Would the person whose imagery is *not* presented have evoked empathy *if it had* been presented? If so, this is the same as acknowledging that even if we ourselves had never existed in order to value the valuing creature (or attend to its image), that creature still would "have" value in the sense we are discussing.

3. Studies show that somewhere between 4 and 10 percent of the people don't have the father they think they have, depending on the sampling methods of different studies (Bellis et al. 2005; for perspective from different historical era, see also Borosini 1913). Yet people don't fail to regard those children as having intrinsic value.

4. Complex self-organizing systems are arranged so as to appropriate, replace, and repurpose the microcomponents that make up the system. We consume nutrients that can be used to replenish the neurotransmitters needed for the brain's ongoing patterns of activity. The B vitamin choline is needed to form acetylcholine, which is a key neurotransmitter for thinking, memory, and other intellectual functions. Dietary calcium and magnesium are needed in the right balance for mood regulation. The system literally seeks out and appropriates microcomponents that can subserve the needed patterns of activity. In recovery from a serious brain concussion, new brain cells are repurposed to take over the function of cells that have been destroyed—an entirely well-documented process (for example, Sandvig et al. 2018).

Chapter 7

1. Why is there an "impulse" to annihilate someone's whole existence, in need of being "controlled" in the first place? A shortage of serotonin by itself wouldn't lead to sudden murder except in a context where a more widely distributed process leads us to fail to count the other's value as important enough to affect our overall motivational state.

2. Regulation of our behavior by concern with others' well-being requires certain minimal yet very specific kinds of amygdala-prefrontal connections, requiring both facilitative and inhibitory activity of serotonin and other neurotransmitters, as shown by Lungu et al. (2007), Gee et al. (2013), Faw (2000b), and others.

3. The hallmark of sudden murder is its "irrationality" even from the egoistic standpoint. In the technical criminological definition of sudden murder, the murderer doesn't commit the crime for any gain or think about the consequences. It represents a state in which *nothing matters*. Even whether I myself am detected and prosecuted doesn't matter, at least for that moment. Nothing, including one's own goals or desires, has any value.

4. For example, Wohlschlager and Beckering (2002) show that when someone is facing another subject who raises the left hand, the primary subject doesn't raise the right hand in imitation—which would be the natural response if responding to an *inanimate* object. Instead, the subject can, if instructed to do so, raise the left hand because they imagine themselves in the place of the facing other, and thus they spontaneously realize that it is the left hand that is to be raised, not the right. This capability was observed even in young children. Wohlschlager and Beckering interpret this to mean that a mirroring subject imagines actions in order to understand what it would be like to literally be in the other's shoes.

5. I discussed this dynamic more extensively in *Eros in a Narcissistic Culture* (1996).

Chapter 8

1. Jeannerod (1994, 1997) shows the sharp differences between this "motor imagery" and the mere receiving of perceptual or enteroceptive sensations. Sensorimotor imagery includes an *initiation of action intentions,* which then generates an efferent signal which in turn can be inhibited in frontal brain areas, resulting in a mere imagining of the action rather than its overt execution. In effect, we gear ourselves up to tell our hands to play a piece of music on an instrument, but then we inhibit the already initiated command from reaching the hands, resulting in a mere imagining of what it would be like to play the piece.

2. For the person this lacking in impulse control, the "neoamygdala"—the outer layer of amygdala that interacts with the prefrontal cortex—has failed to develop in the usual human way and thus fails to connect the rashness of the "old-amygdala" (through the "neo-amygdala") to the prefrontal cortex, which in turn not only *can* regulate the hyperactivation of the amygdala, but normally does so continuously and seamlessly (for example, see Chareyron et al. 2012; Lungu 2007; Tottenham 2009).

3. It is tempting to treat visceral enteroception as if it were the be all and end all of feeling emotions. Cut off the enteroception, some say, and you have the emotion but not the correlative conscious feeling. For example, Damasio (2003) takes essentially this position as a result of his flirtation with contemporary cognitive theory flow charts in his *Looking for Spinoza,* an otherwise very informative book on emotional neurophysiology. What alexithymia shows us is that this "it's all enteroception" explanation is too simple.

4. Anton Lethin (2002, 2004) suggests that this largely inhibited efferent signaling involved in action imagery can even reach the bodily extremities to a certain extent, and at that point it is further inhibited by spinal interneurons. We see the effects of this when musicians, while imagining a musical melody, tend to slightly move their fingers as if to finger the notes.

5. There are a number of different measurement instruments designed to assess the degree of alexithymia (for example, see Bagby et al. 2009; Bermond 1997). These scales are essentially refinements of the earlier Rogers-Gendlin "experiencing scale" (Gendlin 1962/1997, 1982; Klein et al. 1969). These instruments were originally designed to rate subjects on a scale according to how "in touch" they are with their feelings and the extent to which their symbolizations embody what they actually feel. As clients move through the psychotherapeutic process, their therapeutic success correlates with their score on the Experiencing Scale as judged by independent raters—and the independent raters' assessments also correlate strongly with each other, suggesting some degree of validity for the ratings and the resulting scale.

Chapter 9

1. It would be beyond my scope to discuss the addictive trap in detail here, but a good starting point for such an investigation is to study the way the SEEKING system is triggered in addictive behaviors. It isn't just the pleasurable outcome of a behavior that becomes addictive, but the behavior itself. An excellent way into understanding the role of SEEKING here is offered by Alcaro et al. (2021), Markou et al. (1998), and others of their associates. From a neuroscientific standpoint, they show that a *narrowing of the context* for SEEKING behavior is one of the precursors to addiction; the exploratory or SEEKING activity becomes restricted in such a way that, instead of generally wanting to explore the world, the addict reaches the point where only one tiny slice of the world—playing internet games, or triggering hunger in an eating disorder, for example—this one avenue of behavior becomes the only context available for expression of the SEEKING system. The SEEKING system then needs increasing amounts of this one behavior in order to allow its activation, since the body's self-organization adjusts for the abnormal amount of stimulation in the same way that serotonin receptors can spontaneously shrink in response to too much serotonin being artificially dumped into the synapses with drugs like ecstasy. More and more of the drug is then needed even to feel normally OK.

Chapter 10

1. This "existential a priori" (Binswanger 1963) then was incorporated into Gadamer's "hermeneutics" (Gadamer 1971)—the idea that our perception of

reality is always interpretive, that facts tend to be selected or even distorted to fit preconceived categories of experience.

Chapter 11

1. Kuhn shows that even the geocentric worldview could have been maintained if only granted the ad hoc hypothesis of "epicircles" to explain the inconsistent motions of the planets. The facts could still have been interpreted to fit the geocentric view.

2. To assert that a value is *really real* would constitute what many philosophers call "moral realism," the idea that some things—or more to the point, some people and the outcomes that affect them—"really do" have value, independently of whether some other given person does or doesn't recognize or acknowledge this value. In that case, we would be saying more than just "I value X," but something more like "In my view, *anyone* with a capacity for empathy who directs their attention toward X in a way that really understands X's valuing dimension—the fact that X is a valuing creature—*would* value X." In effect, we would be universalizing a view about an intrinsic value.

Conclusions

1. Similarly, we discussed earlier the Hodson et al. (2009) finding that authoritarian personality (using Altemeyer's "Right Wing Authoritarianism" scale) correlates with the "Agreeableness" dimension of the Big Five Personality Inventory. The Agreeable authoritarian empathizes quite well with individuals, members of one's own clan, and those who "look like us" and yet can disregard the value of entire races, religions, ethnicities, and even opposing political camps. These latter categories aren't close at hand, and thus don't compel easy imagery. But regardless of any hatred or dismissal of those who become "othered," the authoritarian still empathizes with those who are close at hand—friends, relatives, the imagistically familiar "clan." The closer to the circle centering around or associated with the "self," the more the authoritarian empathizes. This "expanded egoism" seems almost the opposite of the other-directedness of the depressed person's value feelings.

2. Even if someone posits values in some "ultimate" sense that has nothing to do with subjective valuations (for example, "The Revolution" or "The Balance of Nature" or "God's Plan"), they still must be using "value" in some sense that has a *commonality of meaning* with the sense in which subjective valuations both of oneself and of valued others have value. The commonality is defined relative to the value of valuing creatures themselves and their well-being. Try though we may, we can't have a coherent value system without attention to values created by subjec-

tive valuations. Even if I were to define value in some completely "supra-personal" way—for example, that the Revolution "has value" whether it benefits people or not—I still have to admit that at least some values in the *subjective* sense also have value. Even ethical egoists must grant this, although of course egoists will make an attempt (incoherently, in my view) to index this value to just *one particular* being's subjective valuations.

3. If expanded still further, the valuing of others would lead to the universalized sense of "having value" that we discussed earlier—the "universalized" value of any and all valuing creatures, by virtue of the fact that any rational creature capable of empathy would value those creatures' well-being *if attention were appropriately directed*. In this sense, the lives of child laborers in slave-like sweat shops may have as much or more prima facie value than my maximizing the profits of my garment business, based on the fact that they themselves are also subjects. Whether in a specific instance their prima facie value outweighs the value of my dinner at a fancy restaurant will depend on which *overall valuational viewpoint* we adopt, which in turn will depend on coherence assessments of competing viewpoints.

To acknowledge the value of even some valuing creatures—which may initially be narrowly focused in favor of close friends, family, or clan—can in this way eventually lead to the more generalized attitude that "any intelligent creature capable of empathy would value X if attention were directed to X's valuing dimension." This would be clearly a case in which I would be affirming that something "has value" rather than merely "being valued" (by me or by some other particular subject).

4. The failure to value humanity as a universal class requires incoherent convolutions of twisted logic and carefully targeted ignoring of evidence. New experience tends to be pigeon-holed into preconceived categories, as evidenced for example by low scores on the "Openness" dimension of the Big Five Personality Inventory used by Hodson et al. In other words, the *exploratory drive* (a function of the SEEKING system) is dampened and inhibited, but only in those compartmentalized respects.

5. This doesn't mean that any given one of those resulting prima facie values will necessarily be the decisive values *in the final analysis*. To stop a bully may require making the bully unhappy. It isn't that the bully's happiness has no prima facie value; but this value unfortunately is in conflict with other values. With this standard caveat, we can say that, to the extent that a value system is non-nihilistic, it implicitly affirms the prima facie well-being of others. We can then explore what happens with rare deviations in how the brain is wired, such as in alexithymia, narcissistic disturbance, or sociopathy.

References

Adler, Alfred (1961). *Understanding Human Nature.* New York: Fawcett.
Adorno, Theodor, Else Frenkel-Brunswik, Daniel Levinson, and R. Nevitt Sanford (1964). *The Authoritarian Personality.* New York: Wiley.
Afford, Peter (2012). Focusing in an Age of Neuroscience. *The Folio* 2012: 66–83.
Alcaro, Antonio, Anthony Brennan, and David Conversi (2021). The SEEKING drive and its fixation. *Frontiers in Human Neuroscience* 12. https://www.frontiersin.org/articles/10.3389/fnhum.2021.635932/full.
Alexander, Laith, Hannah Clarke, and Angela Roberts (2019). A focus on the functions of area 25. *Brain sciences* 9 (6), 129. https://doi.org/10.3390/brainsci9060129.
Altemeyer, Robert (2008). *The Authoritarians.* Manitoba: Cherry Hill.
Applebaum, Anne (2020). *Twilight of Democracy: The Seductive Lure of Authoritarianism.* New York: Doubleday.
Archibald, S. J., C. A. Mateer, and K. A. Kerns (2001). Utilization behavior: Clinical manifestations and neurological mechanisms. *Neuropsychology Review* 11: 117–130.
Arendt, Hannah (1959). *The Human Condition.* Chicago: University of Chicago Press.
Arendt, Hannah (1963). *Eichmann in Jerusalem: A Report on the Banality of Evil.* London: Faber & Faber.
Arendt, Hannah (1968). *The Origins of Totalitarianism.* New York: Harcourt/Harvest.
Aristotle (1966). *Nicomachean Ethics.* New York: Bobbs-Merrill.
Ataria, Yochai, and Shogo Tanaka (2020). When body image takes over the body schema: The case of Frantz Fanon. *Human Studies* 43: 653–665.
Aurell, Carl G. (1984). Perception: A model comprising two modes of consciousness. Addendum II: Emotion incorporated. *Perceptual and Motor Skills* 59: 180–182.
Aurell, Carl G. (1989). Man's triune conscious mind. *Perceptual and Motor Skills* 68: 747–754.
Auxier, Randall (1995). The wind we inherited: God and secular America. *Personalist Forum* 112: 95–124.
Ayer, A. J. (1946). *Language, Truth and Logic.* London: Gollantz.

Ayer, A. J. (1965). On the analysis of moral judgments. In *Philosophical Essays*. New York: St. Martin's.

Bagby, Robert Michael, Lena C. Quilty, Graeme J. Taylor, Hans J. Grabe, Oliver Luminet, Ramiro Verissimo, Iris de Grotte, and Stijn Van Heule (2009). Are there subtypes of alexithymia? *Personality and Individual Differences* 47: 413–418.

Becker, Ernest (1973). *The Denial of Death*. New York: Free Press.

Bègue, Laurent, Jean-Léon Beauvois, Didier Courbet, and Dominique Oberlé (2015). Personality predicts obedience in a Milgram paradigm. *Journal of Personality* 83: 299–306.

Bermond, Bob (1997). Brain and alexithymia. In A. Vingerhoets. F. Van Bussel, and J. Boelhouwer (Eds.), *The (Non-) Expression of Emotions in Health and Disease* (115–129). Tilburg: Tilburg University Press.

Bettleheim, Bruno (1959). Feral children and autistic children. *American Journal of Sociology* 64: 455–467.

Bickhard, Mark (2000). Motivation and emotion: An interactive process model. In R. Ellis and N. Newton (Eds.), *The Caldron of Consciousness: Motivation, Affect and Self-organization* (161–178). Amsterdam/Philadelphia: John Benjamins.

Binswanger, Ludwig (1963). *Being in the World*. New York: Basic Books.

Bird, Geoffrey, and Richard Cook (2013). Mixed emotions: the contribution of alexithymia to the emotional symptoms of autism. *Translational Psychiatry* 3:e285. doi: 10.1038/tp.2013.61.

Blake, Aaron (2021). "Pure insanity": Here's one of the craziest conspiracy theories the Trump team pushed. *Washington Post,* June 15, 2021.

Borosini, Victor (1913). The problem of illegitimacy in Europe. *Journal of Criminal Law and Criminology* 4: 212–236.

Bowles, Samuel, and Herbert Gintis (2013). *A Cooperative Species: Human Reciprocity and Its Evolution*. Princeton: Princeton University Press.

Boyd, Robert (1997). "The fear trigger: The trusty little amygdala helps keep us out of harm's way." Spokane, Washington: *The Spokesman-Review,* Nov. 19.

Brand, Gerd (1967). Intentionality, reduction, and intentional analysis in Husserl's later manuscripts. In J. Kockelmans (Ed.), *Phenomenology*. Garden City: Doubleday, 197–217.

Bråten, Stein, Ed. (2007). *On Being Moved: From Mirror Neurons to Empathy*. Amsterdam/Philadelphia: John Benjamins.

Bråten, Stein. (2013). *Roots and Collapse of Empathy.* Amsterdam/Philadelphia: John Benjamins.

Bryer, Bernadette Nelson, Jean Miller, and Pamela Krol (1987). Childhood sexual and physical abuse as factors in adult psychiatric illness. *American Journal of Psychiatry* 144: 1426–1430.

Buford, Thomas (2011). *Self-Knowledge: An Essay in Social Personalism*. Lanham, Maryland: Lexington Books.

Bush, George, Phan Luu, and Michael I. Posner (2000). Cognitive and emotional influences in anterior cingulate cortex. *Trends in Cognitive Sciences* 4 (6) 215–222.

Camazine, Scott, Jean-Louis Deneubourg, Nigel Franks, James Sneyd, Guy Theraulaz, and Eric Bonabeau (2001). *Self-Organization in Biological Systems*. Princeton: Princeton University Press.

Campos, Alfredo, Matty Chiva, and Marylène Moreau (2000). Alexithymia and mental imagery. *Personality and Individual Differences* 29: 787–791.

Cartwright, Duncan (2014). *Psychoanalysis, Violence and Rage-Type Murder*. London: Routledge.

Casey, Edward (2021). *Turning Emotion Inside Out*. Evanston: Northwestern University Press.

Chan, David (2012). *Beyond Just War: A Virtue Ethics Approach*. Basingstoke: Palgrave-Macmillan.

Chareyron, Loïc J., Pierre B. Lavenex, David G. Amaral, and Pamela B. Lavenex (2012). Postnatal development of the amygdala: A stereological study in macaque monkeys. *Journal of Comparative Neurology*. June 15: 520(9): 1965–1984.

Colombetti, Giovanna (2014). *The Feeling Body: Affective Science Meets the Enactive Mind*. Boston: MIT Press.

Cornell, Ann Weiser, with Barbara McGavin (2005). *The Radical Acceptance of Everything*. Berkely, Calif.: Calluna Press.

Cornell, Drucilla (1995). *At the Heart of Freedom*. Princeton: Princeton University Press.

Csikszentmihalyi, Mihaly (1990). *Flow: The Psychology of Optimal Experience*. New York: Harper.

Daly, Anya (2021). The declaration of interdependence! Feminism, grounding and enactivism. *Human Studies* 44: 43–62.

Damasio, Antonio (1999). *The Feeling of What Happens*. New York: Harcourt Brace.

Damasio, Antonio (2003). *Looking for Spinoza*. New York: Harcourt.

Damasio, Antonio (2021). *Feeling and Knowing: Making Minds Conscious*. New York: Pantheon.

Davidson, Richard J., Katherine M. Putnam, and Christine L. Larson (2007). Dysfunction in the neural circuitry of emotion regulation—A possible prelude to violence. *Science* 289 (5479): 591.

Davis, Kenneth, and Jaak Panksepp (2018). *The Emotional Foundations of Personality*. New York: W. W. Norton.

De Beauvoir, Simone (1948/1976). *The Ethics of Ambiguity*. New York: Kensington Press/Philosophical Library.

Depraz, Natalie, Francisco Varela, and Pierre Vermersch (2003). *On Becoming Aware: A Pragmatics of Experiencing*. Amsterdam: John Benjamins.

De Preester, Helena, and Veroniek Knockaert (2007). *Body Image and Body Schema*. Amsterdam: John Benjamins.

De Waal, Frans (2006). *Primates and Philosophers: How Morality Evolved.* Princeton: Princeton University Press.

De Waal, Frans (2008). Putting the altruism back into altruism: The evolution of empathy. *Annual Review of Psychology* 59: 279–300.

Doige, Norman (2007). *The Brain that Changes Itself.* New York: Penguin.

Donoghue, John P. (2002). Connecting cortex to machines: Recent advances in brain interface. *Nature Neuroscience Supplement* 5 (November 2002): 1085–1088.

Dostoyevsky, Fyodor (1864/2004). *Notes from Underground.* New York: Vintage.

Dunlop, Boadie W., and Charles B. Nemeroff (2007). The role of dopamine in the pathophysiology of depression. *Archives of General Psychiatry* 64: 327–337.

Duriez, Bart, and Bart Soenens (2009). The intergenerational transmission of racism: The role of right-wing authoritarianism and social dominance orientation. *Journal of Research in Personality* 43: 906–909.

Durkheim, Emile (1893/2013). *The Division of Labor in Society.* New York: Palgrave Macmillan.

Ellis, Ralph D. (1995). *Questioning Consciousness.* Amsterdam/Philadelphia: John Benjamins.

Ellis, Ralph D. (1996). *Eros in a Narcissistic Culture.* Den Haag/Berlin: Kluwer/Springer.

Ellis, Ralph D. (1999). The dance form of the eyes: What cognitive science can learn from art. *Journal of Consciousness Studies* 6: 161–175.

Ellis, Ralph D. (2005). *Curious Emotions: Roots of Consciousness and Personality in Motivated Action.* Amsterdam: John Benjamins.

Ellis, Ralph D. (2008a). In what sense is "rationality" a criterion for emotional self-awareness? *Consciousness and Cognition* 17: 972–973.

Ellis, Ralph D. (2008b). The phenomenology of alexithymia as a clue to the intentionality of emotion. In Louis Charland and Peter Zachar (Eds.), *Fact and Value in Emotion* (181–192). Amsterdam/Philadelphia: John Benjamins.

Ellis, Ralph D. (2013). Neuroscience as a human science. *Human Studies* 36: 491–507.

Ellis, Ralph D. (2017). *The Moral Psychology of Internal Conflict.* Cambridge: Cambridge University Press.

Ellis, Ralph D. (2021). How my piano uses Gendlin's focusing method. In Jared Kemling (Ed.), *The Cultural Power of Personal Objects* (303–318). New York: SUNY Press.

Ellis, Ralph D., and William Faw (2010). Concluding comments. In Peter Zachar and R. D. Ellis (Eds.), *Categorial versus Dimensional Approaches to Emotion: A Seminar on the Theories of Panksepp and Russell.* Amsterdam/Philadelphia: John Benjamins.

Ellis, Ralph D., and Natika Newton (2010). *How the Mind Uses the Brain.* Chicago: Open Court.

Emory University Health Sciences Center (2006). Emory study lights up the political brain. *Science Daily,* January 31.

Faw, William (2000a). My amygdala-orbitofrontal circuit made me do it. *Consciousness & Emotion* 1: 167–179.

Faw, William (2000b). Consciousness, motivation, and emotion: Biopsychological reflections. In R. D. Ellis and N. Newton (Eds.), *The Caldron of Consciousness: Motivation, Affect, and Self-organization.* Amsterdam: John Benjamins.

Faw, William (2003). Pre-frontal executive committee for perception, working memory, attention, long-term memory, motor control, and thinking: A tutorial review. *Consciousness and Cognition* 12: 83–139.

Federal Bureau of Investigation (1964). Counterintelligence Program Internal Security, Disruption of Hate Groups, National Knights of the Ku Klux Klan (Freedom of Information and Privacy Acts). https://vault.fbi.gov/cointel-pro/White%20Hate%20Groups/cointelpro-white-hate-groups-part-03-of-14-1.

Foucault, Michel (1994). *The Order of Things: An Archeology of the Human Sciences.* New York: Vintage.

Fox, Michael D., Randy L. Buckner, Matthew P. White, Michael D. Greicius, and Alvaro Pascual-Leone (2012). Efficacy of transcranial magnetic stimulation targets for depression is related to intrinsic functional connectivity with the subgenual cingulate. *Biologicqal Psychiatry* 72: 595–603.

Frankl, Viktor (1959). *Man's Search for Meaning.* Boston: Beacon.

Freeman, Walter (2012). *Mass Action in the Nervous System.* Amsterdam: Elsevier.

Freud, Sigmund. (1925/1959). *Beyond the Pleasure Principle.* New York: Bantam.

Frijda, Nico H. (2006/2007). *The Laws of Emotion.* London: Erlbaum.

Gabbay, Vilma, B. A. Ely, Qingyang Li, S. D. Bangaru, A. M. Panzer, C. M. Alonso, F. X. Castellanos, and M. P. Milham (2013). Striatum-based circuitry of adolescent depression and anhedonia. *Journal of the American Academy of Childhood and Adolescent Psychiatry* 52: 62–641.

Gadamer, Hans G. (1971/1975). *Truth and Method.* New York: Seabury.

Gallagher, Shaun (1986). Body image and body schema. *Journal of Mind and Behavior* 7: 541–554.

Gallagher, Shaun (2006). *How the Body Shapes the Mind.* Oxford: Clarendon.

Gallagher, Shaun (2020). *Action and Interaction.* Oxford: Oxford University Press.

Gallese, Vittorio, Luciano Fadiga, Leonardo Fogassi, and Giacomo Rizzolatti (1996). Action recognition in the premotor cortex. *Brain* 119: 593–609

Gee, Dylan G., Kathryn L. Humphreys, Jessica Flannery, Bonnie Goff, Eva H. Telzer, Mor Shapiro, Todd A. Hare, Susan Y. Bookheimer, and Nim Tottenham (2013). A developmental shift from positive to negative connectivity in human amygdala-prefrontal circuitry. *Journal of Neuroscience* 33 (10): 4585–4593.

Gendlin, Eugene (1962/1997). *Experiencing and the Creation of Meaning.* Toronto: Collier-Macmillan/Chicago: University of Chicago Press.

Gendlin, Eugene (1978/1982/1990). *Focusing.* Toronto: Bantam.
Gendlin, Eugene (1992). Thinking beyond patterns: Body, language, and situations. In B. den Ouden and M. Moen (Eds.), *The Presence of Feeling in Thought.* New York: Peter Lang.
Gendlin, Eugene (1996). *Focusing-oriented Psychotherapy: A Manual of the Experiential Method.* New York: Guilford.
Gendlin, Eugene (2017). *A Process Model.* Evanston: Northwestern University Press.
Gendlin, Eugene (2018). *Saying What We Mean* (Edward Casey and Donata Schoeler, Eds.). Evanston: Northwestern University Press.
Gendlin, Eugene (2000). The "mind"/"body" problem and first-person process. In R. Ellis and N. Newton (Eds.), *The Caldron of Consciousness: Motivation, Affect and Self-organization* (109–118). Amsterdam/Philadelphia: John Benjamins.
Gibson, James J. (1986). *The Ecological Approach to Visual Perception.* New York: Routledge/Psychology Press.
Gilligan, Carol (1982). *In a Different Voice: Psychological Theory and Women's Development.* Cambridge, Mass.: Harvard University Press.
Goleman, Daniel (1996). *Vital Lies, Simple Truths: The Psychology of Self Deception.* New York: Simon & Schuster
Greenberg, Jeff, Sheldon Solomon, and Tom Pyszcynski (1997). Terror management theory of self-esteem and cultural worldviews: Empirical assessments. *Advances in Experimental Social Psychology* 29 (S 61): 139.
Griffin, Cáit, Michael V. Lombardo, and Bonnie Auyeung (2016). Alexithymia in children with and without autism spectrum disorders. *Autism Research* 9: 773–780. doi: 10.1002/aur.1569.
Harlow, Harry F. (1950). Learning motivated by a manipulation drive. *Journal of Experimental Psychology* 40: 228–234.
Harvey, Charles (2016). Human (un)kind and the rape of the world. *Philosophy in the Contemporary World* 23: 93–102.
Harvey, Charles (2020). Insatiable: Why everything is not enough. *Philosophy in the Contemporary World* 28: 69–89.
Heidegger, Martin (1927/1962). *Being and Time.* New York: Harper & Row.
Held, Richard, and Alan Hein (1963). Movement-produced stimulation in the development of visually guided behavior. *Journal of Comparative and Physiological Psychology* 56: 872–876.
Held, Richard, and Alan Hein (1958). Adaptation of disarranged hand-eye coordination contingent upon re-afferent stimulation. *Perceptual and Motor Skills* 8: 87–90.
Herman, Judith (1992/1997). *Trauma and Recovery: The Aftermath of Violence—from Domestic Abuse to Political Terror.* New York: Basic Books.
Hibbing, John R., Kevin Smith, and John Alford (2013). *Predisposed: Liberals, Conservatives, and the Biology of Political Differences.* New York: Routledge.

Hicks, Brian, R. F. Kreuger, W. Iacome, M. McGue, and C. J. Patrick (2004). Family transmission and heritability of externalizing disorders: a twin-family study. *Archives of General Psychiatry* 61 (9): 922–928.

Hill, Elisabeth, Sylvie Berthoz, and Uta Frith (2004). Brief report: Cognitive processing of own emotions in individuals with autistic spectrum disorder and in their relatives. *Journal of Autism and Developmental Disorders* 34: 229–235. doi: 10.1023/b:jadd.0000022613.41399.14.

Hobbes, Thomas (1651/2019). *Leviathan*. New York: W. W. Norton.

Hodson, Gordon, Sarah Hogg, and Cara McInnis (2009). The role of "dark personalities" (narcissism, Machiavellianism, psychopathy), Big Five personality factors, and ideology in explaining prejudice. *Journal of Research in Personality* 43: 686–690.

Howard Patrick (2012). How literature works. In N. Friesen, C. Henriksson, and T. Saevi (Eds.) *Hermeneutic Phenomenology in Education: Practice of Research Method, vol. 4*. Rotterdam: Sense Publishers. https://doi.org/10.1007/978-94-6091-834-6_11.

Hsee, Christopher, and Bowen Ruan (2016). The pandora effect: The power and peril of curiosity. *Psychological Science* 10: 1–8.

Huffington Post (2016). Huffpolster; Most Republicans still won't say Obama was born in the U.S. Huffington Post 9/21/16. http://www.huffingtonpost.com/entry/trump-birther-poll_us_57e27935e4b0e80b1b9f30c0.

Hume, David. (1740/1955). *Treatise of Human Nature*. New York: Bobbs-Merrill.

Husserl, Edmund (1900/2001). *Logical Investigations*. New York: Humanity Books.

Husserl, Edmund (1913/1931). *Ideas* (W. R. Boyce Gibson Trans.). London: Collier 1931; from *Ideen zu einer Reinen Phänomenologie und Phänomenologischen Philosophie*, 1913.

Husserl, Edmund (1936/1970). *The Crisis of European Sciences and Transcendental Philosophy* (David Carr trans.). Evanston: Northwestern University Press.

Ihde, Don (1998). *Philosophy of Technology*. Manchester: Paragon House.

Jackson, Frank (1986). What Mary didn't know. *Journal of Philosophy* 83: 291–295.

James, William (1884). What is an emotion? *Mind* 9 (34): 188–205.

James, William (1904/1968). Does "consciousness" exist? In John McDermott (Ed.), *The Writings of William James*. New York: Random House, 169–170.

James, William (1907/1979). *Pragmatism*. Cambridge, MA: Harvard University Press.

Jeannerod, Marc (1994). The representing brain: Neural correlates of motor intention and imagery. *Behavioral and Brain Sciences* 17: 187–244.

Jeannerod, Marc (1997). *The Cognitive Neuroscience of Action*. Oxford: Blackwell.

Kagan, Jerome, and Mitchell Berkun (1954). The reward value of running activity. *Journal of Comparative Physiological Psychology* 47: 108–10.

Kano, Michiko, and Shin Fukudo (2013). The alexithymic brain: The neural pathways linking alexithymia to physical disorders. *Biopsychosocial Medicine* 7: 1–9.

Kauffman, Stuart (1993). *The Origins of Order.* Oxford: Oxford University Press.
Kelly, Raymond C. (2000). *Warless Societies and the Origin of War.* Ann Arbor: University of Michigan Press.
Kiesler, Donald (1973/2017). *The Process of Psychotherapy: Empirical Foundations and Systems of Analysis.* New York: Routledge.
Kiesler, Donald (1996). *Contemporary Interpersonal Theory and Research.* New York: John Wiley.
Klein, Marjorie H, Phillipa L. Mathier, Eugene T. Gendlin, and Donal J. Kiesler (1969). *The Experiencing Scale: A Research and Training Manuel, Vol. 1.* Wisconsin Psychiatric Institute.
Kohut, Heinz (1985). *Self Psychology and the Humanities.* New York: W. W. Norton.
Kornfield, Meryl, and Mariana Alfaro (2022). 1 in 3 Americans say violence against government can be justified. *Washington Post,* January 1, 2022.
Kramer, Eli (2021). Meditating on the vitality of the musical object: A spiritual exercise drawn from Richard Wagner's metaphysics of music. In Jared Kemling (Ed.), *The Cultural Power of Personal Objects* (319–340). New York: SUNY Press.
Kuhn, Thomas (1962/1970). *The Structure of Scientific Revolutions.* Chicago: University of Chicago Press.
Lakoff, George (2008). *The Political Mind: Why You Can't Understand 21st Century Politics with an 18th Century Brain.* New York: Penguin/Viking.
Lambie, John. (2008). On the irrationality of emotion and the rationality of awareness. *Consciousness and Cognition* 17: 946–971.
Landgrebe, Ludwig. (1966). *Major Problems in Contemporary Philosophy.* New York: Ungar.
Langness, L. L. (1977). *Other Fields, Other Grasshoppers.* Philadelphia: J. B. Lippincott.
LeDoux, Joseph (1996). *The Emotional Brain: The Mysterious Underpinnings of Emotional Life.* Simon & Schuster.
Lee, Richard (2015). The hunters: Scarce resources in the Kalahari. In James Spradley and David McCurdy (Eds.), *Conformity and Conflict: Readings in Cultural Anthropology.* London: Pearson.
Lethin, Anton. (2002). How do we embody intentionality? *Journal of Consciousness Studies* 9 (8), 36–44.
Lethin, Anton. (2004). Exposing the covert agent. In R. Ellis and N. Newton (Eds.), *Consciousness and Emotion: Agency, Conscious Choice, and Selective Perception* (157–180). Amsterdam: John Benjamins.
Levinas, Emanuel (1969). *Totality and Infinity.* The Hague: Martinus Nijhoff.
Levine, Joseph (1983). Materialism and qualia: The explanatory gap. *Pacific Philosophical Quarterly* 64: 354–361.
L'hermitte, Francois, Bernard Pillon, and Michel Serdaru (1986). Human autonomy and the frontal lobes Part I: Imitation and utilization behavior. *Annals of Neurology* 19: 326–334.

Lombardo, Michael V., Jennifer L. Barnes, Sally J. Wheelwright, and Simon Baron-Cohen (2007). Self-referential cognition and empathy in autism. *Public Library of Science One* 2:e883. doi: 10.1371/journal.pone.0000883.
Lorenz, Konrad (1963/2002). *On Aggression*. London: Routledge.
Luce, Phillip Abbott (1960). *The White Citizens Councils of Mississippi*. Master's Thesis, Ohio State University.
Lungu, Ovido, Tao Liu, Tobias Waechter, Daniel T. Willingham and James Ashe (2007). Strategic modulation of cognitive control. *Journal of Cognitive Neuroscience* 19: 1302–1315.
Lyotard, Jean-Francois (1984). *The Postmodern Condition: A Report on Knowledge*. Minneapolis: University of Minnesota Press.
Mack, Arien, and Irvin Rock (1998). *Inattentional Blindness*. Cambridge, Mass.: MIT Press.
Markou, Athina, Thomas R. Kosten, and George F. Koob (1998). Neurobiological similarities in depression and drug dependence: A self-medication hypothesis. *Neuropsychopharmacology* 18: 135–174.
Maslow, Abraham (1962/1970). *Motivation and Personality*. New York: Harper & Row.
May, Rollo (1950/2011). *The Meaning of Anxiety*. New York: Martino.
May, Rollo (1969). *Love and Will*. New York: W. W. Norton.
May, Rollo (1972/1998). *Power and Innocence*. New York: W. W. Norton.
McCaghy, Charles (1980). *Crime in American Society*. New York: Macmillan.
Merleau-Ponty, Maurice (1942/1963) *The Structure of Behavior* (A. Fischer trans.). Boston: Beacon. original French edition 1942.
Merleau-Ponty, Maurice (1945/1962). *Phenomenology of Perception* (Colin Smith trans.). New York: Humanities. Original French edition 1945.
Milgram, Stanley (1974). *Obedience to Authority: An Experimental View*. New York: HarperCollins.
Mill, John Stuart (1863/2015). *Utilitarianism*. London: Parker, Son & Bourn.
Montagu, Ashley (1971). *Touching: The Human Significance of the Skin*. New York: Harper & Row.
Montgomery, Kay C. (1954). The role of the exploratory drive in learning. *Journal of Comparative Physiological Psychology* 47: 60–64.
Moti, Nissani (1990). A cognitive reinterpretation of Stanley Milgram's observations on obedience to authority. *American Psychologist* 46: 1384–1385.
Mutz, Diana (2018). Status threat, not economic hardship, explains the 2016 presidential vote. *Proceedings of the National Academy of Sciences*, May 2018, 115 (19) E4330–E4339; DOI: 10.1073/pnas.1718155115.
Natsoulas, Thomas (1993). What is wrong with appendage theory of consciousness. *Philosophical Psychology* 6: 137–154.
Neisser, Ulric (1976). *Cognition and Reality*. San Francisco: Freeman.
Newton, Natika (1996). *Foundations of Understanding*. Amsterdam: John Benjamins.

Newton, Natika (2000). Conscious emotion in a dynamic system: How I can know how I feel. In R. Ellis and N. Newton (Eds.), *The Caldron of Consciousness: Motivation, Affect, and Self-organization* (91–108). Amsterdam: John Benjamins.

Newton, Natika (2017). Understanding and self-organization. *Frontiers in Systems Neuroscience* 11: 8. doi: 10.3389/fnsys.2017.00008.

New York Times (1993). James R. Venable, 92, leader of Klan group. January 21 Obituaries.

Norman, Don (1977). The transformation of conscious experience and its EEG correlate. *Journal of Altered States of Consciousness* 3: 2.

Olson, Steve (2003). *Mapping Human History: Genes, Race, and Our Common Origins.* Boston: Mariner.

Panksepp, Jaak (1998). *Affective Neuroscience.* New York: Oxford University Press.

Panksepp, Jaak (2000). The neuro-evolutionary cusp between emotions and cognitions: Implications for understanding consciousness and the emergence of a unified mind science. *Consciousness & Emotion* 1: 17–56.

Panksepp, Jaak (2011). Cross-species affective neuroscience decoding of the primal affective experiences of humans and related animals. *PloS (Public Library of Science) ONE* 6 (8): e21236. doi:10.1371/journal.pone.0021236. https://en.wikipedia.org/wiki/PLOS_ONE.

Panksepp, Jaak (2012). In defense of multiple core affects. In P. Zachar and R. D. Ellis (Eds.), *Categorial versus Dimensional Approaches to Emotion: A Seminar on the Theories of Panksepp and Russell.* Amsterdam/Philadelphia: John Benjamins. 31–70.

Panksepp, Jaak, Jason Wright, Máté Döbrössy, Thomas Schlaepfer, and Volker Coenen (2014). Affective neuroscience strategies for understanding and treating depression: From preclinical models to three novel therapeutics. *Clinical Psychological Science* 2 (4): 472–494.

Picciolini, Christian (2020). *Breaking Hate: Confronting the New Culture of Extremism.* New York: Hackett Books.

Pierson, Don (2013). Depression-awareness campaign aids Bradshaw too. *Chicago Tribune,* Oct. 3, 2003.

Posner, Michael I. (1990). Hierarchical distributed networks in the neuropsychology of selective attention. In A. Caramazza (Ed.), *Cognitive Neuropsychology and Neurolinguistics: Advances in Models of Cognitive Function and Impairment.* New York: Plenum, 187–210.

Prasad, Monica, Andrew J. Perrin, Kieran Bezila, Steve G. Hoffman, Kate Kindleberger, Kim Manturuk, and Ashleigh Smith Powers (2009). "There must be a reason": Osama, Saddam, and inferred justification. *Sociological Inquiry* 79: 142–162.

Pytell, Timothy (2017). Is it OK to criticize a saint? On humanizing Viktor Frankl. *Psychology Today Blog.* https://www.psychologytoday.com/us/blog/authoritarian-therapy/201703/is-it-ok-criticize-saint-humanizing-viktor-frankl.

Rank, Otto (1924/1929/1994). *The Trauma of Birth*. New York: Dover. Original German edition *Das Trauma der Geburt* 1924.

Rank, Otto (1929/1936/1978). *Truth and Reality*. New York: W. W. Norton. Original German edition *Warheit und Wirklichkeit* 1929.

Retz, Wolfgang, Petra Retz-Junginger, Tillmann Supprian, Johannes Thome, and Michael Rösler (2004). Association of serotonin transporter promoter gene polymorphism with violence: relation with personality disorders, impulsivity, and childhood ADHD psychopathology. *Behavioral Sciences & the Law* 22: 415–425.

Ricoeur, Paul (1950/1966). *Freedom and Nature: The Voluntary and the Involuntary*. Evanston: Northwestern University Press.

Rogers, Carl (1951). *Client Centered Therapy: Its Current Practice, Implications, and Theory*. London: Constable.

Rogers, Carl (1959). A tentative scale for the measurement of process in psychotherapy. In E. A. Rubenstein and M. B. Parloff (Eds.), *Research in Psychotherapy*, 96–107. American Psychological Association.

Rogers, Carl, Ed. (1967). *The Therapeutic Relationship and Its Impact: A Study of Psychotherapy with Schizophrenics*. Madison: University of Wisconsin Press.

Rosentiel, Tom (2010). *Public Sees a Future Full of Promise and Peril*. Pew Research Center.

Sandvig, Ioanna, Ingrid Lovise Augestad, Asta Kristine Håberg, and Axel Sandvig (2018). Neuroplasticity in stroke recovery. The role of microglia in engaging and modifying synapses and networks. *European Journal of Neuroscience* 47: 1414–1428.

Sartre, Jean-Paul (1943/1965). *Being and Nothingness: An Essay on Phenomenological Ontology* (Trans. Hazel Barnes). New York: Washington Square Press.

Scheler, Max (1954/1970). *The Nature of Sympathy*. Hamden: Archon Books.

Schlesinger, Louis B. (2004). Classification of antisocial behavior for prognostic purposes: Study the motivation, not the crime. *Journal of Psychiatry & Law* 32: 191–219.

Schmidt, Lawrence (1995). *The Specter of Relativism*. Evanston: Northwestern University Press.

Shevrin, Howard (2001). Event-related markers of unconscious processes. *International Journal of Psychophysiology* 42: 209–218.

Singer, Peter (1981/2011). *The Expanding Circle*. Princeton: Princeton University Press.

Skinner, B. F. (1968). *Walden Two*. New York: Macmillan.

Slote, Michael (2014). *A Sentimentalist Theory of the Mind*. Oxford: Oxford University Press.

Snyder, Timothy (2017). *On Tyranny*. New York: Duggon/Random House.

Solomon, Robert (1976). *The Passions: Emotions and the Meaning of Life*. New York: Hackett.

Spitz, René A., and Katherine M. Wolf (1946). Anaclitic depression: An inquiry into the genesis of psychiatric conditions in early childhood. *P.A. Study of the Child, II.* New York: International University Press.

Stamenov, Maxim, and Vittorio Gallese (Eds.) (2002). *Mirror Neurons and the Evolution of Brain and Language.* Amsterdam/Philadelphia: John Benjamins.

Stein, Edith (1916/1989). *The Problem of Empathy.* Washington: ICS Publications.

Stolorow, Robert (2018). *The Power of Phenomenology.* New York: Routledge.

Stolorow, Robert, with George Atwood (1994). *The Intersubjective Perspective.* Lanham, Md.: Jason Aronson/Rowman & Littlefield.

Stout, Martha (2005). *The Sociopath Next Door: The Ruthless versus the Rest of Us.* New York: Broadway Books.

Sundararajan, Louise (2001). Alexithymia and the reflexive self: Implications of congruence theory for treatment of the emotionally impaired. *The Humanistic Psychologist* 29: 223–248.

Taylor, Jack, and Jeffrey French (2015). Oxytocin and vasopressin enhance responsiveness to infant stimuli in adult marmosets. *Hormones and Behavior* 75: 154–159.

Tottenham, Nim, Todd A. Hare, and B. J. Casey (2009). Developmental perspective on human amygdala function. In P. J. Whalen and E. A. Phelps (Eds.), *The Human Amygdala.* New York: Guilford, 107–117.

Tremblay, Lescia K., Claudio A. Naranja, Simon J. Graham, Nathan Hermann, Helen S. Mayberg, Stephanie Hevenor, and Usoa E. Busta (2005). Functional neuroanatomical substrates of altered reward processing in major depressive disorder revealed by a dopaminergic probe. *Archives of General Psychiatry* 62(11): 1228–1236.

Unamuno, Miguel de (1972). *The Tragic Sense of Life.* Princeton: Princeton University Press.

Varela, Francisco, Evan Thompson, and Eleanor Rosch (1991/1993). *The Embodied Mind.* Cambridge Mass.: MIT Press.

Wade, Richard (1967). *Slavery in the Cities.* Oxford: Oxford University Press.

Warren, Earl (1977). *The Memoirs of Chief Justice Earl Warren.* New York: Doubleday.

Watt, Douglas (1998). Affect and the "hard problem": Neurodevelopmental and corticolimbic network issues. *Consciousness Research Abstracts: Toward a Science of Consciousness, Tucson 1998:* 91–92.

Watt, Douglas (2000). The centrencephalon and thalamocortical integration: Neglected contributions of periaqueductal gray. *Consciousness & Emotion* 1: 91–114.

Weiss, James, Joseph Lamberti, and Nathan Blackman (1960). The sudden murderer: A comparative analysis. *AMA Archives of General Psychiatry* 2: 669–678.

West, Cornel (1979). Schleiermacher's hermeneutics and the myth of the given. *Union Theological Seminary Quarterly Review* 34: 71–84.

Westen, Drew (2008). *The Political Brain.* New York: Public Affairs.

White, Robert W. (1959). Motivation reconsidered: The concept of competence. *Psychological Review* 66: 297–333.
Wilentz, Sean (2002). From Justice Scalia, a chilling vision of religion's authority in America. *New York Times*, July 8, 2002.
Wilkerson, Isabel (2020). *Caste*. New York: Random House.
Wohlschläger, Andreas, and Harold Bekkering (2002). The role of objects in imitation. In M. Stamenov and V. Gallese (Eds.), *Mirror Neurons and the Evolution of Brain and Language*. Amsterdam: John Benjamins, 101–114.
Yalom, Irvin (1980). *Existential Psychotherapy*. New York: Basic Books.
Yardley, Elizabeth, David Wilson, and Adam Lynes (2013). A taxonomy of male British family annihilators, 1980–2013. *Howard Journal of Criminal Justice* 53: 117–140.
Yehuda, Rachel, Sarah Halligan, and Robert Grossman (2001). Childhood trauma and risk for PTSD. *Development and Psychopathology* 13: 733–753.
Zachar, Peter (2000a). *Psychological Concepts and Biological Psychiatry*. Amsterdam/Philadelphia: John Benjamins.
Zachar, Peter (2000b). Child development and the regulation of affect and cognition in consciousness: A view from object relations theory. In R. Ellis and N. Newton (Eds.), *The Caldron of Consciousness: Motivation, Affect, and Self-organization*. Amsterdam: John Benjamins, 205–222.
Zachar, Peter, and Ralph D. Ellis (2012). *Categorial versus Dimensional Approaches to Emotion: A Seminar on the Theories of Panksepp and Russell*. Amsterdam/Philadelphia: John Benjamins.
Zeigler-Hill, Virgil (2013). Neuroticism and negative affect influence the reluctance to engage in destructive obedience in the Milgram paradigm. *Journal of Social Psychology* 153: 161–174.
Zikopoulos Basilis, Malin Hoistad, Yohan John, and Helen Barbas (2017). Posterior orbitofrontal and anterior cingulate pathways to the amygdala target inhibitory and excitatory systems with opposite functions. *Journal of Neuroscience* 37: 5051–5064.
Zito, Salena (2016). Taking Trump seriously, not literally. *The Atlantic*, September 23.

Index

action readiness, 50, 142, 147, 209
addiction, 27, 62, 72, 86, 166–67, 230
Adler, Alfred, 45
Adorno, Theodor, 90, 92, 94, 98, 100, 179, 202, 205, 216
afferent vs. efferent nervous signals, 104, 119, 143–44, 147
Afford, Peter, 20, 47–48
Agreeableness, 67, 93–96, 108–109, 113
  correlated with authoritarianism, 108–109, 113
alexithymia, 22, 31, 33, 85, 88, 137–50, 230
alienation, 12, 31, 45, 52–53, 55, 62–63, 72, 74, 78, 80, 90, 102, 187–89, 200, 201, 211, 217
Altemeyer, Robert, 90, 92, 93–94, 98, 100, 193, 202, 205
alternative truth, 180
amygdala, 57, 58, 59, 99–100, 126, 227, 228, 229
anger, 6, 35, 99–100, 123–24
anomie, 31, 127, 167, 171, 182
appendage approach to consciousness, 9
Applebaum, Anne, 86
Arendt, Hannah, 2, 80, 84–87, 96, 98–99, 121, 126, 134, 174–75, 178–81, 213

Aristotle, 167
attention
  in moral development, 205
  involuntary, 5, 58, 92, 104, 107, 143
  selective, 1–2, 6, 11, 19, 58, 90–92, 130, 133–34, 137, 139, 148, 172, 174, 191, 213
  voluntary, 15, 17–18, 19, 32
Aurell, Carl G., 9, 19
authoritarian personality (*see also* Right Wing Authoritarianism), 80, 88, 90, 92–94, 96–101, 109, 113–14, 130, 134, 179, 193, 202, 205
autism, 22
Auxier, Randall, 202
Ayer, A. J., 139, 173, 176, 182, 196

Bagby, Robert, 141–42, 230
Baldwin, James, 44, 187
banality of evil, 80
basic emotions, 7, 10, 16–18, 28–29, 50–57
Becker, Ernest (*see also* terror management theory), 179, 181, 201, 216
Bègue, Laurent, 113
behaviorism, 2, 38, 47, 49, 50, 176
Bermond, Bob, 142, 230

Bickhard, Mark, 8, 21, 41, 202
Big Five personality inventory, 92–94, 108, 231–32
Binswanger, Ludwig (*see also* existential a priori), 17, 174, 191, 230
blockages to action, 61
Bradshaw, Terry, 72–74
Bräten, Stein, 113, 115
Bush, George, on prefrontal-amygdala relationship, 97, 99

CARE system (in brain), 51, 55, 68–69, 121, 124, 126, 176, 199, 204–205, 220
causation, 26, 31, 92, 98, 118, 141–42, 145–47, 203–204, 217, 224
Chan, David, 91
change blindness, 19
Chareyron, Loïc, 229
Colombetti, Giovanna, 20, 21, 36, 39, 223, 224
commensurability of different values, 186, 198, 202, 220
community, 22, 24, 52–54, 79–80, 84–85, 180, 187–88
conformism, 71, 80, 101, 176, 227
consciousness and brain, relation between 4–6, 9–11, 20, 37, 40, 50, 107, 117–18, 147
conspiracy theories, 1, 8, 14, 38, 78, 85, 89–92, 181, 216, 220–21
Cornell, Ann Weiser, 34–35, 61, 111, 197
Cornell, Drucilla, 206

Daly, Anya, 8, 21, 225
Damasio, Antonio, 9, 18, 50, 57, 117, 119, 141, 143–44, 210, 229
Davis, Kenneth, 14, 29, 38, 50, 67, 96, 193, 227
De Beauvoir, Simone, 23, 182, 185, 196, 212

De Preester, Helena, 226
De Waal, Frans (*see also* natural selection), 215
deconstructionism, 174, 175
Depraz, Natalie, 32–33, 48, 224
depression and SEEKING system suppression (*see also* lethargy), 39, 73–75, 212–13
Doige, Norman, 18, 26
Donoghue, John, 118–19
dopamine, 27, 62, 73, 108, 111
Dostoyevsky, Fyodor, 146
drugs, anti-depressant, 62, 230
Duriez, Bart, 92, 205
Durkheim, Emile, 31
dynamical systems, 6, 26–27, 59, 209–10, 223

ecological psychology, 19, 223
efferent vs. afferent nervous signals, 104, 119, 143–44, 147
emotion and motivation, distinction between, 6–7
emotion, conflicting definitions of, 7–8
emotional consciousness, 48, 50, 137–38, 140–46
emotional expression in music, 7, 67–74, 83–84, 104–106, 120–21, 142, 153, 196–97, 219
emotivist theory of ethics, 139, 173, 176, 196
empathy, 20, 39, 41–42, 55, 94–95, 102, 108–109, 113–15, 122, 133, 167–68, 177–78, 183, 206, 217
enactive meaning, 39–46, 51, 66, 74, 78–79, 87–90, 117–20, 126, 151, 166, 198–200, 207, 221
enactivism, 3–6, 10–14, 16–21, 26–28, 36–42
enactivity of perception, 5, 14, 19, 104, 107, 144
enteroception, 32, 141–48, 229

erotic love, 200
Euthyphro, 23
existential "themes," 8–10, 16–17, 20, 53, 63, 188
existential a priori, 15–18, 138, 149, 191–95
existentialism, 12, 15–17, 20, 23–25, 28–30, 48, 54, 62–63, 124, 138, 166, 174, 187–90
experiencing scale, 47–48
explanatory gap, 11
exploratory drive, 2, 12, 14, 18, 24, 49, 51, 55, 56, 69, 90, 97, 98, 101, 177, 180, 192, 193
  and SEEKING, 12, 18, 24, 29, 38–39, 51, 56–58, 71, 88–92, 96–98, 120, 167, 177–78, 193

face, in Levinas, 206
family annihilators, 128–29
Faw, William, 59, 228
FEAR system (in brain), 51, 53–54, 57–58, 99–100
fear, 3, 7, 45, 49, 51, 53–54, 57, 58, 80, 99–100, 141–42, 181, 211
felt sense, 7, 12, 26, 32–36, 52–53, 58, 61–62, 75–76, 140, 145–47, 153–58, 169–70
focusing (in Gendlin's sense), 12, 31–36, 47–48, 61, 76, 145, 147, 194, 197
  and dreaming, 147
Foucault, Michel, 174
Frankl, Viktor (*see also* logotherapy), 21, 28, 60–61, 62, 63, 164, 207
Freeman, Walter, 18
Freud, Sigmund, 49
Frijda, Nico, 18, 50, 57, 142, 164, 167, 209, 210., 227
frustration as trigger for anger, 16, 79, 146
Fukudo, Shin, 144

functional blindness, 5, 104

Gabbay, Vilma, 62
Gadamer, Hans G. (*see also* hermeneutics), 174, 179, 191, 230
Gallagher, Shaun, 8, 19, 21, 26, 36, 48, 210, 223, 226
Gallese, Vittorio (*see also* mirror neuron system), 39, 115
Gendlin, Eugene, 8, 11–12, 20–21, 26, 30, 32–34, 37–38, 40–42, 47–48, 52–54, 58, 65, 75, 103–104, 115, 118–20, 123, 146–49, 153, 186, 230
Geworfenheit, 187
Gibson, James J., 19, 210
Gilligan, Carol, 206
Goleman, Daniel, 207
Grand Scheme value systems, 23, 44, 63–64, 69–71, 78–93, 98, 121–22, 135, 184–86, 202–203
Greenberg, Jeff (*see also* terror management theory), 181, 200, 201, 207
grief, 10, 53, 72, 73

hard problem of consciousness, 11
Harlow, Harry, 56, 225, 226
Harvey, Charles, 45
hate crime murders, 129–31
hedonistic reinforcement vs. basic emotion, 54
Heidegger, Martin, 12, 17, 36, 39, 44, 59, 70, 99, 100, 174, 187, 223–24
hermeneutic circle, 14, 101, 173–74, 191–95, 200–203, 221
hermeneutics, 2, 10, 91, 101, 138, 151, 174, 185, 191–205, 221
Hibbing, John, 99–100, 191
historicism, 174

Hobbes, Thomas, 48, 79, 121, 219–20
Hodson, Gordon, 92–94, 108–109, 113, 133–34, 193
Homunculus problem, 4
Howard, Patrick, 197
Hsee, Christopher, 57
Hume, David, 14, 170, 177–81, 206
Husserl, Edmund, 11, 36, 39, 174, 223–24, 228

Ihde, Don, 10
image dependence, 106–13
Implicit preconscious processes, 21, 25–27, 34, 37–38, 40–44, 51, 54–55, 66–74, 79, 83–92, 109, 118–19, 129, 140, 146, 192, 198, 209, 214
inattentional blindness, 5, 19
indexicals, problem of, 183–84
inhibition, role in motor imagery, 104–105, 143–44, 147, 229
inner conflict, 12–14, 38, 42, 49, 61, 101, 111, 126, 138, 151, 179–81, 187, 189, 191, 194–95, 200, 211
inspiration and the SEEKING system, 51, 61, 67, 72, 108, 186, 212
inspiration, baseline level of, 25, 28–29, 43, 70–72, 77, 88, 108, 116–17, 131, 203
instrumental reinforcement, 48
instrumental values, 13, 23, 41–46, 55, 65–66, 72, 83–85, 89, 93, 117, 151–52, 160–61, 198–200, 203–207
intentional meaning, 32, 141, 143–47, 169–70
interactivism, 8, 20, 28, 41, 48, 167, 202
introversion, 67
is-ought problem, 168

Jackson, Frank, 13

James, William, 5, 9–10, 223–24
Jeannerod, Marc, 40, 105, 118–19, 131, 144, 146, 227, 229

Kano, Michiko, 144
Kauffman, Stuart, 26–27, 224, 225
Kiesler, Donald, 20, 47, 54
Klein, Marjorie, 20, 47, 230
kneejerk response, 5
knowledge argument (Frank Jackson's), 13–14
Kohut, Heinz, 78
Kramer, Eli, 121
Kuhn, Thomas, 10, 29, 174, 231

L'hermitte, Francois, 40
Lakoff, George, 96
Lambie, John, 140–41
Landgrebe, Ludwig, 174
LeDoux, Joseph, 3, 240
lethargy component of depression, 34, 57, 61–62, 73, 111
Levinas, Emanuel, 52, 132–33, 206
Levine, Joseph, 11
life world, 11 and passim
limbic area, 26, 50
Liu, Tao, 99, 228, 229
logotherapy, 21, 60
Lungu, Ovido, 99, 228, 229
LUST system (in brain), 51, 68, 199
Lyotard, Jean-Francois, 174

Mack, Arien, 5, 19
Maslow, Abraham, 121
Merleau-Ponty, Maurice, 1, 5, 11, 19, 38, 119, 210, 223–24, 225
Milgram, Stanley, 112–13, 179
Mill, John Stuart, 185
mind-body problem, 9–12
mirror neuron system, 19–21, 39–41, 115, 131–33, 119, 131
  suppression of, 131–33

moral development, 42, 55, 98, 121, 149–50, 160, 171, 177, 181, 204–206
moral realism, 196–97
motor cortex, 9, 37, 105, 119, 143–44
   role in mirror neuron system, 39, 106, 131
motor imagery, 37, 39, 104–105, 143–44, 229

narcissism, 24, 77–78, 134, 200, 213
Natsoulas, Thomas, 9, 225
natural selection, 28–29, 57, 115, 152
Nazism, 3, 22, 78, 80, 87, 89, 100
negative value experience, 106–13
negativity bias, 191
Neisser, Ulric, 19, 223
neural plasticity, 18, 26, 59, 100, 105, 148, 210
neurophenomenology, 32
Newton, Natika, 19–21, 26, 36, 37, 40, 131, 144, 210, 223, 224, 227
nihilism, 80, 86–87, 90, 92, 96, 98, 121, 124, 126–35
   and murder, 126–35
nurturance (*see also* CARE system), 18, 29, 50–51, 54–55, 57, 68, 112, 115, 177, 204

Olson, Steve, 85
Openness, 88, 92, 94, 96–97, 193, 227

PANIC system (*see also* separation distress), 25, 28, 38, 51, 52–55, 72, 98, 125, 204
   correlation with depression, 59–62, 74
Panksepp, Jaak, 9, 14, 18, 24–25, 28–29, 38–39, 49–62, 79, 96, 108, 112, 119, 125, 144–46, 177, 193, 199, 219, 226, 227

perceptual imagery dependence, 109–11
periaqueductal gray area (PAG), 50, 58, 144
philosophy of science, 10–11, 29, 174
Picciolini, Christian, 21–22, 29, 53, 79–80, 85, 97
PLAY system (in brain), 51, 70, 73, 167, 219
poetry, 75–77
Posner, Michael, 19
posttruth culture, 178–82
pragmatism, 5, 9–10
Prasad, Monica, 97, 192–93
prefrontal cortex, 13, 26, 58, 99–100, 205, 227, 228, 229
proprioception, 32, 107, 119, 140–44, 148
psychopathy, 94, 121, 127, 135, 166, 168, 184, 205
PTSD (*see also* trauma), 62

Rachmaninoff, Serge, 67–68
racism, 12, 93–97, 108, 110, 133–34, 138, 178, 193, 195, 205, 216, 217
RAGE system (in brain), 51, 57–58, 79, 125
Rank, Otto, 49, 107
relativist-emotivist view of values, 173
Ricoeur, Paul, 191
Right Wing Authoritarianism (*see also* authoritarian personality), 80, 88, 90, 92–94, 96–101, 109, 113–14, 130, 134, 179, 193, 202, 205
Rock, Irvin, 5, 19
Rogers, Carl, 33, 47, 230
Ruan, Bowen, 57

sadness, 2434–35, 60–62, 73, 77
Sartre, Jean-Paul, 84, 109, 185
Scheler, Max, 41, 52, 219, 228

Schmidt, Lawrence, 174
SEEKING system, 3, 24, 28–29, 38–39, 43, 49, 51, 55–63, 67, 69, 71, 73–75, 98, 212–13
  correlated with "Openness," 96–98, 193
  role in moral development, 120–21, 177, 193
  selective dampening of, 86–88, 96–98
selective alexithymia (*see also* alexithymia), 88
self-deception, 1, 37, 38, 59, 91, 101, 138, 189, 217, 219
self-maintaining structure (*see also* dynamical systems, self-organization), 26, 225
self-organization, 6, 26–27, 59, 209–10, 223
sensorimotor imagery, 104, 107, 119, 143–44, 148
sentimentalism (in ethics and political philosophy), 55, 139
separation distress (*see also* PANIC system), 24, 28, 38, 51, 52–55
serotonin, 27, 62, 125
Shevrin, Howard, 210
simulation theory vs. action imagery, 39
Singer, Peter, 206
Skinner, B. F., 48, 76
Slote, Michael, 9, 55, 224
Snyder, Timothy, 90
Soenens, Bart, 92, 205
Solomon, Robert, 30
Solomon, Sheldon (*see* terror management theory)
Stamenov, Maxim, 115
Stein, Edith, 41, 52, 228
Stolorow, Robert, 30, 41, 45, 54, 62–63, 213
Stout, Martha, 127
sudden murder, 123–28

Sundararajan, Louise, 31–32, 140–41
symbolization, 33–36, 65, 75–77, 103–105
  and action imagery, 104–107, 117–22
  and embodiment, 75–77
  in poetry, 76, 197

targeted inhibition of exploratory drive, 90
technology, philosophy of, 10–11
terror management theory, 200–203
thrownness, 187
Tottenham, Nim, 229
tragic paradox, 77
transcendental ego, 59
trauma (*see also* PTSD), 45, 53, 54, 63, 73, 100, 101, 181
trigger stimulus, 9–10, 13, 16–17, 32, 52–53, 55, 59, 63, 74, 79, 109, 111, 137–38, 141–42, 147, 204

utilization behavior, 40

Varela, Francisco, 19, 36, 223
veneer theory of moral behavior, 121
voluntary movement, 119

Watt, Douglas, 38, 50, 57–58, 210, 224
West, Cornel, 36, 191
Westen, Drew, 96
White Citizens Councils, 181
white nationalism (*see also* racism), 26, 29, 31, 53, 79–80, 85, 90, 178, 220
White, Robert, 14, 49, 164, 225, 226
wild boy of Aveyron, 121
Wilkerson, Isabel, 101

Yalom, Irvin, 30, 63, 207, 213

Zachar, Peter, 210, 226

www.ingramcontent.com/pod-product-compliance
Lightning Source LLC
Chambersburg PA
CBHW020645230426
43665CB00008B/328